The Gloss of Harmony

Anthropology, Culture and Society

Series Editors:
Professor Vered Amit, Concordia University
and
Professor Christina Garsten, Stockholm University

Recent titles:

THE GLOSS OF HARMONY

The Politics of Policy-Making
in Multilateral Organisations

Edited by Birgit Müller

First published 2013 by Pluto Press
345 Archway Road, London N6 5AA

www.plutobooks.com

Copyright © Birgit Müller 2013

The right of the individual contributors to be identified as the authors
of this work has been asserted by them in accordance with the Copyright,
Designs and Patents Act 1988.

British Library Cataloguing in Publication Data
A catalogue record for this book is available from the British Library

ISBN   978 0 7453 3375 5   Hardback
ISBN   978 0 7453 3374 8   Paperback
ISBN   978 1 8496 4948 3   PDF eBook
ISBN   978 1 8496 4950 6   Kindle eBook
ISBN   978 1 8496 4949 0   EPUB eBook

Library of Congress Cataloging in Publication Data applied for

10   9   8   7   6   5   4   3   2   1

Typeset from disk by Stanford DTP Services, Northampton, England
Printed and bound by CPI Group (UK) Ltd, Croydon, CR0 4YY

Contents

Series Preface

Anthropology is a discipline based upon in-depth ethnographic works that deal with wider theoretical issues in the context of particular, local conditions – to paraphrase an important volume from the series: *large issues* explored in *small places*. This series has a particular mission: to publish work that moves away from an old-style descriptive ethnography that is strongly area-studies oriented, and offer genuine theoretical arguments that are of interest to a much wider readership, but which are nevertheless located and grounded in solid ethnographic research. If anthropology is to argue itself a place in the contemporary intellectual world, then it must surely be through such research.

We start from the question: 'What can this ethnographic material tell us about the bigger theoretical issues that concern the social sciences?' rather than 'What can these theoretical ideas tell us about the ethnographic context?' Put this way round, such work becomes *about* large issues, *set in* a (relatively) small place, rather than detailed description of a small place for its own sake. As Clifford Geertz once said: 'Anthropologists don't study villages; they study *in* villages.'

By place, we mean not only geographical locale, but also other types of 'place' – within political, economic, religious or other social systems. We therefore publish work based on ethnography within political and religious movements, occupational or class groups, among youth, development agencies and nationalist movements; but also work that is more thematically based – on kinship, landscape, the state, violence, corruption, the self. The series publishes four kinds of volume: ethnographic monographs; comparative texts; edited collections; and shorter, polemical essays.

We publish work from all traditions of anthropology, and all parts of the world, which combines theoretical debate with empirical evidence to demonstrate anthropology's unique position in contemporary scholarship and the contemporary world.

Professor Vered Amit
Professor Christina Garsten

1
Introduction – Lifting the Veil of Harmony
Anthropologists Approach International Organisations

Birgit Müller

All eyes were turned to Rio de Janeiro in June 2012. The world was watching as the United Nations Conference on Sustainable Development Rio+20 unfolded, where 45,000 people, representatives of states, civil society, business, international organisations and specialised agencies were to define and to commit to 'The Future We Want'. Faced with climate change, mounting social inequality, hunger and a frantic race to grab land, minerals, fossil fuels and genetic resources, thus with environmental, social and economic problems that are globally interconnected, this Earth Summit brought together state delegations, civil society organisations and private business with often diametrically opposed interests and aspirations. In spite of fundamental differences in outlook on free trade, economic growth and corporate control, the outcome document was consensual. Without confronting the problems of the present and their causes the document proposed that 'the green economy in the context of sustainable development and poverty eradication ... could provide options for policymaking but should not be a rigid set of rules'.[1] It reaffirmed and recalled what had been adopted twenty years earlier (Chartier et al., 2012), and it tried to steer the world in the 'right' direction without requiring firm commitments. Yet, by looking into the future it also acted on the problems of the present by framing and consolidating them in particular ways.

In this book, we do not want to join in the concert of voices that evaluate the performance of international organisations, instead we are looking at the mechanisms of governance that emerge from the paradox of entrusting relatively powerless and underfunded

1

organisations with tackling some of the essential problems of our time. We are interested in how international organisations actually do shape the world in often unexpected and unpredictable ways, sometimes following agendas that are hardly made explicit.

Since their creation, the agencies of the United Nations (UN) have existed in the tension of appeasing political and economic conflicts between states often highly unequal in power and resources, and standing as warrants for universal rights that should be valid for all citizens of the world (Kennedy 2006: 206). In their attempts to act on conflicts over resources, territory and market shares, on environmental destruction, hunger and illness, they tried to assume a position above and beyond the interests of particular states, while being shaped not only by state interests but also by the power relations and supra-state actors of the era of globalisation such as multinational corporations, international networks of non-governmental organisations (NGOs) and representations of indigenous peoples. Paradoxically, while over the last twenty years states have called on the UN and its specialised agencies to address an ever wider range of problems, they refused to increase the funds dedicated to the organisations. As the demands and expectations increased the UN system acquired a more global legitimacy, while its funds were cut and its financial autonomy shattered (Devin and Placidi-Frot 2011).

This volume brings together the insights anthropologists have gained in different international organisations of the UN system. It focuses on the commonalities and differences of mechanisms of international governance through different scales. The chapters look not only at the official objectives and unintended consequences of international governance but also at how international organisations involve collective and individual actors in their policy-making, absorb critique, attempt to neutralise political conflict, and create new political fields in competition and collusion with local actors and national governments. The authors analyse mechanisms ranging from audit and self-monitoring through to bestowing honour and shame with which international organisations influence national and local governance and evaluate their own performance. The common thread that runs through all the contributions to this volume is the tension between the normative idealistic aspect of the organisation (do good, bring peace, be just), the mechanistic technical one (order, control, audit), and the political and economic interests that are played out there as well as the frustrations and the impetus for change that the actors in these organisations experience.

By focusing on international organisations with anthropological research methods that take into account the micro-social processes, the complexities of agency and interests, the chapters point to the disarticulation between practices of and in these organisations and their rationalising models.

The authors focus here on agencies of the UN that address some of the most fundamental problems that the world confronts today but that have no constraining mechanisms at their disposal to impose compliance with their rules, guidelines and recommendations, and operate on the principle of consensus of the nation states that are their members. These agencies have the mandate to fight environmental destruction (UNEP – UN Environmental Programme), hunger (FAO – Food and Agriculture Organization) and the loss of biodiversity (CBD – Convention on Biological Diversity), to defend the rights of economically and socially marginalised people – refugees (UNHCR – UN High Commissioner for Refugees), ethnic minorities (League of Nations), indigenous peoples (UNDRIP – UN Declaration on the Rights of Indigenous Peoples), prisoners (UN Committee Against Torture), to return cultural artefacts to the nations that claim them as their national heritage (UNESCO – UN Educational, Scientific and Cultural Organization) and to give recognition to Traditional Indigenous Knowledge (WIPO – World Intellectual Property Organization).

HOW ANTHROPOLOGISTS APPROACH INTERNATIONAL ORGANISATIONS

International organisations invaded fields of anthropological enquiry as their impact came to be felt where anthropologists did research. Through their advisors, projects and funds they were active in parts of the world where anthropologists have traditionally done fieldwork among 'indigenous' and rural populations. But also in the newer fields of anthropological enquiry, in enterprises, urban settings, tourism, state organisations, in the domain of intellectual property rights and cultural policies, the guidelines, codes of conduct and other soft laws produced by international organisations have had an impact on practices and policies. In recent years the organisations themselves – as circuits of power where normative frameworks are produced and globally diffused, resources are distributed and knowledge circulated through transnational expert networks – have also become fields of anthropological enquiry.

From paradoxes and tensions encountered at the local level, anthropologists moved thus to the organisation itself that appeared at first as a *terra incognita*, whose workings, networks, mechanisms of power and symbolic relations had to be explored without relying a priori on discourses produced in the official documents or departments of communication. They explored the headquarters of the organisations, analysed the mechanisms of governance in daily practice, and followed the construction of an institutional identity in images and language. They observed closely the interactions, uncovered dissent among and between groups, the emergence of disputes and the formation of consensus. Most of the time, they did not find their most precious materials in the official transcripts of sessions. They gleaned them in chance encounters (Hertz 2010), spontaneous interactions and by careful observation (MacDonald 2010). The strength of the anthropological approach is to take the time to understand, to dare to deconstruct the seemingly obvious by observing daily interactions and routines, to engage with actors while keeping a distance: 'The institution, far from being treated as a formal structure should be thought of as a space of confrontation between representations: in this space paths cross in pursuit of power' (Abélès 2011: 20). Images and discourses that international organisations project toward the outside world are the culmination of long processes of negotiation and harmonisation. Anthropologists are particularly interested in what happens upstream and outside the formal negotiations, in subjective and controversial representations of different actors and in the logics that guide their interactions. They explore not only the content of texts, regulations and standards, but also their 'social life' as they were drafted by known actors around tables in specific institutions (Mosse 2005: 19) and the history of their reception.

How can the anthropological ideal of doing 'participant observation' be accomplished? How does the anthropologist acquire an intimate knowledge of the organisation and the actors in a field that is so ephemeral, dispersed, complex and often opaque? Anthropologists who have ventured to explore international organisations and their practices have had to mobilise their skill of carefully observing interactions, those that seemed mundane and ordinary as well as others heavily loaded with symbolic meaning and issues of power. They showed their capacity for methodological innovation by making written documents speak by following the production of highly formalised and often opaque texts, and analysing websites and materials promoting the organisations. They adapted to the locations of multilateral negotiations that become centres of intense interactions for short periods. They followed the institutional players to their different sites of action, always in search of relationships that allow a level of communication that would bring them closer to the subjectivities and singularities of each interlocutor. The goal was not only to understand how international organisations think (Douglas 1986; Garsten and Jacobsson 2011), in the sense of their institutional culture, but rather to explore how people think and act inside the organisation (Abélès 2011). How do institutional actors produce consistent and harmonised representations of the organisation and its goals, or contribute to the tensions and contradictions within it?

The method and, consequently, the material that can be collected, depend on the angle taken by the research and the conditions of access to the field. Although anthropologists seek to work in an inductive manner, that is, they make the subject of their research evolve from their fieldwork, the choice of the angle structures the materials collected. Researchers interested in international organisations as places where they can study intercultural relations, discursive regimes (Groth 2012) and modes of globalised communication, chose headquarters for their fieldwork. To explore the formal and informal rules of conduct and subtle power plays during long periods of negotiation, they immersed themselves with institutional actors in the extremely slow and repetitive negotiating and learning processes (see Fresia, Bendix, Cowan, Bellier – all in this volume). Other anthropologists follow global controversies throughout the organisation, for example, on environmentally sustainable development (Goldman 2005), agricultural techniques (Müller 2011 and this volume), cultural artefacts (Hauser-Schäublin this volume) or the influence exerted by large private companies (MacDonald 2010). They study the emergence of new collective actors (Bellier 2008 and this volume) – organisations of indigenous peoples, farmers, women, etc. – at the UN, exploring the sites where dialogue and interaction takes place. Others have chosen to trace 'associations' between international officials, private consultants and members of NGOs that revolve around and circulate inside the organisation (Badaró 2011) and to analyse more closely the devices and arrangements of formal international meetings (Bendix, Fresia, Kelly – all this volume; also Kelly 2009). By analysing international governance, many anthropologists look at these organisations not as confined entities but as *dispositifs* (Foucault 1994) (assemblages or apparatus) that constantly attract new players, involving them as interlocutors, consultants and experts and formatting them through forms of calculation, technical reasoning and capacity building (Müller 2009; Li 2007). Others look at how international organisations produce normative frameworks and diffuse them all over the world, how they distribute resources and circulate knowledge through transnational expert networks (MacDonald this volume) effecting relationships of power and control from the metropolis to the remotest parts of the world.

Access to places where interactions take place and where relationships of trust can be established is crucial for anthropological fieldwork. When an international organisation is powerful, it has mechanisms to impose its standards and decisions at the global level, and to affect the interests of big business and capital, as a consequence it becomes difficult to get access. Discretion is required and the doors to the negotiating rooms are closed to the external observer. Anthropologists are then asked to 'do fieldwork without taking note'[2] (Dematteo 2011). In contrast, the weak areas of international governance, such as the section of the WIPO dealing with traditional knowledge, studied by Regina Bendix (this volume), often seek to exchange with anthropologists to circumscribe their fugitive objects and find ways and means of transforming them into legal objects. Asked to act as an expert on cultural knowledge, Bendix used her role to highlight how the delegates themselves went through processes of acculturation inside WIPO.

To access their field site, anthropologists assume the most diverse roles, often combining research with expertise (Fresia this volume) or engagement with distanced analysis (Randeria and Grunder 2011). As observers they are rarely disconnected from the issues in debate. Their moving between closeness and distance means that the organisation often expects a certain degree of allegiance and discretion. For some, the difficulty consists of getting access to information in relatively closed organisations, for others, who were able to immerse themselves, the challenge is to keep their distance and to negotiate a way out of their expert role (Mosse 2005, 2008).

Anthropological inquiries do not specifically seek to identify the malfunctioning of the international system; they address the practices and effects of international governance, its intended and unintended consequences, structured and unstructured ignorance, games of light and shadow, its content but also its shortcomings, its voids, its ambiguities and contradictions. Anthropologists place at the heart of their approach, the analysis of how these organisations construct worldviews and practices that spread throughout the world while simultaneously being shrouded with contradiction, slowness and paradox. Despite the differences in fieldwork and approach, a convergence emerges of some institutional mechanisms observed. The chapters in this volume explore how international organisations that have no constraining mechanisms at their disposal find ways and means to make the world governable without directly governing it. How do they reach a common reading of world affairs and project themselves into the future? How does this consensus about the State of the World affect the lives of people on the ground?

MAKING A WORLD THAT IS GOVERNABLE

International organisations advise on 'best practices' and good governance, and try to shape government policies and practices according to what they present as 'universal' standards. David Mosse has critically pointed out that these 'universal' principles, the singular common-sense models, the agreed international standards of governance, and the financial guidelines and benchmarks tend to be oriented towards the interests of selected players (Mosse 2005: 7). 'Free'-market-based solutions are promoted so as to ensure that market behaviour will be shaped to fit a legal, political and economic environment suited to global investors (Soederberg 2003:17–18). While it is the preserve of governments to agree on common norms and standards, and to reach a consensus on the text that is ultimately written, in order to recreate reality and reframe, measure and simplify it takes a far larger group of actors, what David Mosse (2005: 6) called a 'transnational epistemic community'. A common language has to be found that puts the reality created into words. Regina Bendix shows (this volume) how government officials and members of NGOs negotiated at the WIPO about the protection of 'indigenous intellectual knowledge'. They tried to resolve – to this day unsuccessfully – the contradiction that Marilyn Strathern (1996) pointed out, between cultural and intellectual property rights. Cultural property of indigenous peoples is considered 'authentic because it can be shown to have been handed on' over different generations (Strathern 1996: 24). Intellectual property, the domain of WIPO, is claimable precisely because it has not been shared and has not been handed on. Government representatives and representatives of indigenous peoples have engaged over years in a protracted process, redefining the various traditional cultural expressions as a new legal object expressing property relations and leading a legal life of its own. Step by step, the negotiation rounds struggle to achieve shared norms of interpretation. Thereby the world to be governed is transformed from heterogeneous cultural realities into registers of knowledge that become an official document to be approved and offered to the member states for adoption and that become the basis for making financial claims on multinational corporations.

Anthropologists suggested reading 'backwards' from the documents produced by these organisations (Mosse 2005), describing them as assemblages of discourses and practices, following their trajectories and histories. They were able to show that coherent policy narratives in the organisations studied are often produced, without a master plan, from an existing repertoire created in preceding sessions and meetings by a large variety of actors from governments, international administrations, NGOs and corporations. Drafts are tamed until they become acceptable and polite, cleansed of their conflictive elements and rendered 'technical' (Müller 2009; Riles 1999, 2000). The importance lies in the narrative that is maintained, as Marion Fresia (this volume) shows.

She analyses how a consensus was imagined, negotiated and constructed in the executive committee of the UNHCR until the subtleties of form disguise oppositions that are sometimes fundamental. Wealthier countries want to keep out refugees who put a strain on their social security system while upholding some general humanitarian ideal. Poorer countries that house a lot of refugees refuse to adhere to high ideals unless they receive financial compensation. She observed over a period of several months how a small group of diplomats and lawyers from the secretariat of the UNHCR elaborated, through arduous discussions, a soft and uncommitted text, Conclusion no. 107 on Children at Risk. While her assumption was that donor countries would have more weight over the negotiations, she found that power relationships among delegates were clearly in favour of some non-donor countries, which took a keen interest in the negotiations, were very supportive of each other, acted *en bloc* and constituted a quite homogeneous and stable coalition that claimed financial compensation. Reconstructing the personal trajectories and networks of diplomats and experts enabled her to understand how debates pursued in other forums of the UN were introduced into the debate on refugee children, thus contributing to the consolidation of an institutional culture and a common code that went beyond the framework of the organisation. This world of texts negotiated almost to the letter created, paradoxically, a fuzziness that can be filled by interests and power relations.

Mechanisms of governance in international organisations use linguistic tools that produce a seemingly neutral expert discourse, which draws on numerous statistical indicators and an abstract, vague and naturalising vocabulary. Several studies by socio-linguists (Cusso and Gobin 2008; Rist 2002; Siroux 2008) have recently demonstrated how this new global language operates 'through impersonal verbal and nominal constructions, the absence of identifiable authors, an apparent neutrality and a propensity to use a vague lexical field with positive connotations' (Siroux 2008: 20). In these discourses, statistical 'facts' work not only as elements of proof but also become political objectives in themselves. This type of discourse depoliticises political issues through 'neutralisation' (Bourdieu 1982: 155), a process that dominant groups have used to naturalise economic inequalities. The description of reality that these neutral expert discourses offer is almost 'clinical' (Cusso and Gobin 2008: 7): a diagnostic is established and a remedy found, which reduces the problem to a single cause and to a single way of dealing with it. These harmonised discourses, global norms and standards affirm a consensus while creating ambiguity (Ilcan and Phillips 2003; Müller 2009).

In its comprehensive effort to categorise and measure 'hunger', 'food' and 'agricultural production' the FAO, for example, has contributed to a system of governance that relies on 'normalising' the hungry. That is, the hungry person is transformed into a statistical unit and part of the 850 million 'hungry' who need to be fed in order to fulfil the commitment of the World Food Summit 1996 to halve the number of the 'hungry' by 2015. This style of reasoning produced particular ways of finding out the 'truth' about peoples, populations, commodities and nutrition. As Susan Ilcan and Lynn Phillips point out, these become new objects of inquiry and eventually the known objects, disrobed of their mystery (Ilcan and Phillips 2003: 450). Hunger, intellectual property, bio-safety and even free trade are treated as technical problems for which technical solutions can be found. The global discourse about the fight against poverty through 'good governance' redefines the relationship between the state and the citizens and promotes 'a new harmony' between rich and poor who, together, could develop their capacity for solving the problems at issue. The socio-linguist Francine Mestrum (2008: 27) observed in the global discourses on poverty a progressive shift towards the non-monetary dimensions of poverty. Differences in revenue appear in the statistics but are absent in the programmatic discourses, which focus on improving poverty indicators in the domains of health, education, housing, etc., through 'capacitating' the poor themselves. Hence, the discourse of 'good governance' focuses on the capacities of the poor rather than on the practices through which one social group impoverishes another (Li 2007: 7). What needs to be protected is less the income of the people, but their capacity to earn it. The income becomes thus the responsibility of the individuals themselves, rather than an object for social and political struggle over exploitation and the access to resources. Guidance is offered to individuals and communities to 'empower' themselves.

Analysing these mechanisms Peter Bille Larsen (this volume) points to the omnipresence of prescriptive practices and devices leading to what he terms an 'international guidance culture'. Looking at guidelines in the environmental governance field, which has few enforceable rules to combat climate change, ocean pollution and loss of biodiversity, he conceptualises the ways in which guidelines inform and affect the lives of international civil servants, state agencies and local communities. Rather than assuming that environmental governance has been rendered technical and politically impotent by guidelines, he suggests that the idea of technicality displaces ideas of power and politics. As 'techno-political devices', guidelines combine legitimacy, representation and prescription. They imply change without pointing fingers at current problems – merely suggesting other ways of doing things. Guidelines are thus future-oriented, while consolidating particular ways of thinking, framing and talking about the problems of the present. What appears as soft text may become hard reality as Birgit Müller shows (this volume) in her analysis of the instrumentalisation of the UN Voluntary Guidelines on Food Security to undermine the Nicaraguan food sovereignty law.

DISSOLVING CONFLICT – CREATING HARMONY

Studies in international relations tend to analyse international organisations either as battlegrounds for government interests, as mere structures where mostly the strongest countries set the rules of the game and determine its outcome (Keohane 2007), or as players in their own right who possess a 'rational-legal authority' that gives them power (Barnett and Finnemore 1999: 700). When anthropologists study how people act and think inside international organisations however, these organisations appear at the same time more active than a simple forum or battleground and also more contradictory and ambiguous and less 'rational'. Exploring the emic category of 'broker', which the organisations use to characterise themselves, has become a means for understanding how international organisations set about achieving consensus and devise mechanisms to keep open conflict over power and resources out of their general assemblies. Rather than affirming themselves as effective decision-makers with regard to controversial issues, the agencies of the UN establish themselves as 'brokers' who mediate conflicts between governments, private sector and civil society organisations who mediate conflicts. In the most basic sense of the term, a broker is an intermediary between buyer and seller who helps to negotiate economic transactions to the satisfaction of both parties. 'A broker … brings about communication for profit' (Boissevain 1974: 148) and thus depends on this role. The role that many UN adminis-trations have been called on to play between donor and receiver countries in recent years closely resembles this economic broker role.

As the funds attributed to UN organisations have considerably diminished since the beginning of the 1990s, these organisations have been reduced in many cases to brokering projects financed by individual donor states with the receiver countries. The political equality that all states have in the assembly thus becomes negotiable through the modes of financing of the projects, through the 'donor-driven approach'. Instead of intervening on world agriculture and nutrition, the FAO for instance tends to act as a development agency split between those who can claim the status of being 'developed' – who are thus outside of its realm of influence – and those who have to be 'developed'. It partakes thus in 'the will to improve' (Li 2007) that it shares with other development agencies. As an institutional development broker (Bierschenk and Olivier de Sardan 1993; Mosse 2005) it thus also translates between the expectations, ideas and worldviews of the donor and the receiver, and positions itself in such a way as to become indispensable for the transaction. Many UN organisations have started to go beyond the role of an intermediary and claim the role of 'strong broker' or 'objective broker', basing their strength on 'competence' and 'knowledge', in short on the capacity of being an expert, who can claim a superior normative and technical authority over donor and receiver countries alike.

Attempting a genealogy of human rights governance from the League of Nations of the inter-war period to the UN today, Jane Cowan shows (this volume) how the broker role has changed. States under scrutiny have shifted from being the object of international supervision to being primarily a subject that self-reports. By encouraging critical self-accounting the Universal Periodic Review process of the UNHCR wants the state under review primarily to 'interiorise' human rights principles while submitting to the friendly, cooperative and non-politicised scrutiny of others. In the past, international bureaucrats of the League of Nations negotiated over minority problems behind closed doors and used opacity to obtain concessions from Minority States. Today, in the UN, transparency is an explicit value. The international bureaucracy helps states in the performance of 'transparency', which, however, often hides as much as it reveals. Etiquettes of speaking, acronyms, and an intense haggling around terminology and word choice lead to heavily coded, and often opaque and 'technical' texts (Merry 2006; Riles 2000).

Does this emphasis on technicality and form make the processes in the UN therefore less political? As all the contributions to this volume point out, state actors continue to advance their geopolitical interests strategically in the realm of the UN. However, they are supposed to do so in a 'non-politicised' way. The term 'non-politicised' is ambivalent, as Cowan points out, and seems to rule out an open confrontation between conflicting notions about how to best organise society. Openly antagonistic debates between states hardly exist in the muted diplomatic atmosphere of the UN. The Universal Periodic Review process, conceived as a consensual space for sharing best practices, plays on the register of morality, exemplifying what Cowan, following Chantal Mouffe (2005), calls 'post-political forms of regulation and government'. Political tensions and antagonisms about projects for society drop back behind the search for a compromise, for the smallest common denominator. In this striving for harmony opponents are defined not in political but in moral terms (Mouffe 2005), they cannot be envisaged as 'adversary' but only as morally inadequate, immature. Once the compromise is found and put down in words, 'agreed text' is created and controversy is erased. Isaiah Berlin's observation is relevant here: 'Where ends are agreed, the only questions left are those of means, and these are not political but technical, that is to say, capable of being settled by experts or machines, like arguments between engineers or doctors' (Berlin 1969 [1958]). The moral principle then easily disappears behind technical procedures.

This mechanism becomes apparent in the UN Committee Against Torture, which uses elaborate technical procedures to uphold the moral standard that using torture on helpless prisoners is wrong. Tobias Kelly (this volume), analysing the monitoring mechanisms in the UN Committee Against Torture, shows how the 'shame of torture' easily 'dissipates' within the 'bureaucratic regime' of the commission. The monitoring process does not look at individual cases but at policies, procedures and institutional arrangements. Rather than judging and contesting the self-evaluations produced by the states under review, the UN Committee Against Torture suggests technical solutions, such as training police officers, prison guards, soldiers, lawyers and the general public in the prevention of torture and ill-treatment. Its mechanisms of monitoring look less into the imperfect past but rather project themselves into a better future. The concrete violation of the human rights of individual prisoners thus disappears very easily behind human rights procedures.

Not all agencies in the UN system, however, assume the position of a neutral broker detached from concrete and complex realities. The UNESCO committee for the return and restitution of cultural objects that Brigitta Hauser-Schäublin analyses (this volume) understands itself as a committed broker that performs advocacy on behalf of countries whose cultural artefacts have been looted, expropriated or stolen to end up in private and public art galleries abroad. The cultural artefacts – centuries-old ritual objects, sculptures, manuscripts – that the committee seeks to restore to the countries they came from, had become 'disembedded' from their cultural context and were transformed into valuable commodities. As collectors' items, they took on other functions, meanings and values. These were put into question in the restitution process, which reasserted the sacred character of the object, the 'identity', 'heritage' and belonging' that the artefact embodied, not legal proceedings or collectors' value. The claimants used moral arguments and evoked the suffering from former colonial domination while the holder of the artefact – museums and art collections and the mostly more powerful states representing them – drew on arguments of legality and legitimacy. The broker role of UNESCO consisted of getting the 're-enchanted' artefact returned and of saving the face of the holder by rephrasing the return as a donation or a permanent loan. In contrast to the task of the human rights bodies discussed above, whose value-loaded but intangible object seemed to escape definition, let alone supervision, the intervention of UNESCO was concerned here with concrete material objects, bearing witness to a complicated history of domination and oppression that the holder states were eager to forget and to erase. The holder states were thus ultimately persuaded to relinquish them to uphold the gloss of harmony.

The role of a neutral broker and expert stands in tension with the normative mandate of the UN to promote individual human rights. On the one hand, UN agencies refer to their role as guardians of human and social rights to claim moral high ground when dealing with individual states. On the other hand, policy guidelines for realising these rights are the result of intense haggling and compromise in a diplomatic arena where states search for the lowest common denominator. Contestation is thus brought into the arena of international organisations not so much through its own democratic mechanisms but from the outside, by a whole set of actors that gravitate towards the organisations and are drawn into its realm.

PARTICIPATION AND ACTOR BUILDING ACROSS SCALES

Networks of engaged individuals and groups have been instrumental for the creation of many agencies of the League of Nations and later of the UN (Kott 2011). The UN Charter, unlike that of the League of Nations fashioned just a few decades earlier, already in 1945 provided for consultation with NGOs 'concerned with matters within their competence' (United Nations 1945: Art. 71). Organisations with consultative status were valued as interlocutors because of the moral and intellectual input they could bring to UN deliberations. In the 1970s and 1980s, the scenario changed and more and more social movements started to carry their concrete problems of practice, their struggles and aspirations into the arena of the UN, culminating in the large UN Summits of the 1990s. By the end of the decade of the 1990s, however, 'civil society actors felt increasingly that they were in serious and growing danger of being co-opted to serve watered down intergovernmental agendas rather than advancing their own visions and objectives' (McKeon 2009: 11). They felt that they ran the risk of being drawn into the same mechanism of 'rendering technical' that dampens political controversies among states inside the organisation. 'Dialogue' with civil society threatened to become a mode of governance which neutralised political antagonisms and required careful strategising on the part of civil society organisations to avoid legitimising policies they did not agree with and that they were unable to influence effectively. Especially in the numerous processes of participation and consultation over the internet that international organisations have put in place, 'citizens' were consulted as individuals stripped of their context and collective attachment, and thus ultimately disempowered (Müller 2011). This technique of governance works 'by deflecting attention from the system itself onto the individual' (Shore and Wright 2011:16). Individuals and groups consulted as experts by the organisation became in the process indirectly responsible for the technical solutions that the organisation had to offer. Paradoxically though, as the expert role was generalised and everybody could become 'a responsible expert' (Phillips 2007), the organisation acted as the ultimate arbitrator of which expertise was valid.

As a consequence, the mechanisms of consultation and control formulated in terms of partnership, transparency and accountability create new power games in the field of ethical policies that can open as many opportunities for marginalised groups as they can become means for controlling them. When civil society observers and participants in international meetings learn the rules of conduct of the institutions that tolerate and increasingly involve them, 'precise, consistent and smooth behaviours' are instilled (Van Vree 1999), restraining expressions of affect and emotion. However, by appropriating these rules and participating in the creation of a common language, non-state actors, representatives of farmers' organisations, indigenous and women's organisations are trying to use the rules of the game of international institutions for their own purposes in their relation to the nation state.

Irène Bellier shows (this volume) how the representatives of indigenous peoples around the world have invested in the UN arena over the years, making the organisation a tool that allowed them to make their voices heard. The local populations that have been victims of oppression, exploitation at the national level, and whose traditional livelihood and environment have been destroyed, transformed themselves into international actors. They became 'peoples' with a shared subjectivity, involved in the construction of knowledge about themselves and in the production of standards, and demanded recognition of their collective rights. In the process, they learned the functioning of the UN agencies and became skilled at moving within their structure. Meanwhile, their self-representation has adapted to institutional expectations, and the UN has absorbed some of the edge of their demands thus reducing their potential for protest.

Discourses and concepts used at the international level structure national policy interventions and public policy, and travel to the more remote sites where anthropologists observe their impact at local and state levels (Bellier 2007; Müller and MacDonald in this volume). The strength of rules and standards produced at the international level and used locally depends not only on their coercive power but also on how they are integrated into daily practice, becoming so familiar that they 'shap[e] the rules people carry in their heads' (Merry 2006). Processes of international governance thus produce a whole spectrum of cultural and political closures and opportunities – 'from the extremes of society-wide approval to major resistance' – while 'most social activity occurs in the spaces in between' (Goldman 2005: 25).

By analysing not only the social life of documents in the headquarters of international organisations but also how they are used in projects on the ground, anthropologists show how seemingly technical issues are re-politicised in the life of the projects. What is experienced as anti-politics (Ferguson 1990), as the dissolving of conflict in a discourse of harmony, is thus less an essence than a recurring practice of international organisations that has to be studied 'at work'.

A striking example of such a re-politicisation, is the use of the Voluntary Guidelines for the Right to Food by opposition parties and the national representation of the FAO in Nicaragua (Müller this volume) to weaken the Nicaraguan food sovereignty law. As Birgit Müller shows (this volume), on the national and local level the FAO of the UN ceases to play the 'neutral broker' between donor and receiver countries, advocates and opponents of industrial farming models and large-scale investments in agriculture, and instead claims for itself a superior moral and legal authority. The FAO thus partakes in 'the will to improve' (Li 2007) that it shares with other development agencies and that impacts not only the human communities but also the types of food grown, the seeds and the soil. While claiming to empower and involve local communities it assumes, on the local level, an organisational void that needs to be filled and a problem that needs to be solved. 'Hunger', diagnosed and measured as child stunting, triggers an institutional response justified by a discourse of urgency and moral superiority. Only if local actors can draw on social networks and organisations of their own can they uphold their own interests and use and modify the corpus of global best practices to their own advantage.

Ken MacDonald observed a similar 'globalisation of everyday life' in the remote Pakistani villages where the International Union for the Conservation of Nature (IUCN) put into practice models developed at the CBD destined to make biodiversity conservation pay for itself. He shows (this volume) how local communities and environments are 'imaginatively brought into being' in the sites of conservation policy. Following a managerial logic that annihilates context, the IUCN redefined and categorised the local actors, attempted to reconfigure their understanding of biodiversity, to restructure access and use rights and to define a problem which had not previously existed. Without any previous local research the IUCN intervened in a Himalayan village proposing a 'cash for wildlife' swap to the inhabitants if they ceased to ritually hunt ibex (wild mountain goats). The ibex thus became a precious and rare commodity and the villagers who had been 'hunters' were redefined in terms of guardians of biodiversity or poachers. The local actors were thus reinserted into a new social structure that was from the outset conflictual. The programme welcomed by the most powerful villagers created the 'reality' of an endangered rare species it had previously described. Under the surface of project goals such as 'sustainability', 'self-reliance' or 'capacity building', value-laden concepts, systems of morality and practical tasks oriented to value-based goals were hidden that operated to the disadvantage of many people they were intended to benefit. Those disadvantaged had a hard time defending their interests as the underlying meaning of these rationalisations – namely that you can buy 'nature' for money – was obscured under the appearance of bureaucratic neutrality and global significance.

What does the gloss of harmony do to the conflicts, problems and tensions of the contemporary world? The obvious effect seems to be that everybody continues talking, albeit in a very formalised fashion. The narrative continues. Often the minimal objective is maintained to keep a subject on the agenda even if it is far from being resolved. The Declaration of Rio+20 can thus be read as a catalogue of vague principles that are 'recognised', 'reaffirmed', 'stressed' and 'underlined' rather than as a roadmap towards 'The Future We Want' to bring about. For better or for worse, it empowers the international bureaucracy, allows it to affirm its expertise, to play the role of an indispensable broker and keeper of an institutional memory of 'agreed text' and of fundamental values. Less obviously, by covering the geopolitical tensions between states with the veil of harmony, it opens political space for civil society groups and social movements that affirm themselves as political contrarians to carry conflicted realities back into the muted diplomatic arena. Paradoxically, while civil society organisations are required to conform to the style and language of the institutions, it is their potential for naming and contesting concrete realities that makes them indispensable because this enlivens the institutions. Most problematically, perhaps, the 'gloss of harmony' and homogenised discourse of international organisations constitutes a formidable challenge for local governance if it is asserted with a claim to superior moral and technical authority and with financial incentives. It is at the level of local practice that the gloss evaporates.

ACKNOWLEDGEMENTS

I would like to thank the European Science Foundation and the Wenner Gren Foundation for generously funding the Paris Workshops on the Anthropology of International Organizations in 2008 and 2010 respectively that brought together most of the authors of this volume. I would like to thank the authors for the stimulating discussions and the collaborative effort that made this book possible.

NOTES

1. 'The Future We Want', resolution adopted by the General Assembly of the United Nations, 66/288, 11 September 2012, para. 56.
2. 'Faire de l'ethnographie sans ethnographier.'

BIBLIOGRAPHY

Abélès, Marc (ed.) (2011) Des anthropologues à OMC: Scènes de la gouvernance mondiale (Paris: CNRS Éditions).
Badaró, Máximo (2011) 'Le régime d'invisibilité des experts', in Marc Abélès (ed.) Des anthropologues à OMC: Scènes de la gouvernance mondiale, pp. 82–110 (Paris: CNRS Éditions).
Barnett, Michael N. and Martha Finnemore (1999) 'The politics, power, and pathologies of international organizations', International Organization 53(4): 699–732.
Bellier, Irène (2007) 'Partenariat et participation des Peuples Autochtones aux Nations Unies: Intérêt et limites d'une présence institutionnelle', in C. Neveu (ed.) Démocratie participative, cultures et pratiques (Paris: L'Harmattan).
Bellier, Irène (2008) 'Le développement et les Peuples Autochtones: Conflits de savoirs et enjeux de nouvelles pratiques politiques', in V. Geronimi, I. Bellier, J.-J. Gabas, M. Vernières and Y. Viltard, Savoirs et politiques de développement: Questions en débat à l'aube du XXIè siècle (Paris: Karthala).
Berlin, Isaiah (1969 [1958]) 'Two concepts of liberty', in Isaiah Berlin, Four Essays on Liberty (Oxford: Oxford University Press). Available at: http://www.

wiso.uni-hamburg.de/fileadmin/wiso_vwl/johannes/Ankuendigungen/Berlin_twoconceptsofliberty.pdf (consulted March 2013).

Bierschenk, Thomas and Jean-Pierre Oliver de Sardan (1993) 'Les courtiers locaux du développement', *Bulletin de l'APAD* 5: 71–76.

Boissevain, Jeremy (1974) *Friends of Friends: Networks, Manipulators and Coalitions* (Oxford: Basil Blackwell).

Bourdieu, Pierre (1982) *Ce que parler veut dire: L'économie des* échanges *linguistiques* (Paris: Fayard).

Chartier, Denis, Jean Foyer and the collective ECOVERIO (2012) 'Rio+20: La victoire du scénario de l'effondrement?', *Écologie et Politique* 45: 117–130.

Cusso, Roser and Corinne Gobin (2008) 'Du discours politique au discours expert: Le changement politique mis hors débat?', *Mots: Les langages du politique* 88: 5–11.

Dematteo, Lynda (2011) 'Les maîtres du clair-obscur: Transparence et secret dans la communication', in Marc Abélès (ed.) *Des anthropologues à l'OMC: Scènes de la gouvernance international* (Paris: CNRS Éditions).

Devin, Guillaume and Delphine Placidi-Frot (2011) 'Les evolutions de l'ONU: Concurrences et integrations', *Critique internationale* 53(Oct.–Dec.): 21–42.

Douglas, Mary (1986) *How Institutions Think* (New York: Syracuse University Press).

Ferguson, James (1990) *The Anti-Politics Machine: Development, Depoliticization, and Bureaucratic Power in Lesotho* (Cambridge: Cambridge University Press).

Foucault, Michel (1994 [1977]) 'Le jeu de Michel Foucault', in *Dits et écrits*, vol. II, pp. 298–329 (Paris: Gallimard).

Garsten, Christina and Kerstin Jacobsson (2011) 'Transparency and legibility in international institutions: The UN Global Compact and post-political global ethics', *Social Anthropology* 19(4): 378–393.

Goldman, Michael (2005) *Imperial Nature: The World Bank and Struggles for Social Justice in the Age of Globalization* (New Haven, CT: Yale University Press).

Groth, Stefan (2012) *Negotiating Tradition: The Pragmatics of International Deliberations on Cultural Property* (Göttingen: Universitätsverlag Göttingen).

Hertz, Ellen (2010) 'Excessively up at the International Labour Organisation: Notes on "Notes of Proceedings"', in MAPS Working Papers 9, University of Neuchâtel.

Ilcan, Susan and Lynne Phillips (2003) 'Making food count: The global governance of food and expert knowledge', *Canadian Review of Sociology and Anthropology* 40(4): 441–461.

Kelly, Tobias (2009) 'The UN Committee Against Torture: Human rights monitoring and the legal recognition of torture', *Human Rights Quarterly* 31(3): 777–800.

Kennedy, Paul (2006) *The Parliament of Man: The Past, Present, and Future of the United Nations* (Toronto: HarperCollins).

Keohane, Robert (2007) 'Designing multilateral institutions: Interests and power', Castle Lecture Series: Institutional Design and Power', Yale University, 29 October.

Kott, Sandrine (2011) 'Les organisations internationals, terrains d'étude de la globalisation: Jalons pour une approche socio-historique', *Critique Internationale* 52(July–Sept.).

Li, Tania Murray (2007) *The Will to Improve: Governmentality, Development and the Practice of Politics* (Durham, NC: Duke University Press).

MacDonald, Kenneth Iain (2010) 'Business, biodiversity and new "fields" of conservation: The World Conservation Congress and the renegotiation of organisational order', *Conservation and Society* 8(4): 256–274.

McKeon, Nora (2009) *The United Nations and Civil Society: Legitimating Global Governance – Whose Voice?* (London: Zed Books).

Merry, Sally Engle (2006) *Human Rights and Gender Violence* (Chicago: University of Chicago Press).

Mestrum, Francine (2008) 'La pauvreté multidimensionnelle: La dynamique sémantique dans le discours de la Banque Mondiale', *Mots. Les langages du politique* 88(Nov.): 25–37.

Mosse, David (2005) 'Global governance and the ethnography of international aid', in David Mosse and David Lewis (eds) *The Aid Effect: Giving and Governing in International Development* (London: Pluto Press).

Mosse, David (2008) 'Conference review: The anthropology of international institutions', *Anthropology Today* 24(5): 24.

Mouffe, Chantal (2005) *On the Political* (London: Taylor and Francis).

Müller, Birgit (2009) 'Rendre technique un débat politique: Controverses autour des biotechnologies agricoles au sein de la FAO', *Tsantsa* 14: 27–36.

Müller, Birgit (2011) 'The elephant in the room: Multi-stakeholder dialogue on agricultural biotechnology in the FAO', in Davide Però, Cris Shore, Sue Wright (eds) *Policy Worlds: Anthropology and the Anatomy of Contemporary Power* (Oxford: Berghahn Books).

Phillips, Lynne and Susan Ilcan (2007) 'Responsible expertise: Governing the uncertain subjects of biotechnology', *Critique of Anthropology* 27(1): 103–126.

Randeria, Shalini and Ciara Grunder (2011) 'The (un)making of policy in the shadow of the World Bank: Infrastructure development, urban resettlement and the cunning state in India', in Davide Però, Cris Shore and Sue Wright (eds) *Policy Worlds: Anthropology and the Anatomy of Contemporary Power* (Oxford: Berghahn Books).

Riles, Annelise (1999) 'Models and documents: Artefacts of international legal knowledge', *International and Comparative Law Quarterly* 48(4): 809–830.

Riles, Annelise (2000) *The Network inside Out* (Ann Arbor, MI: University of Michigan Press).

Rist, Gilbert (ed.) (2002) *Les Mots du pouvoir, sens et non-sens de la rhétorique internationale* (Paris: Nouveaux Cahiers de l'IUED).

Shore, Cris and Susan Wright (2011) 'Conceptualizing policy: Technologies of governance and the politics of visibility', in Davide Però, Cris Shore and Sue Wright (eds) *Policy Worlds: Anthropology and the Anatomy of Contemporary Power.* Oxford: Berghahn Books.

Siroux, Jean-Louis (2008) 'La dépolitisation du discours au sein des rapports annuels de l'Organisation mondial du commerce', *Mots. Les langages du politique* 88(Nov.): 12–23.

Soederberg, Susanne (2003) 'The promotion of "Anglo-American" corporate governance in the south: Who benefits from this new international standard?', *Third World Quarterly* 24(1): 7–28.

Strathern, Marilyn (1996) 'Potential property: Intellectual rights in property and persons', *Social Anthropology* 4(1): 17–32.

United Nations (1945) Charter of the United Nations and Statute of the International Court of Justice. Available at: http://www.un.org/en/documents/charter/index.shtml (consulted March 2013).

Van Vree, Wilbert (1999) *Meetings, Manners, and Civilization: The Development of Modern Meeting Behaviour* (Leicester: Leicester University Press).

Part I
Making a World That is Governable

2

The Power of Perseverance

Exploring Negotiation Dynamics at the World Intellectual Property Organization

Regina F. Bendix

Sitting on the backbenches of the grand meeting room in Geneva's World Intellectual Property Organization (WIPO) headquarters, behind state delegations and alongside representatives from observing organisations, I was struck by the peculiarities of this field site. The WIPO meeting rooms and halls presented, it seemed, the reverse challenge of multi-sited ethnography (Marcus 1995). Rather than following actors along the trajectories of their networks, I sat among hundreds of actors who had brought with them components of the one or more 'fields' they inhabited otherwise in their lives. Much like the ethnographer, each of them was engaged in adapting their comportment to this setting; delegates were engaged in a learning process and, like the ethnographer, they pursued a goal: delegates sought to grasp the moves and turns of the subject under negotiation and (re-)present their portfolio in as convincing a manner as possible, while the ethnographer sought to understand just how this learning and strategising unfolded. This chapter thus undertakes a reflection on the challenges and opportunities of conducting qualitative research in international institutions, using the Intergovernmental Committee for Genetic Resources as a case in point for research dynamics more applicable to this type of 'field' more generally.

The Intergovernmental Committee for Genetic Resources, Traditional Knowledge and Traditional Cultural Expressions/ Folklore (IGC) took up its work in 2001. As a result, the WIPO, which had previously dealt with regulatory mechanisms such as copyright and patent law, took on decision-making over the complex collective good known as 'culture'. I began to follow the IGC's activities digitally[1] in 2003, became intrigued (though no less concerned) by these negotiations, which seek to delineate a 'legal life' for cultural knowledge and traditional expressions, firming up implicit values and ownership. I had the opportunity to meet with the IGC's secretary at an international ethnological conference in 2004. He invited conversation with cultural researchers, indeed, he was positively eager to access expertise on the matters discussed within the IGC, as well as feedback on the processes within the IGC. With a group of colleagues in ethnology, law and economics, we formed a research group broadly concerned with the constitution of cultural property and cultural property rights, and, while we investigate a number of arenas, from local to international, my ethnographic entry point and special focus within this group has been the IGC. I applied for observer status for our research group at the IGC, which was granted for the IGC's biannual meeting in 2006 during which I undertook a first participatory observation.[2]

I begin with a brief consideration of the more recent methodological literatures on fieldwork within changing global parameters for anthropology and related fields and a characterisation of WIPO's IGC. I will then offer initial reflections on what I consider the particularity of fieldwork in international institutions. Specifically, I will argue that understanding the learning of the ethnographer within this setting parallels that of the subjects under investigation. Issues such as the temporal pace, the enculturating component present at each session, and the complex communicative parameters participants can draw on all crucially contribute to an understanding of international negotiations. Given the profound importance of language – oral and translated, written, digitalised as well as non-verbal – components of the ethnography of communication are arguably methodologically most suitable for this setting.

INTERNATIONAL INSTITUTIONS AND ANTHROPOLOGICAL FIELDWORK

Extant studies on international organisations have begun to provide guidance for researchers working in settings such as this WIPO committee (e.g. Shore and Wright 1997; Shore et al. 2011). One of the prominent and indeed important focuses has been policy, and hence it is often the questions of how to handle the – generally heavily paper-based – data analytically rather than the nature of fieldwork itself that has been problematised and theorised. Although even engaging fieldwork manuals often makes for an odd, fish-out-of-water reading experience, confronting this field still makes patently obvious that key notions of anthropological fieldwork, such as locality and intimacy (Appadurai 1997: 115–116), need to be newly conceptualised. How did others arrive at their data, how did the 'fieldworker–field' dynamic play out?[3] This information is as relevant for this international setting as it was for Whyte's street corner society. Recourse to the growing body of work on the European Union (Abélès 1992; Shore 2000, 2005; Shore and Wright 1997) yield few insights on how those authors worked, that is, what role they took in the halls of Brussels or within administrative offices of particular delegates. Nor is there a clarification on how access was gained for participant observation. Access is, however, a crucial issue as is evident from case studies on organisational culture more generally.[4] While institutions such as WIPO and other UN (United Nations) sub-organisations are essentially 'public', a path toward legitimating one's presence both to partake in events and meet individual delegates is nonetheless required, not least because such organisations and international meetings in particular are guarded and require, depending on site and issue, measures of security clearance.[5] Document analysis, as noted above, is mentioned repeatedly as an avenue to pursue in the extant ethnographic literature – and it also forms part of our engagement with WIPO's IGC. Yet the documents only gain depth and meaning if one has insights into the processes that brought them forth, the relationships and the hierarchies among those who produced them, and the difference between what reaches document-stage and what remains in the evanescent realm of oral communication.[6]

How can international negotiations be approached as a 'field' as conceptualised in qualitative anthropological research? How can the protagonists' very lack of shared cultural background and shared linguistic competences in settings such as the IGC be set aside so as to open an ethnographic view into the field of expectation and interaction they co-create during a week or more of joint negotiating?[7] And what is the contribution of such an ethnography to the larger understanding of institutions engaged in an unfolding, ever more complex global governance? The anthropological study of international organisations and international political institutions has grown considerably in recent decades, even if many analyses have only been presented at conferences, not yet having reached the stage of publication.[8] The literature on the methodological approaches used to examine this international stage is nevertheless sparse. Lisa Markowitz (2001) framed this type of field as necessitating a form of *studying up* in reference to Laura Nader (1969).[9] Ellen Hertz (2010) has thoroughly reflected on the notion of 'studying up', its reception within anthropology and perhaps most crucially, what or where exactly this 'up' might be. Based on the case of a meeting within the International Labor Organization, she concluded: 'The aura of height that we associate with international organizations, their institutionalized ethereality, deserves to be taken seriously but not at face value' (2010: 19).

My ethnographic evidence was gathered in part through mingling among old hands and newcomers at WIPO sessions. I was 'studying up', which made me reconsider the suggestion that 'participant observation is a research technique that does not travel well up the social structure' (Gusterson 1997: 115). Instead my experience confirmed the view that participant observation has always been marked by status tensions that arise between the fieldworker and their object of study, regardless of the 'up', 'down' or 'parallel' relation (see Gullestad 2006; Hannerz 2006). Above all, it is important to consider the method of 'fieldwork' in its entirety and expand its core component of participant observation to include the spectrum of research settings that late modernity affords, and within which 'up' and 'down' as potential socio-spatial relations between fieldworker and field no longer suffice. The attempt to understand the workings of international organisations in particular ultimately requires research tools able to determine the interconnectedness of actors in all directions. Vered Amit noted how difficult it often is for anthropologists to accept the extension of their method to new fields. She attributed this to the fact that the discipline derives a good deal of its legitimacy from the methodology of fieldwork (2000: 5; cf. also Schmidt-Lauber 2009). Similarly, actors at international institutions achieve legitimacy for the group they represent by 'being there' – communicating directly via Twitter or blogs. During participant observation in 2006, I noted two middle-aged Andean non-governmental organisation (NGO) representatives taking photos of each other within the setting to be presented at home.

An international negotiation thus represents an opportunity for what one might term an inverse multi-sited ethnography. George Marcus (1995) outlined the methodological need to follow dispersed communities in his much cited 'Ethnography in/of the world system' as an emergent, multi-sited approach. Gisela Welz, building on Marcus's work and the terminology from Carol Breckenridge and Arjun Appadurai's (1996: 50–52) 'cosmopolitan ethnography', spoke of 'moving targets'. Politically occasioned diasporas, labour migration and corporate networks are constellations that suggest a spatially and increasingly digitally mobile ethnographer. But how do such multi-sited studies differ in terms of fieldwork from the type of spatially localised but highly heterogeneous setting that one works in within an international institution? And how useful are such studies for reconceptualising 'participant observation' – a method which, among other things, serves to make visible all that is self-understood and nearly invisible, an approach that gains insight through the distance between observer and observed (Hauser-Schäublin 2003: 37)? Exemplary multi-sited work (e.g. Briggs and Mantini-Briggs 2003; Ribeiro 1995) still works with intensive social relationships which are built into a necessarily fragmented field. There is far less opportunity to reflect on self and other than is the case in classic, stationary fieldwork and, as those observed are in motion themselves, one gets to observe their habits only in fragments as well. There are, however, certain aspects that are constant, as Sarah Strauss, in a study of quite different nature, argued: one can follow the practice, 'as it is realized by people, in books and pamphlets, in motion pictures and tv' (2000: 181). The linkages Marcus thought of can thus be followed in all their 'glocalized' (Marcus 1995) ramifications, nonetheless leading to transnational practice. In following networks of people, practices and ideas, one will find that the localised sense of the self-evident makes way for new practices and habits within interwoven networks.

Seeking to re-theorise 'the field' for anthropology in the mid 1990s, Akhil Gupta and James Ferguson (1997: 35) argued that spatial sites were giving way to political locations. International institutions, especially in their concretised form during negotiations, are of course a highly political location, yet simultaneously they are also spatially manifest. Indeed, the UN and its many subsidiary branches have put great care into the construction of often quite spectacular buildings and symbol-laden meeting rooms. It is hard to imagine a 'thicker' field, when one adds to this material dimension the latent and manifest 'knowledges'[10] brought to negotiations by participants from all over the world, and the communicative connections into the variegated worlds that participants represent. The challenge, then, is to narrow the scope so as to make it possible to carry out meaningful research within such a setting. Before turning to the concrete fieldwork experience at WIPO's IGC and the further reflections on fieldwork resulting from it, I will introduce the IGC.

WIPO's IGC AS A CASE IN POINT FOR THE ETHNOGRAPHY OF INTERNATIONAL ORGANISATIONS

Too many idealists, too many cynics, too little awareness, too much incompetence: this is how Justin Hughes, then head of the United States Delegation to the WIPO, summed up the reasons why an intergovernmental WIPO committee broadly concerned with cultural property rights has made little appreciable progress in ten years of work.[11] Experts in international law would characterise the proceedings of this working body less harshly. They would tend to agree, however, that, even given the customary slow pace of international negotiating, the IGC is exceptional in its minimal progress. There are good economic reasons for minimal results in this case of international rapprochement (Lankau et al. 2010). But a further reason for it is very likely also the complexity of the topic of negotiation, that does not readily fit under the usual, already complex categories of intellectual property (also known as IP).

WIPO became a sub-organisation of the UN with its headquarters in Geneva in 1974. Conventions to protect intellectual property rights have their beginnings in 1886, with the Berne Convention for the Protection of Literary and Artistic Work (copyright) and the 1883 Paris Convention for the Protection of Industrial Property (patents). WIPO was founded in 1970, initially having a mandate from its predecessor organisation (the United International Bureau for the Protection of International Property) to promote the protection of intellectual property rights. With their incorporation into the UN, the mandate grew to include the promotion of economic development. The World Trade Organization (WTO) is focused on the regulation of trade between participating countries. These are just two of the arenas where actors concerned with matters touching on property rights for culture may become active. Another is, for instance, the Convention on Biological Diversity (CBD), where issues relating to indigeneity and traditional knowledge are also pursued.

WIPO thus broadly serves as a framework within which *rights to knowledge* – which has become subject to ownership – can be negotiated. Christopher May summarises the principles involved in the two of the most well-known types of intellectual property rights: copyright and patents: 'Intellectual Property Rights express the legal benefits of ownership, most importantly: the ability to charge rent for use; to receive compensation for loss; and to gather payment for transfer' (2007:4). The difference between patents and copyrights are certainly relevant for the realm of traditional cultural expressions and traditional knowledge, as patents protect an idea and copyright protects the expression of an idea:

> Although this simple distinction has become increasingly difficult to draw for a law of intellectual property, the balance between private rewards and the public interest in having relatively unrestricted access to knowledge and/or information has generally been traditionally expressed through time limits on Intellectual Property Rights, which is to say unlike material property, Intellectual Property Rights are formally only temporary rights. Once their time has expired, the knowledge enters the public realm of freely available material that can be used without authorisation by, or payment to, an owner. (May 2007: 4–5)

For students of culture there might be an immediate paradox in finding rights to aspects of culture such as traditional knowledge or cultural expressions negotiated under the auspices of intellectual property rights: cultural processes are communal and shared and the artefacts emerging from them are at least in part owed to such communal tradition and dynamic (Noyes 2006). For intellectual property lawyers the issue also harbours its paradoxes: patent and copyright laws were established to encourage individuals to invent and to create. In granting benefits for such creativity, the market of ideas was to be stimulated – which has had a sizeable economic impact. Yet with cultural property, one mostly faces 'knowledge' or 'ideas' that already exist, and whose communal owners or carriers demand for it to be protected against individuals or corporations seeking to appropriate it under intellectual property rights terms, without sharing the benefits with the original owners.

Two major motors can be identified behind such international cultural property negotiations: developing nations that recognise within culture a resource attractive to industrialised states, and minority groups across the globe who understand cultural property rights also as a tool to redress their position in relation to a state's majority culture. In this regard, WIPO's description of the issues is likely already problematic in the eyes of some: 'Traditional knowledge (TK), genetic resources (GRs) and traditional cultural expressions (TCEs, or "expressions of folklore") are economic and cultural assets of indigenous and local communities *and their countries*' (emphasis added).[12] There are further factors adding fuel to this discussion, such as global colonial and postcolonial histories, and the illicit traffic in culture. A more fundamental issue still is the mimetic nature of humans: we copy cultural facets from our neighbours both present and past (Cantwell 1993). The very faculty to imitate is at the basis of human creativity and regulation has unforeseeable consequences.

WIPO's General Assembly established the IGC in 2000 with the mandate to undertake 'text-based negotiations with the objective of reaching agreement on a text of an international legal instrument (or instruments) which will ensure the effective protection of traditional knowledge (also known as TK), traditional cultural expressions /folklore and genetic resources.'[13] The point of departure was predominantly in the realm of biotechnology and increased awareness of what has been termed 'biopiracy' on the part of the pharmacological industries, which has also increasingly drawn the attention of concerned cultural anthropologists (e.g. Hayden 1998, 2003). Matters concerning the interrelationship of biological resources and traditional knowledge had come into WIPO's view during the late 1990s with regard to intellectual property and genetic resources under the more general heading of biological diversity and biotechnology. During the same time span, WIPO had also undertaken fact-finding missions on innovations and creativity with regard to traditional knowledge, as the question of considering new beneficiaries, 'including the holders of indigenous knowledge and innovations' came into view (WIPO Secretariat 2000: 2). The linkage to indigenous plant and healing knowledge and questions of intellectual property in the realm of genetic resources is obvious, but traditional knowledges span, of course, into other areas of life as well and can be of relevance to other industries with interest in developing and patenting new products. Work on the third element, 'expressions of folklore', later called 'traditional cultural expressions', goes back to 1978 when WIPO jointly with UNESCO began to draft 'Model Provisions for National Laws on the Protection of Expressions of Folklore Against Illicit Exploitation and Other Prejudicial Actions', which were adopted in 1982; regional consultations in the area of folklore followed. These parallel and yet intertwined endeavours led, ultimately, to the proposal and establishment of the IGC for genetic resources, traditional knowledge and traditional cultural expressions(WIPO Secretariat 2000: 2–3).

Twice a year, the IGC assembles more than 300 delegates. A great deal of IGC negotiation time has gone into defining the terms 'traditional knowledge' and 'traditional cultural expression' (also known as TCE) and countless WIPO documents attest to this effort.

Yet, to paraphrase Justin Hughes again: it appears somewhat absurd to have government officials try to define, for instance, traditional cultural expressions, when folklorists and anthropologists have said for decades that they cannot be properly defined.[14] This does not, however, keep national delegates, consulting experts and participating observers from contributing ever new shades, expansions and refinements to the terms. Some delegates want to make sure that a special form of expressive behaviour practised only in their country be included, others insist on marking differences between public and secret aspects of folklore, yet others strive for generalisations satisfactory to all.

In October 2011, the WIPO General Assembly renewed the IGC's mandate for another two years, in order for them to undertake 'text-based negotiations with the objective of reaching agreement on a text of an international legal instrument (or instruments) which will ensure the effective protection of traditional knowledge (TK), traditional cultural expressions (TCEs)/folklore and genetic resources.'[15]

Since summer 2010, additional intercessional meetings were added to speed up the drafting of documents. The IGC was not held to any specific procedural rules other than those established for WIPO work in general, and anyone who ploughs their way through the documents generated in preparation for and in summation of IGC sessions will note that a great deal of time was spent in an effort to clarify procedure. Again, this may be connected with the matter to be negotiated, because genetic resources, traditional knowledge and traditional cultural expressions attract an unusually wide array of participants, and the WIPO leadership has made it clear that this breadth and the voices thus represented are important – even though in the end it is still just the national delegates who will be able to vote. As with other WIPO committees, WIPO facilitates, in addition to member states' delegates, and 'in conformity with the budgetary allocations . . . the participation of representatives of developing countries and certain countries of Europe and Asia' (WIPO Secretariat 2000: 4). Representatives of relevant intergovernmental organisations, as well as accredited international and regional NGOs, are invited in an observing capacity. The concerns of this IGC have resulted in an unusually high participation precisely of such groups, including representatives of indigenous organisations; thus a voluntary fund was established in 2006, to support travel and lodging.

While international organisations are of interest to anthropology and related fields as a matter of course, IGC meetings are perhaps of particular disciplinary relevance. Cultural research has assisted in the conceptualisation and valuation of cultural excerpts – through ethnographic description, collection and exhibition – and thus contributed to the double resource nature of culture: traditional knowledge and traditional cultural expressions figure as both economic and identity resources, with actors claiming one or both, depending on what is at stake. Valdimar Hafstein, among others, has led the way into this realm with his dissertation on the negotiation of the intangible cultural heritage convention in UNESCO (Hafstein 2004, 2009). Cultural expressions, and to a lesser extent excerpts of cultural knowledge, have been turned into commodities for a long time, but the IGC also represented to me a juncture where this process was rendered visible and should – as a cultural practice in and of itself – receive ethnographic treatment. In the course of research, it became apparent that little happened with regard to arriving at mutually agreeable cultural property regulation. Yet the few things that happened stretched over many days, which allows for ethnographic introspection useful for understanding the particulars of this particular location. In what follows, I draw from field notes to reflect the nature of the setting on a sample negotiation day, before turning to methodological reflections.

WHAT HAPPENS AT THE IGC: EXCERPTS FROM A SAMPLE DAY

The meeting begins with various formal steps – the election of officers, adopting the agenda, adopting the report of the ninth session, and accrediting of organisations requesting observer status. Then all the delegations who wish to do so read out opening statements. Headsets are prepared at every seat, so that the simultaneous translations of these seemingly innocuous greetings can be understood in a selection of world languages. It is rare for an opening intervention to put forth unveiled interests and preferred outcomes; those who opt to speak are generally sufficiently familiar with UN-protocol and associated habits of speech to package in code the posture their government or organisation has instructed them to take. On this day, the better part of the morning, after beginning a good half hour later than announced, is taken up by a selection of presentations by indigenous groups and communities about their work and concerns. An Andean community organisation pleads for maintaining community integrity, demands that legislation develops based on customary law and sees prior informed consent as a crucial foundation for cultural property trade; a person representing Crimean Tatars from the Ukraine demands that groups ought to have a chance to register as indigenous; and a Bangladeshi delegate enthusiastically shows a PowerPoint presentation of an ongoing project registering all traditional cultural expressions and evaluating their potential economic worth. Though different in temperament, all of these speakers have adopted vocabulary that in differential ways stresses legal, economic and ethical facets entailed in the IGC's task. I later learn that the Indigenous Caucus offers introductory sessions for newcomers to the IGC, precisely to familiarise them with the language, the issues discussed so far, and the options open to present their concerns.

During a break, I chat with a young Japanese representative who asks me whether I think that these negotiations are really only about the protection of indigenous cultural rights or whether what is at stake is 'all'. What he means by 'all' becomes evident when, during a later intervention, he voices Japan's opposition against a rights-based approach because 'this may restrict the enriching of national culture'. He points to the long and global history of intercultural borrowing and, only half jokingly, states 'if China retroactively withdrew rights to borrow, much of Japanese culture would be inaccessible'.

The session proper opens in the afternoon. The Indonesian Ambassador I Gusti Agung Wesaka Puja presides and every so often makes an effort to speed up the dragging proceedings. Yet on this day few spontaneous exchanges erupt. During coffee breaks, bigger and smaller groups take shape. People talk rather more intensively than is feasible in the meeting proper, for in the meeting room, seats are facing forward toward the window front and the dais on which the chair and the WIPO secretaries assisting him are seated. Nations are placed in alphabetical order – hence the United States find themselves between Uruguay and the United Republic of Tanzania, France sits with Fiji, Finland, Gabon and Gambia, and China is flanked by Chile and Colombia. The WIPO secretary tells me that efforts are made not to have inimical nations seated next to one another. Delegates can use these name plates as 'flags' to announce their intention to speak by placing the sign vertically, though some delegates also raise their hand. Various seats remain empty, as delegates disappear to take part in a special meeting, for instance of Group B, which is another name for the industrialised nations, of the Indigenous Caucus, the African or the Asian Group or perhaps the Group of Island Nations.

Every so often, a member of the secretariat walks through the rows and collects USB sticks in order to download the wording of the opening statements – later they will be worked into the documentation of this session and made digitally available. Indeed, as a researcher I find that a number of delegates, in particular those with observer status, are more than willing to share their statements with me in the same fashion when I ask for them. There is little curiosity over what a researcher would be doing at this meeting, some of these backbenchers representing observing organisations are researchers themselves, unlike the members of national delegations, who are far more often trained in law and/or economics. I can ask questions about the work of my seat neighbours and will do so more as time progresses, though absorbing the setting and the levels of communication is ethnographically taxing – formal and oral, via microphone and via headphones in interpretation, informal and oral, via email or chat function between delegates seated far apart but in the same interest groups, and via reams of printed-out papers.

Once the opening statements conclude, the actual agenda items are tackled. The documents generated during previous IGCs have been available for commentary, so as to make progress toward shaping documents that find common agreement. As the discussion of the agenda item 8 'Traditional Cultural Expressions/ Folklore' begins, it becomes palpable that we will not get beyond reiterations of the commentaries as well as commentaries on others' commentaries within the circulated documents: the Columbian delegate argues for a binding instrument and refers to a circulated proposal. He would like an international definition of terms and while he calls for moral rights and penal terms, he also sees the need for competent, scientific registers in order to be able to determine whether something has been abused. He voices positive acceptance of Norway's statement on disclosure of patent matters. The USA are called and cede to China; the Chinese delegate notes her country's passage of an intangible heritage and cultural copyright law; she seeks clarification on the term 'misappropriation', as well as its scope. For China, it is impossible to judge the value of folklore, hence value should not be a precondition. Now the USA calls for an elaboration and *refinement of the draft which will deepen the understanding of the members of the IGC. The chair, seemingly ironic, thanks the USA for their noble commitment. And so the afternoon continues.*

During this particular day, a Japanese delegate finally exclaims that content and definition of the core terms under negotiation are still amiss: 'We lack common understanding – hence it is premature to talk about legally binding principles.'[16]

ASSETS AND OPPORTUNITIES IN FIELDWORK AT INTERNATIONAL ORGANISATIONS

Deceleration

This Japanese intervention encapsulates what is at issue in most, if not all, international negotiations. There is no shared language, no shared cultural background and thus also no shared communicative norm beyond what some – but not all – delegates have acquired during a career of working within such international settings and what, in the course of a given committee, is built as a shared frame of reference in the course of years, or sometimes even decades. Substantive negotiations thus always necessitate procedural negotiations, that is, work on what Foucault called the conduct of conduct (1994: 237). This results in sluggish proceedings, that drag on almost unbearably, decidedly worse than what one is familiar with from national parliaments. Within a national governing body, there is room for outspoken, even aggressive posturing, depending on a given state's internal political tradition. The foundation for the type of international negotiation unfolding here, however, is based on verbal demonstrations of respect and politeness, precisely because there is insufficient knowledge of one another's customary boundaries of verbal argument.[17]

The negotiating and renegotiating of the IGC's procedural framework appears endless and delegates from some states take the opportunity to return to procedure whenever progress toward the actual issues at stake seems too fast to them. Even four years later, in 2010, when the IGC has made progress to actual text-based negotiation, there are time and again instances where delegates manage to stall proceedings, insisting on minute changes in formulation which can result in drastic changes in impact – such as a change from 'should' to 'could' – and which thus again gives rise to lengthy debate.[18]

As an ethnographer, I experience this 'discovery of slowness'[19] as an asset for fieldwork in and with international organisations on two levels. First, on the level of fieldwork, slowness allows the ethnographer an incremental enculturation into the setting and its mechanisms. In tandem with the neophyte international diplomat or NGO representative whose agency the ethnographer is documenting and trying to understand, she or he acquires insight into proper negotiation habits, learns to decode communicative styles and uncovers the levels of competence and influence held by different categories of delegates, WIPO personnel and interpreters.[20] Second, on the analytic level, much as in Sten Nadolny's novel of the same title, the main protagonist's seemingly disabling characteristic – a disposition to slowness of thought and action – turns into a powerful asset. He who is slow and can afford to wait ultimately wins over those who are in a hurry. Negotiators on the international stage similarly win when refraining from rash actions; success is measured in years or even decades, not days. Obedience to this tactic could be witnessed time and again during the opening days of the IGC and the digital protocol made available for each session. Every delegation had the opportunity to offer a formal greeting to the chair, and, while some delegations used this segment to formulate what they hoped to see accomplished during the meetings, others – particularly representatives of the industrial states favouring little or no cultural property protection – nonetheless engaged in lengthy greetings. The chair of the December 2010 ICG meeting – himself part of the African group – decided to cut the greetings so as to gain more time for actual negotiating.[21]

The practices and dynamics of international negotiation follow basic ground rules. Years of working with a specific topic of negotiation, and stable personages involved, contribute specificity to the nature of oral exchanges and shape the look of written documentation. Laying open this specificity and its variations, in turn, is what ethnography can add to the understanding of negotiation dynamics and of international organisations. There is a vast literature on national and international negotiation practices,[22] yet ethnography is uniquely positioned to lay bare the experiential dimension within such settings, which, in turn, has a considerable impact on how decisions are (or are not) arrived at. The slowness of progress would appear to be in favour of the ethnographer who seeks to understand agency on the global stage. With the decelerated tempo and the co-presence of so many 'worlds' within one room, international institutions may be a site that ideally answers the concerns Arjun Appadurai has voiced with regard to fieldwork in the era of globalisation: 'For the human sciences, the main threat posed by the discourse of globalization is the possibility of phenomena too large, *too quick*, too all-encompassing to succumb to our gaze' (1997:115, my emphasis).

Multiple Contexts and Knowledges Assembled in One Site

What else can be gained from the stationary study of what can only be partial aspects of an international centre, where far-flung networks flow together? I would strongly argue in favour of complementing the multi-sited tracing of networks with the intensive analysis of the situated practice within an international meeting – an event which, in gentle allusion to Clifford Geertz, might be termed a 'thick site'. While these sites may indeed appear less than transparent during fieldwork itself, they remain of an essentially loose texture, in part in response to the fact that the actors involved fluctuate constantly.[23] Focusing on the communicative possibilities and practices allows one to trace the influences of various networks as they seek to influence what is happening in this room. William Fisher (1997: 459), calling for innovative methods to deal with the culture of NGOs, also argued that studying the 'chaotic, public spectacle' of international meetings and conferences is essential for understanding how the strands of networks actually operate. Initial work of this nature has been done by Hafstein (2004). Sally Merry has called for the same in the arena of conventions in the realm of international law (2006: 108–9). She points to the ethical issues that arise from the involvement of the researcher.

It may appear superficial to attempt to treat as one field all the converging fields within one Geneva conference room. Certainly, individual actors will not draw on all contexts of their lives back home during their stay. Yet cognitively, delegates do bring many sites from all over the globe with them to the Geneva conference room that is anchored in space and time. While maintaining communicative contact with those whom they represent, these heterogeneous actors create a face-to-face community during the week of the meeting. This meeting, in turn, achieves concreteness in its printed and digital distribution, and accumulates weighty historicity over time – the amount of paper generated by the IGC in more than a decade of work would be staggering, if one bothered to print it out. Thus, while participants arrive with divergent backgrounds and specific concerns in their baggage, they depart with the perspectives and practices as well as with draft papers generated during the meeting. These, in turn, will have an effect within their networks at home.

This is, indeed, the considerable effect of what the very slow process of the IGC appears to have: what is discussed over and over in draft form within IGC meetings is brought back into far-flung settings. For instance, efforts to register traditional cultural expressions and traditional knowledge have sprung up from Australia to India, in preparation for new legal norms that may be implemented. These are already permitting some stakeholders to assert ownership claims over their traditional cultural expressions – now circumscribed via registration – and thus threaten potential 'borrowers' (from creative and health industries, for example) with lawsuits. In the process of registering, such practices are also 'marked', much as are, for instance, intangible practices listed by UNESCO – a crucial component in the further reification of habitual cultural practices which requires scholarly attention (e.g. Hafstein 2009). The analyses of legal gaps prepared for the IGC, available online on the WIPO site, as much as publications by scholars such as Silke von Lewinski, who have themselves served as national delegates at the IGC (Lewinski 2004), offer information to constituencies far from Geneva. Information is surely the most powerful weapon for those seeking to understand what is at stake. Why some countries push for cultural property legislation and others have an equal, if not bigger, interest in forestalling it.

'It's Communication'[24]

To overcome all that they do not share, ICG delegates have to speak and listen, write and gesture. Communication is the major skill required in international negotiation, and in our group's work in Geneva, we have relied on the *ethnography of speaking* as developed by Dell Hymes, as a framework for approaching the IGC's meetings, within which terms such as 'speech community' and Hymes' model of *framing* and *analysing* the 'speech event' are central and easily captured in the mnemonic device SPEAKING: setting and scene, participants, ends or the purpose and outcome of the event, the act sequence, instrumentalities such as forms and style of speech, the norms of interpretation established within the group and the genre of the speech event (Hymes 1974). Keeping these parameters in mind, the IGC (or any other negotiation round) can be grasped as a time-bound speech event co-created by a heterogeneous and porous speech community. It is possible to follow the enculturation of individual delegates into the workings of international negotiating not least, as indicated, alongside one's own communicative enculturation as participant observer.

Most actors arriving at the IGC are generally equipped with the same tools to participate in this speech community: a briefcase containing either only stacks of documents or also a laptop, the inevitable USB stick holding relevant interventions, and a headset built into the seat. The secretaries and other WIPO employees provide constancy to the proceedings, as they to an extent 'traditionalize' the communicative rules, particularly through the documents that they prepare and circulate. They also have to be open to requests for change, not least as the chair of the meeting changes with every second meeting.

An ethnographic documentation of such a speech event demands a close focus on different types of speaking, and the weight each is given. In this particular context, opening interventions are given much time and rhetorical flourish but little weight, final interventions cut to the point, and depart from culturally patterned rhetoric toward a far harsher common language. Indeed, in IGC meetings in 2008 and 2009 (not least due to the problematic chairing style of a newly elected chair) the final day and a half of the meeting saw a heating up of conflicting procedural requests to the point where there was not even a formal closure. Conversely, the meeting in December 2010 was unusually harmonious, guided by a chair who took time to consult with special interest groups and gave them in turn time to work separately, so that on the last day a high-powered national delegate shared cookies from one of the more expensive Geneva *patissiers* with members not necessarily within his interest group. During the closing plenary, leave-taking interventions of an unusually personal and personable nature were offered. Negotiating as a cultural practice in principle unfolds in a great many cultural varieties, and yet it is clear that there is a UN repertoire of possibilities of speaking and negotiating to which participants have to adapt. The IGC is a particularly liberal forum that allows representatives of all kinds of observing organisations and communities to speak, but even the utterances of those delegations adapt within a very short time to that which is proper for this time and place.

The setting demands of all those present not only multi-linguality but also dexterity in handling spoken, written and digital communication. The multilinguality is further enhanced by simultaneous translation, which is, at the same time, also a constitutive component of the negotiation ambience. The fact that translators are called interpreters in this setting is a telling, semantic nuance,[25] and numerous participants that we interviewed reflect cogently on language use, speech acts and interpretive acts. This dimension of international negotiation is from my point of view a highly fruitful area of further work – including analysis of the considerable body of rules as well as secondary literature in international law on matters of translation and interpretation. During the IGC meeting in December 2010, for instance, I noted the following in my field diary during a separate meeting aiming to narrow and sharpen a set of future work tasks:

> Observing the English interpreter, I am amused at her handling of 'speaking for the chair'.[26] She quite frequently weaves into her interpretation a 'says the chair', perhaps to simply clarify in the mêlée of voices that it is not her opinion or some other delegate's intervention but rather the opinion of vice chair of the IGC meeting and chair of this editing meeting. But her lively gestures and emphatic intonation also make a fairly clumsy if not incompetent chair sound even more so, as his speech is monotonous, showing little inflection or engagement but rather a kind of forced 'keeping to a task' that exceeded his diplomatic skills.[27]

Interpreters generally sit in cabins, behind glass, and are not always visible, but Room B at WIPO permits for a simultaneous view of interacting delegates and interpreters, and thus it is possible to grasp the plight as well as agency of interpreters who have available a very limited number of pre-circulated statements. During sessions devoted to editing documents – which the WIPO IGC has been holding increasingly in the course of the last two years – interpreters need to competently translate delegate interventions, chair comments and decisions, and written documents that are being edited by a select group or – as has occurred with increasing frequency – the entire IGC assembly. The interpreters' booths, much like the press box in some other such settings, would, correspondingly, constitute an excellent field position, though interpreters themselves tend to downplay or not acknowledge their role in the negotiation process at all – not least as their professional ethos demands absolute neutrality.[28]

Participants, however, do not appear 'lost in translation' but rather register complaints in every session, as documents are not translated into all languages (though over the years of our observing, the numbers of languages offered has increased). Translation is also an integral part of the transcription and thus the fixation of negotiation processes and results. While the simultaneous translation is usually offered in six languages, IGC documents were initially published online in English, French and Spanish only; at present the number has increased to six, and now includes Arabic, Chinese and Russian. The earlier practice is reflective of a postcolonial pragmatism that assumes most of the world to be competent in at least one of these languages, colonisation by England, France, and Spain respectively having resulted in them becoming second or official languages in many modern nation states. But interventions by delegates show how short-sighted this assumption is. Complaints regarding the extra expenses that accrue to those countries, due to additional translation work involved in preparing for the sessions, is regularly voiced. Simultaneous interpretation is offered for most of the day, but during the most animated discussions of the meeting (generally in the evenings) the interpretation gets sparser, as the contracts of the interpreters cover a limited set of hours.

One of the components in Hymes' scheme – the shared norms of interpretation – can be considered nearly absent in an international negotiation: they are, ultimately, what a negotiation round is struggling to achieve. Once shared norms have been arrived at, a finished document could be approved and offered to the WIPO General Assembly, which in turn would then hopefully recommend it to its member states for adoption. The delegates of the IGC continue to produce texts that exceed the length for a diplomatically acceptable document. This points once again to what I described early on in this chapter: reaching agreement over cultural property rights attains a level of complexity that will likely stymie progress for years to come.

Spatial Intimacy

The communicative strands of an IGC meeting are fluid and, despite certain sets of parameters, their outcome cannot be foreseen. This is in strong contrast to the materiality and permanent Gestalt of the WIPO building in Geneva. The glass structure, visible from afar, and the interior design and decor leave their mark on the 'habitus' of the participants, as they experience it with both the senses and the mind. The material dimension and the symbolic significance of artwork, colours, and overall design is a further productive dimension for understanding the subtle, and not so subtle, ways in which participants from all over the world are accommodated into this setting. Gaining entry into the building and finding one's predetermined seat either at a comfortable desk or among the crowded backbenches (in the case of observing NGOs) key participants into the nature of the setting. Participants learn which floors and offices are open to them and how to make use of the space. In the same building are other WIPO committees and the building complex itself is located in the vicinity of offices or even headquarters of other international organisations.

Geneva is a rather small city in comparison to metropolises hosting UN headquarters and subsidiary institutions such as Paris or New York. Yet even in those cities, delegates will quickly come to know which hotels and guesthouses are chosen by what delegations, and in which sites located outside of the WIPO building interest groups prepare their joint positions. Global aspirations and disparities will map themselves onto a relatively small part of a city. Encounters on – in Geneva's case – scenic trams with other delegates will render the city into a space within which one views the world through the goals and communicative bubble co-created at the IGC.[29]

The large WIPO meeting rooms turn into a spatially intimate setting due to the structured work of communication. This also contributes to the weakening of the status groups within an IGC meeting. There are, of course, some age differences and an ethnographer will quickly be able to recognise whether a delegate is as new to the setting as herself. The dress code is business-like for men and women, and is only rarely broken by delegates choosing native dress. There develops a short-term familiarity over the course of a meeting that cuts across status groups, forged by setting, task and the democratic if western-patterned nature of the proceedings. Some NGO observers and indigenous community representatives have achieved seniority in terms of the longevity of their commitment vis-à-vis some of the young, one-time national delegates. The representative of the Tulalip Tribes of Washington State, for instance, has been present since the IGC took up its work and has a correspondingly long institutional memory. Nation states, by contrast, often staff their IGC delegations with younger lawyers, as they apparently regard the IGC as a training ground where diplomatic neophytes can be familiarised with the formalities and communicative style of international negotiations.

CONCLUSION

Language and speech are the essence of negotiation; it seems thus more than sensible to make communicative practice a centre-piece of research. The communicative and material space establish a field, as I have illustrated, permitting types of ethnographic work that contribute significantly to an understanding of how international organisations work. Decision-making at this level is slow, but the dynamic behind this slowness is fierce. It bundles not only the variety of human agency present within the site, but also the will and agency of all those fields present and presented through the delegates. I have suggested an ethnographic approach to this setting with a focus on temporal, communicative and spatial modalities, as well as on the 'thickness' of contexts echoing within this one site. This promises data especially for developing an understanding of international management and administration. The term 'regime' has acquired much popularity in recent anthropological writing. It is closely linked to the realisation that governance styles bring forth international and global transformations, implemented by regimes and thus shaping networked life in late modernity. Conclaves such as those of the WIPO IGC meetings provide a localised field research opportunity within which the formation of such regimes can be documented in an emergent and flexible committee culture. Certainly this cannot be the only site where it is possible to study the unfolding of international governance, but it is one that is suited to the tools of ethnography, particularly the ethnography of communication and linguistic anthropology more generally. The IGC is indeed a highly heterogeneous field in its composition and countless other potential fields come together there. However, from the Geneva centre it then diffuses along multiple networks decision-making patterns that leave their mark on the many fields represented here.

ACKNOWLEDGEMENTS

Many thanks go to Birgit Müller for inviting me to participate in this volume and my appreciations to the anonymous reviewers who offered keen and helpful critiques for both the French and this English version. The research on which this chapter builds was funded by the *Deutsche Forschungsgemeinschaft* as part of the research group DFG FOR 772 'The Constitution of Cultural Property', funded for 2008–14. Our website gives information on the goals of this endeavour (see: http://cultural-property.uni-goettingen.de/?lang=en). WIPO was one of the first areas within which we pursued our research questions, though there are also others (see Bendix et al. 2010). A preliminary version of the present chapter was presented at the American Anthropological Meetings 2009 in Philadelphia, and incipient results have also been discussed with members of the Göttingen Center for Modern Humanities (ZTMK). The chapter expands on an initial publication in German (Bendix 2009) and is based on my own fieldwork in Geneva in December 2006 and 2010, as well as on productive discussions with Stefan Groth, who has completed longer periods of fieldwork in Geneva at WIPO as part of the Göttingen research team (Groth 2010a, 2010b, 2012).

NOTES

1. All materials are available at: http://www.wipo.int/tk/en/igc/ (consulted 24 August 2012).
2. Some of the fieldwork in Geneva was carried out by several members from our research team who come from different disciplines. The present chapter will not further elaborate on the advantages and complications of interdisciplinary field research; first reflections on interdisciplinarity as it has unfolded in our group can be found in Bendix and Bizer (2011).
3. Mosse's (2011: 63–65) reflection on the social convergence of expert and anthropologist in the field of development is one of the few contributions in the ethnography of policy considering fieldwork concerns. But even here we receive more information on the problems unfolding with the field once a draft of the resulting study was circulated among those researched.
4. A number of contributors to Gellner and Hirsch's collection (2001) mention the question of access both to an organisation and to individuals circulating within it. The very diversity of organisational formats considered here – from museums to hospitals, civil organisations to laboratories – already multiplies the question of access and accountability. The international organisation setting is, arguably, quite different again due to its continually emergent nature on the backdrop of organisational parameters set by the course of world political history rather than, or at the very least more so, than a specific goal (such as museum exhibition, health care, local political goals or research).
5. Gaining access for our group, as described above, proved uncomplicated, as this particular WIPO IGC is particularly welcoming to observers. This grants only access to the general meeting and the hallways, however. Gaining access to the constituent subgroup meetings is a matter of making contacts and how such contacts view the relevance of a particular subgroup meeting.
6. Riles' superb *The Network Inside Out* (2001) in essence helps us to recognise the production of such hierarchies and linkages. In seeking to lay open the aesthetics of bureaucratic practices through her monograph, her work is already quite a few steps beyond what I seek to make palpable here – the characteristics of entering and being within an international organisation and the nature of participant observation that can result from it.
7. As one of the major researchers in EU settings, Marc Abélès, stated:

> Another central issue is that of linguistic pluralism, and the way that varying the language of negotiation tends to neutralise political debate. Shifting from one official language to another is a constant reminder of the diversity of traditions and histories which have formed the national identities of member countries. (Shore and Abélès 2004:10)

8. Many of the anthropologists working in this field identify themselves as applied anthropologists. The Society for Applied Anthropology's journals have printed articles on related issues, indeed, one could go as far back as papers dealing with 'collective bargaining' in the area of labour negotiation (Garfield and Whyte 1950), though the question of field methodology is not addressed here either. Development anthropology is another subdiscipline where clear ties between the study of international organisations and work within their structures can be identified. Christoph Brumann and Tim Allen organised a European Association of Social Anthropologists (EASA) panel on the 'Anthropology of the United Nations' in 2008; George Marcus and Marc Abélès presented their project 'Collaborative Ethnography Inside the World Trade Organization' in a panel at the annual AAA conference in 2009. Both panels focused on the results of research but not on how the respective data were collected. In other disciplines, such as international relations or sociology, data has been published on the modalities of negotiation and how these have changed, but methodological considerations appear to be lacking here as well.

9. This claim would need to be specified more closely; since the late 1960s, there has been an enormous growth in service sector work located within and contributing to international interconnectedness (Hannerz 2002). Practitioners within these fields may reveal in their habitus remarkable parallels to the corporate and scientific leadership that Nader had in mind when she coined the term, but their power potential differs, and correspondingly the relationship of the fieldworker to such fields will need to adjust.

10. Although it is unusual, I opt to work with 'knowledges' in the plural as a range of knowledge spheres is juggled within international negotiation. The chapter addresses this multiplicity not least because actors within this setting rarely reflect it: there are different bodies of knowledge concerning the nature of negotiation; there is also considerable difference in substantive 'expertise', depending on the disciplinary training of delegates and their status (legal, economic, anthropological, indigenous). Ethnography in this setting should focus on the command of such knowledges and the capacity of actors to make strategic use of them.

11. Justin Hughes, Senior Advisor to the Undersecretary of Commerce for Intellectual Property, Head of United States Delegation to the WIPO, and Professor of Law, Cardozo School of Law, gave the keynote address during the eighth annual 'IP/Gender: Mapping the Connections' symposium at American University's Washington College of Law in Washington, DC, on 1 April 2011. The full conference can be heard as webcast on demand via http://tiny.cc/tco0e (consulted 10 April 2011).

12. See: 'Traditional Knowledge, Genetic Resources...' at: http://www.wipo.int/tk/en/ (consulted 15 March 2011).

13. 'Intergovernmental Committee', at: http://www.wipo.int/tk/en/igc/ (consulted 15 March 2011).

14. There is always a lag between scholarly knowledge production and knowledge transfer to various publics. But in the realm of international negotiations it is particularly painful to witness actors highly trained for instance in law or economics working with concepts of culture that have been deconstructed in ethnographic disciplines since the Second World War.

15. See: 'Intergovernmental Committee' at: http://www.wipo.int/tk/en/igc/ (consulted 5 November 2011).

16. Fieldnotes, IGC Meeting from 30 November to 8 December 2006.
17. For a detailed analysis of the linguistic pragmatics of the IGC, see Groth (2012). In a personal communication, Ellen Hertz – having observed a number of international negotiations herself, noted:

> It would be interesting to analyse the qualities of this particular code comparatively across IOs [international organisations]: there's a kind of neutered 19th century gentleman's diplomatic tone to it that I would have a hard time attributing to any one national style : it's rather something like the way Indian diplomats imagine that American diplomats should talk to Chinese diplomats who are themselves trying to get with the Japanese and Russian diplomatic styles ... (email from 12 June 2012)

18. Groth (2012) calls this tactic 'micro-editing'; we first presented this notion in a joint paper at the EASA meetings 2008 (Bendix and Groth 2008).
19. As in Sten Nadolny's (1983) novel about the historical sea captain John Franklin.
20. Riles' (2001) endeavour is, in part, laying bare the knowledge needed to carry out organisational, bureaucratic and negotiating work; the parallels between 'ethnographer learning' and 'diplomat learning' become then quite obvious and might be utilised more effectively in research in international organisations.
21. Field notes, 17th IGC meeting, 6–10 December 2010; cf. also Groth (2012).
22. Consider works by political practitioners such as Fred Iklé (1968) or Henry Kissinger (1994), which would warrant analysis from an ethnographic perspective, as well as the sizeable body of research in political science, sociology, economics and international relations of both qualitative and quantitative nature, of which, again, but a few titles are noted here with the intention of encouraging anthropologists to consider such bodies of literature in terms of interdisciplinary confrontation and cooperation, e.g. Keohane and Nye (1972), Raustiala (2001), Risse-Kappen (1995), Risse (2000), Spector (1994), Thurner et al. (2000).
23. This constellation of a thick field inhabited by fluctuating actors will need to be considered also with regard to the ethnographic writing resulting from the study of international organisations and governance.
24. In humble reference to Bill Clinton's presidential campaign slogan 'It's the economy, stupid', from 1992.
25. Translation is always a form of interpretation, a fact that scholars of translation studies have long been aware of (Venuti 1995).
26. This in allusion to Yankah (1995).
27. Fieldnotes from the IGC meeting at WIPO, 9 December 2010.
28. Stefan Groth has conducted some interviews with interpreters that confirm this assessment, whereas delegates tend to be more aware of their dependency on these professionals, particularly late in the day when interpreters have gone home.
29. There are of course national representatives who live year-round in such cities, and who are delegates for their state or organisation for different issues in different conference rooms. But many delegates only come for this meeting.

BIBLIOGRAPHY

Abélès, M. (1992) *La Vie quotidienne au Parlement européen* (Paris: Hachette).

Amit, V. (2000) 'Introduction: Constructing the Field', in V. Amit (ed.) *Constructing the Field: Ethnographic Fieldwork in the Contemporary World*, pp. 1–18 (London: Routledge).

Appadurai, A. (1996) *Modernity at Large: Cultural Dimensions of Globalization* (Minneapolis: University of Minnesota Press).

Appadurai, A. (1997) 'Fieldwork in the era of globalization', *Anthropology of Humanism* 22(1): 115–118.

Bendix, R. (2009) 'Wenn viele Felder sich in einem Raum vereinen: Feldforschung in internationalen Gremien', in E. Hermann, K. Klenke and M. Dickhardt (eds) *Form, Macht, Differenz: Motive und Felder ethnographischen Forschens*, pp. 333–346 (Göttingen: Universitätsverlag Göttingen).

Bendix, R. and K. Bizer (2011) 'Verbundförderung für interdisziplinäre Gesellschafts- und Kulturwissenschaften: Eine Kritik', *Cultural Property Policy Papers 3*. Available at: http://cultural-property.uni-goettingen.de/publications/?lang=de (consulted March 2013).

Bendix, R. and S. Groth (2008) 'Ways of speaking at WIPO's Intergovernmental Committee on Cultural Property', paper delivered at the EASA Congress, Ljubljana, 26–29 August.

Bendix, R., K. Bizer and S. Groth (eds) (2010) *Die Konstituierung von Cultural Property: Forschungsperspektiven*. *Göttingen Studies in Cultural Property*, vol. 1 (Göttingen: Universitätsverlag Göttingen).

Briggs, C. and C. Mantini-Briggs (2003) *Stories in the Time of Cholera: Racial Profiling during a Medical Nightmare* (Berkeley, University of California Press).

Cantwell, R. (1993) *Ethnomimensis: Folklife and the Representation of Culture* (Chapel Hill, NC: University of North Carolina Press).

Fisher, W.F. (1997) 'Doing good? The politics and antipolitics of NGO practices', *Annual Review of Anthropology* 26: 439–464.

Foucault, M. (1994) *Dits et écrits IV* (Paris: Gallimard).

Garfield, S. and W.F. Whyte (eds) (1950) The collective bargaining process: A human relations analysis', *Human Organization* 9(2): 5–10.

Gellner, D.N. and E. Hirsch (eds) (2001) *Inside Organizations: Anthropologists at Work* (Oxford: Oxford University Press).

Groth, S. (2010a) 'Traditional knowledge and the politics of difference', *Journal of Ethnology and Folkloristics* 4(1): 7–24.

Groth, S. (2010b) 'Perspektiven der Differenzierung: Multiple Ausdeutungen von traditionellem Wissen indigener Gemeinschaften in WIPO-Verhandlungen', in R. Bendix, K. Bizer and S. Groth (eds) *Die Konstituierung von Cultural Property: Forschungsperspektiven*. *Göttingen Studies in Cultural Property*, vol. 1, pp. 177–195 (Göttingen: Universitätsverlag Göttingen).

Groth, S. (2012) *Negotiating Tradition: The Pragmatics of International Deliberations on Cultural Property*. Göttingen Studies in Cultural Property, vol. 5 (Göttingen: Universitätsverlag Göttingen).

Gullestad, M. (2006) 'Reconfiguring scholarly authority: Reflections based on anthropological studies of Norway', *Current Anthropology* 47(6): 915–932.

Gupta, A. and J. Ferguson (1997) 'Discipline and practice: "The field" as site, method, and location in anthropology', in A. Gupta and J. Ferguson (eds) *Anthropological Locations: Boundaries and Grounds of a Field Science*, pp. 1–46 (Berkeley: University of California Press).

Gusterson, H. (1997) 'Studying up revisited', *PoLAR: Political and Legal Anthropology Review* 20(1): 114–119.

Hafstein, V. (2004) *The Making of Intangible Cultural Heritage: Tradition and Authenticity, Community and Humanity*. PhD dissertation, University of California, Berkeley.

Hafstein, V. (2009) 'Intangible heritage as a list. From masterpiece to representation', in L. Smith and N. Akagawa (eds) *Intangible Heritage*, pp. 93–111 (London, Routledge).

Hannerz, U. (2002) 'Notes on the global ecumene', in J.X. Inda and R. Rosaldo (eds) *The Anthropology of Globalization*, pp. 37–45 (Malden, MA: Blackwell).

Hannerz, U. (2006) 'Studying down, up, sideways, through, backwards, forwards, away and at home: Reflections on the field worries of an expansive discipline', in S. Coleman and P. Collins (eds) *Locating the Field: Space, Place and Context in Anthropology*, pp. 23–41 (Oxford: Berg).

Hauser-Schäublin, B. (2003) 'Teilnehmende Beobachtung', in B. Beer (ed.) *Methoden und Techniken der Feldforschung*, pp. 33–54 (Berlin: Reimer).

Hayden, C. (1998) 'Hybrid knowledges: Mexico's niche in the biodiversity marketplace', in G. Heins et al. (eds) *Politik der Natur: Neue Konflikte um Biologische Ressourcen*, pp. 215–232 (Frankfurt: Leske und Budrich).

Hayden, C. (2003) *When Nature Goes Public: The Making and Unmaking of Bioprospecting in Mexico* (Princeton, NJ: Princeton University Press).

Hertz, E. (2010) 'Excessively up at the International Labour Organization: Notes on "Note on the Proceedings TMITI/2007/10"', Working Paper 9-2010/E, Maison d'Analyse des Processus Sociaux, Neuchatel.

Hymes, D. (1974 *Foundations of Sociolinguistics: An Ethnographic Approach* (Philadelphia, PA: University of Pennsylvania Press).

Iklé, F.C. (1968) *How Nations Negotiate* (New York: Harper and Row).

Keohane, R.O. and J.S. Nye (eds) (1972) *Transnational Relations and World Politics* (Cambridge, MA: Harvard University Press).

Kissinger, H. (1994) *Diplomacy* (New York: Simon and Schuster).

Lankau, M., K. Bizer and Z. Gubaydullina (2010) 'Die verborgene Effektivität minimaler Resultate in internationalen Verhandlungen: Der Fall der WIPO', in R. Bendix, K. Bizer and S. Groth (eds) *Die Konstituierung von Cultural Property: Forschungsperspektiven. Göttingen Studies in Cultural Property*, vol. 1, pp. 197–217 (Göttingen: Universitätsverlag Göttingen).

Lewinski, S. v. (ed.) (2004) *Indigenous Heritage and Intellectual Property: Genetic Resources, Traditional Knowledge and Folklore* (The Hague: Kluwer Law International).

Marcus, G.E. (1995) 'Ethnography in/of the world system: The emergence of multi-sited ethnography', *Annual Review of Anthropology* 24: 95–117.

Markowitz, L. (2001) 'Finding the field: Notes on the ethnography of NGOs', *Human Organization* 60(1). Available at: http://www.sfaa.net/ho/2001/spring2001.html (consulted March 2009).

May, C. (2007) *The World Intellectual Property Organization: Resurgence and the Development Agenda* (New York: Routledge).

Merry, S.E. (2006) 'Anthropology and international law', *Annual Review of Anthropology* 35: 99–116.

Mosse, D. (2011) 'Politics and ethics: Ethnographies of expert knowledge and professional identities', in C. Shore and S. Wright (eds) *Anthropology of Policy: Critical Perspectives on Governance and Power*, pp. 50–67 (London: Routledge).

Nader, L. (1969) 'Up the anthropologist – Perspectives gained from studying up', in D. Hymes (ed.) *Reinventing Anthropology*, pp. 284–311 (New York: Pantheon).

Nadolny, S. (1983) *Die Erfindung der Langsamkeit* (München: Piper).

Noyes, D. (2006) 'The judgement of Solomon: Global protections for tradition and the problem of community ownership', *Cultural Analysis* 5: 27–55. Available at: http://socrates.berkeley.edu/~caforum/volume5/vol5_article2.html (consulted March 2013).

Raustiala, K. (2001) 'Compliance and effectiveness in international regulatory cooperation', *Case Western Reserve Journal of International Law* 32: 453–508.

Ribeiro, G.L. (1995) *Transnational Capitalism and Hydropolitics in Argentina* (Gainesville: University Press of Florida).

Riles, A. (2001) *The Network Inside Out* (Ann Arbor: University of Michigan Press).

Risse, T. (2000) 'Let's Argue', *International Organization* 54: 1–39.

Risse-Kappen, T. (ed.) (1995) *Bringing Transnational Relations Back In: Non-state Actors, Domestic Structures and International Institutions* (Cambridge: Cambridge University Press).

Schmidt-Lauber, B. (2009) 'Profil einer volkskundlich-kulturanthropologischen Empirie: Zum (Zu)Stand der Feldforschung im Fach', in S. Windmüller, B. Binder Windmüller, and T. Hengartner (eds) *Kultur – Forschung. Zum Profil einer volkskundlichen Kulturwissenschaft* (Münster: Lit-Verlag).

Shore, C. (2000) *Building Europe: The Cultural Politics of European Integration* (London: Routledge).

Shore, C. (2005) 'Culture and corruption in the EU: Reflections on fraud, nepotism and cronyism in the European Commission', in D. Haller and C. Shore (eds) *Corruption: Anthropological Perspective*, pp. 131–155 (London: Pluto).

Shore, C. and M. Abélès (2004) 'Debating the European Union: An interview with Cris Shore and Marc Abélès', *Anthropology Today* 29(2): 10–14.

Shore, C. and S. Wright (1997) *Anthropology of Policy: Critical Perspectives on Governance and Power* (London: Routledge).

Shore, C., S. Wright and D. Però (eds) (2011) *Policy Worlds: Anthropology and the Analysis of Contemporary Power*. EASA Series vol. 14 (Oxford: Berghahn).

Spector, B.I. (ed.) (1994) *Negotiating International Regimes: Lessons Learned from the United Nations Conference on Environment and Development (UNCED)* (London: Graham and Trotman).

Strauss, S. (2000) 'Locating yoga: Ethnography and transnational practice', in V. Amid (ed.) *Constructing the Field*, pp. 162–194 (London: Routledge).

Thurner, P.W. et al. (2000) 'EU intergovernmental conferences: A quantitative analytical reconstruction and data-handbook of domestic preference formation, transnational networks, and dynamics of compromise during the Amsterdam Treaty negotiations', Arbeitspapiere – Mannheimer Zentrum für Europäische Sozialforschung Nr.60, Mannheim. Available at: http://www.mzes.uni-mannheim. de/publications/wp/wp-60.pdf (consulted November 2012).

Venuti, L. (1995) *The Translator's Invisibility: A History of Translation* (London: Routledge).

Welz, G. (1998) 'Moving targets: Feldforschung unter Mobilitätsdruck', *Zeitschrift für Volkskunde* 94: 177–194.

WIPO Secretariat (2000) 'Matters concerning intellectual property and genetic resources, traditional knowledge and folklore', Document WO/GA/26/6. Available at 'Matters concerning intellectual property and ...': http://www.wipo.int/ meetings/en/doc_details.jsp?doc_id=1460 (consulted 15 March 2011).

Yankah, K. (1995) *Speaking for the Chief: Okyeame and the Politics of Akan Royal Oratory* (Bloomington, IN: Indiana University Press).

3

The Making of Global Consensus

Constructing Norms on Refugee Protection at UNHCR

Marion Fresia[1]

Since the end of the Second World War, the United Nations (UN) and other international agencies have come to play an increasing role in defining global problems as well as the global policies, modes of governance and normative frameworks that should address these problems. In the area of human displacement, the United Nations High Commissioner for Refugees (UNHCR), for instance, has fully participated in the social construction, reproduction and transformation of the 'refugee' category. Created in 1950 on a temporary basis to address the needs of European populations displaced before 1951, the UNHCR is today a permanent institution mandated to ensure the rights of all refugees worldwide.[2] Over the years, it has actively encouraged states to develop national asylum systems that are in line with international refugee law, while contributing to the production, circulation and universalisation of policies, norms and guidelines on refugee protection. The UNHCR is now widely recognised as the 'guardian of the global refugee regime', which includes 'the norms, rules, principles and decision-making procedures that regulate the behaviour of the States in the area of refugee protection' (Loescher et al. 2008: 2). Imbued with this powerful moral authority, which is personalised in the figure of the High Commissioner, the UNHCR has also imposed itself as a main actor in the humanitarian field, with the reputation of being one of the most reactive and operational UN agencies, capable of offering basic services to millions of refugees across the world at short notice. Through its legal and humanitarian activities, the UNHCR thus plays a key role in the governance of human mobility today.

Within refugee and forced migration studies, social and political scientists have extensively discussed the global discourses and policies of the UNHCR, as well as the social consequences of its humanitarian interventions on the ground, especially in camp situations (Agier 2008; Backewell 2007; Harrel-Bond 1986; Turner 2010, among others). This rich/abundant literature has described the UNHCR in an ambivalent manner, either in a realist perspective, as dominated by western interests willing to contain human displacement, or as an agency that has some autonomy vis-à-vis its main funders, capable of advancing its own institutional interests and agenda (Barnett and Finnemore 2004; Loescher et al. 2008). In both cases, the UNHCR is mostly apprehended at a macro-level of observation and little is said about decision-making processes and professional practices within the organisation. Some recent studies have, however, explored some of the internal tensions of the UN agency (Loescher 2001), its professional identity (Fresia 2009; Wigley 2005) or the daily practices involved in resettlement procedures (Sandvik 2010). From that micro-level perspective the UNHCR does not appear to be a homogeneous actor with its own rationale, but an assemblage of legal experts, diplomats and humanitarian workers, with different interests and perceptions as to what the UNHCR's mandate should be, constantly circulating between the headquarters in Geneva and hundreds of field offices around the world. Although the United States and European countries are its main funders, 70 member states form the 'Executive Committee' of the UNHCR. In addition, non-governmental organisations (NGOs) and external consultants are also involved in shaping its agenda, thereby blurring the borders of what constitutes the institution (Valluy 2007).

In line with these recent studies and with ethnographic approaches of international institutions and experts (Abelès 2011; Ambrosetti 2009; Atlani-Duault 2005; Mosse 2011), this chapter seeks to explore the UNHCR from the inside, by looking at how global normative frameworks on refugee protection are socially constructed, produced and rationalised out of the multiplicity of voices, interests and representations that coexist within the agency. While UNHCR's norm-setting activities take place at different institutional scales, I will focus on the normative production of its Executive Committee (ExCom) at headquarters level. UNHCR's ExCom is indeed the only specialised multilateral forum at the global level entrusted with the role of contributing to the development of international standards relating to refugees (Sztucki 1989). Each year, ExCom members negotiate and adopt thematic 'Conclusions' on refugee protection. According to the UNHCR's official narrative, these Conclusions aim to fill gaps in international refugee law and provide international guidance on asylum matters (UNHCR 2005). They are said to have great moral and political authority as they are adopted by consensus by UNHCR's member states (UNHCR 2005). In legal terms, they can be considered 'international soft law', defined as 'norms which, in principle, are not legally binding but can nevertheless have concrete effects' (Snyder 1993: 16). They can be seen as part of a 'transnational legal order' (Merry 2003: 105), characterised by a proliferation of international recommendations telling states what attitudes are appropriate for them to adopt vis-à-vis the people living on their territory, and threatening moral condemnation or shame if they are not respected (Finnemore and Sikkink 1998: 891). In this chapter, rather than analysing the concrete influence that ExCom Conclusions may have on the normalisation of the attitudes of states, I will look at how these Conclusions are conceptualised, written, negotiated and socially constructed. Who are the actors involved in their definition and negotiations? Which types of cognitive framework and expert knowledge do they mobilise and for what purposes? Which techniques are eventually mobilised to build consensus out of an assembly of experts and diplomats with conflicting interests and viewpoints?

Taking an ethnographic approach, I will answer these questions by describing the six-month negotiation process that led to the adoption of the ExCom Conclusion no. 107 in October 2007, on the theme 'Children at Risk'. Employed at that time by UNHCR as an education expert, I had the opportunity to participate in the drafting process of the Conclusion but also to obtain from the ExCom rapporteur the authorisation to observe the negotiations from a research perspective and interview some of its main stakeholders[3] with the condition of preserving their anonymity.[4] My occupation of this position thus 'situates' my interpretations, as I had better access to the preparatory work of UNHCR experts than to the work of diplomats.

This chapter will be built around the reconstitution of the drafting and negotiation processes of ExCom Conclusion no. 107. I will first discuss the framework in which the Conclusion was prepared and highlight how global norms, which are presented as universal and context-free, are actually embedded in specific ideological, cultural and cognitive frameworks as well as in localised networks of actors and power dynamics. I will then turn to the dynamics of the negotiations as such, and look at how the social positions of state and non-state actors were shaped vis-à-vis the Conclusions, and how multiple voices were turned into a consensual narrative through various techniques of bargaining, coalition-building, mediation and depoliticisation. In a last part, building on recent debates on the usefulness of ExCom Conclusions (Barutciski 2010; UNHCR 2008) and on the fact that UNHCR's member states have failed, for the first time since the creation of UNHCR, to adopt a Conclusion in 2010 and 2011, I will discuss the social role of ExCom Conclusions and examine the practical ways in which social actors mobilise them.

DRAFTING A GLOBAL NORM

The UNHCR Executive Committee

The UN General Assembly established the UNHCR Executive Committee in 1958 to act as a control body with regard to the financial and administrative activities of the UNHCR, and also as an advisory body for protection policy. Originally composed of 25 state members chosen by the UN Economic and Social Council for their 'interest and devotion' to the refugee problem, the ExCom progressively grew to include 40 members in the 1980s and finally to 85 members in 2012. While the ExCom members include the main donor states (the USA, some European Union countries and Japan), it also now includes non-donor countries as well as countries that are not signatories to the 1951 Refugee Convention (such as Bangladesh, Thailand or Lebanon). The steady broadening of ExCom is due to increased membership in the UN, and to the UNHCR's willingness to open its doors to countries that have not ratified the Refugee Convention – in the hope that it will convince them to ratify at a later stage (Loescher et al. 2008). ExCom Conclusions were originally perceived as playing an advisory role to the High Commissioner, but since the 1970s, they have also been directed at states and at the larger international community – creating an ambiguity about who is responsible for implementing them (UNHCR 2008: 7). During the 1970s and 1980s, Conclusions were quite short and remained general, but their length and precision steadily increased during the 1990s as the UNHCR's activities expanded and became more bureaucratised.

ExCom Conclusions are officially adopted during the plenary session of the ExCom, which is convened once a year, usually in October. Extremely formal and ritualised, the plenary session takes place in one of the main conference rooms of the Palais des Nations, in Geneva. The meeting lasts several days, during which state delegations speak one after the other to express their positions. ICVA, a consortium of NGOs that specialise in refugee matters, and other international institutions can also participate in the session as observers[5] and express their views, while academics and specialised media can request special authorisation to attend it. Yet this annual meeting is only the end point of a series of informal consultations and bilateral meetings between the UNHCR and its member states that are held all year long with a more limited number of actors. NGOs and other external actors cannot attend these back-stage meetings[6] where real disagreements are discussed and resolved. The ExCom plenary session is therefore only the visible part of the iceberg, which is also why ExCom members like to say that 'a good ExCom should be a boring ExCom'. It is through this process that, between May and September 2007, the Conclusion no. 107 on Children at Risk was negotiated through a number of informal preparatory consultations before being adopted in the plenary session of October 2007.

The Social Fabric of the First Draft

Although the Conclusions are supposed to reflect the deliberations of the UNHCR member states, in practice the legal experts of the Division of International Protection play a dominant role as they both propose possible topics for a Conclusion,[7] *and* write the first draft of the text. As opposed to the representatives of member states, who have a more polyvalent profile, UNHCR staff members appear as the holders of both an expert knowledge (with regard to refugee law) and practical knowledge (related to their field experience). They are thus considered as better able to 'see the need for, and the value of, additional Conclusions' (UNHCR 2008: iii). Some researchers have argued that the expertise held by international organisations provides them with the legitimacy to define the nature of the same problems for which they propose the solutions (Barnett and Finnemore 2004) and allows them to maintain a certain autonomy vis-à-vis their member states. Building on this observation, we will explore how the autonomy of the UNHCR has expressed itself within the framework of its Executive Committee, while being constantly contested, reframed or limited by states.

In January 2007, four themes were proposed to member states for negotiations with the ExCom standing committee: rescue at sea, asylum seekers as victims of human trafficking, refugee self-sufficiency and children at risk. The selection of these themes was linked to a process of internal lobbying whereby various sections within the UNHCR tried to bring to the attention of the Division of International Protection and to member states issues of concern related to their own priorities. Although the legal experts were hoping that the first theme would be chosen – as access to protection and asylum procedures during rescue-at-sea operations has become extremely problematic in the current migratory context and suffers from major legal gaps[8] – member states chose the last theme. Two diplomats explained their choice as follows: 'we wanted to choose the less sensitive topic to avoid confrontations'[9] and 'to avoid making commitments in areas we want to keep our entire sovereignty'.[10] Right from the beginning, there was therefore a clash between two visions of the Conclusions: one presenting them as a moral imperative to advance the refugee protection regime and go beyond existing legislation, and the other more concerned with preserving state sovereignty and good diplomatic relations with peers. A topic appeared on the agenda of the ExCom not only because it addressed 'real' problems of protection but because it was the result of a compromise between what the UNHCR experts wanted to see codified in a text which was to become universal, and the concessions member states were ready to make in terms of international commitments.

This tension between the UNHCR and its member states reappeared many times during the negotiation process and reflects a larger structural contradiction inherent to the UNHCR's mandate, which implies applying pressure on states to protect refugees 'without indisposing the states that created it and thereby jeopardizing its future' (Barutciski 2010: 134). Yet, although the UNHCR experts were not able to impose their topic, they remained the main authors of the first version of the Conclusion and thus of the definition of what was the appropriate attitude states should adopt to protect refugee children 'at risk'. The drafting process was indeed entirely coordinated by the legal experts of the Division of International Protection of the UNHCR, together with the head of the child unit. The latter was a former employee of UNICEF and part of a transnational expert network specialised in child protection, whose members were employed both in UN agencies (UNICEF, UNESCO, UNHCR) and NGOs (Save the Children, Terre des Hommes, Jesuit refugee service, etc.), or who had circulated among these institutions. Flexible and dynamic, this network had all the characteristics of an epistemic community (Haas 1992) in the sense that its members worked, at least temporarily, for the same cause (the protection of children), advancing solutions to what they had defined as a new category of populations at risks: 'children victims of armed conflict'.[11] This network maintained that solutions could only come from a comprehensive and systematic approach to child protection, contained in the notion of 'child protection system'. The head of the UNHCR child unit – who worked in close consultation with his expert network while drafting the Conclusion – made it his priority to include this notion in the text. He also wanted to ensure that the principle of the 'best interest of the child', recognised in the 1989 Convention on the Rights of the Child, became part of the realm of asylum law. More importantly, he thereby wanted to affirm the authority of the UNHCR with regard to determining the best interest of refugee children, especially in repatriation or resettlement contexts (Pouwels 2008). Once the key concepts of *child protection system* and *best interest of the child* were included in the text, the rest was drafted through a consultative approach, which was central to UNHCR bureaucratic practices. Each technical section of the UNHCR's headquarters (education, health, shelter, etc.) was consulted and asked to comment or write a paragraph of the text in relation to their area of expertise. As an 'education expert', I became involved in the process. Like others, I used this opportunity to highlight the main priorities of our unit, which were themselves influenced by our incorporation in a broader inter-agency network of education experts. The chief of the child unit, but also myself and other colleagues were thus all acting as 'entrepreneurs in norms setting' (Finnemore and Sikkink 1998). We hoped to convince member states to transform what we considered the right solutions to child protection in refugee situations into international recommendations. Some of these solutions we already applied in the field. However, none of us were acting or inventing these solutions on an individual basis: we were mobilising models of actions that circulated more widely within inter-agency networks to which we belonged, and in which we were socialised. As we mobilised these models in the refugee context, we contributed to their circulation but we also reinterpreted and rebuilt them in new ways (more appropriate to our operation context).

The majority of the proposals made by the UNHCR technical sections and by NGOs were incorporated in the text. Like other international organisations today, the UNHCR is guided by a holistic and 'rights-based approach', which implies that one basic human right cannot be prioritised over another, as they are all perceived as equally important and interdependent. Difficult to contest, this approach made it challenging to prioritise one right or action over the other and explains why the first draft of the text was rather long and ambitious (14 pages), looking more like a wish list than an attempt to target gaps in international refugee law.[12] Although comprehensive and holistic, recommendations were formulated in a depoliticised manner, without always highlighting the social, cultural and political prerequisites their realisation would involve. As with any other text of universal scope, its content was thus embedded in a legalistic and static view of social reality, and based on the assumption that this social reality could be modified through the simple implementation of a series of technical and institutional measures.

The text placed the child at the centre of attention, simultaneously as a 'victim' but also as an empowered agent 'capable of participation'.[13] It was considered as the holder of individual rights, such as the right to individual protection, health, contraception, homosexuality. Its interests should take precedence before those of his/her group of belonging and, in specific circumstances, it was the UNHCR that was to determine what this interest was (Pouwels 2008). This first draft was thus embedded in a liberal representation of law, childhood, sexuality and family, which is already present in the 1989 Convention on the Rights of the Child. We will now describe how the content of this draft has been contested and reframed during the negotiation phase.

NEGOTIATING THE TEXT

The Scene

Although not legally binding, negotiations over Conclusion no. 107 were tough and took place over a six-month period. This length is quite atypical as compared to other international forums: 'very short when compared to multilateral negotiations but very long and quite unusual within the humanitarian sphere where normative frameworks are usually decided only by a group of rich donor countries'.[14] The negotiations were held in the main conference room of the UNHCR and organised through several one-day sessions. Access was restricted to delegates of member states only. Despite their repeated requests, NGO observers were never allowed to participate, as diplomats feared they would make public the political game that states play during negotiations.[15]

Conclusions were adopted by consensus, which meant that all negotiators potentially had the power of veto. The text was reviewed paragraph by paragraph through several readings. Delegates formulated proposed amendments according to instructions they received from their capital. A paragraph was eventually adopted once there were no more objections. Discussions were moderated and facilitated by the rapporteur of the ExCom, a position designated for a one-year mandate (in 2007 the position was filled by a representative from a North American country). The formal organisation of the negotiations was supported by the Executive Secretariat of the UNHCR, which was also in charge of inserting proposed amendments directly in the text, which was projected on a screen for all to see. Finally, two UNHCR legal experts, those who had been in charge of coordinating the drafting of the first text, were also part of the negotiation process and provided clarification on the text if necessary. These four people (rapporteur, one person from the Secretariat and two UNHCR experts) were sitting on a stage, facing the delegates, who were seated in rows. Despite the rather small size of the room and the fact that most delegates knew each other as Geneva-based members of states' permanent missions to the UN, modes of communication remained impersonal, mediated through translators, earphones and microphones.

The Actors' Performances and Positions

The Diplomats

The diplomats representing the UNHCR member states were the most visible protagonists of the negotiations. Only twenty of the official ExCom members participated in the process, and many of them were represented by lower-level diplomats. Some were specialised in asylum and humanitarian issues, and the others (the majority) had a generalist profile. All the people interviewed had participated in other multilateral negotiations in Geneva and also in New York. Similar to the role that diplomats play in other multilateral forums, the diplomats were not acting as simple representatives of their states (applying instructions), but rather as brokers between various arenas (national and international), translating what could be thinkable and feasible from one to the other (Buchet de Neuilly 2009: 79). Their positions within the negotiation were thus the result of a complex dynamic made up of (1) formal instructions they received from the capital, which were themselves framed by the desire to make international recommendations fit within national legislation; (2) the image and reputation their state may want to defend by advocating a given thematic;

(3) the relations of alliance or debt they may have towards other diplomats; (4) their personality and career strategies, their personal ability to use their margin of manoeuvre during negotiations and the practical knowledge they developed during their socialisation in the diplomatic game (Ambrosetti 2009).

While my initial assumption was that the input from UNHCR donor countries would have more weight in the negotiations, power relationships among delegates clearly favoured some non-donor countries belonging to the Organisation of the Islamic Conference (OIC). These were recently accepted within the ExCom because of the large number of refugees they are currently hosting on their territory.[16] Forming a coalition led by three countries,[17] they were extremely active and used the ExCom arena less to develop international refugee law than to claim their rights to cultural differences and financial assistance (burden-sharing) – a tendency, which has been confirmed by other analysts with regards to other ExCom sessions (Barutciski 2010). The leaders of this group were, for instance, systematically opposed to paragraphs that were too explicitly embedded in liberal conceptions of childhood, family and sexuality, requesting that the notion of the 'best interest of the child' be complemented by statements underlining the importance of the role and the interest of the family as a whole. Likewise, the paragraph asking states to protect 'children who are transgressing social and gender roles', alluding to homosexuality, was contested (as homosexuality is forbidden in many OIC countries). The right to contraception was another issue of debate on which OIC countries allied with the Holy See. Resistance was organised against a paragraph which proposed naturalisation in the country of asylum as a durable solution for refugee children. OIC countries were also able to obtain the inclusion of the 'principle of burden-sharing' in three different paragraphs of the text. This refers to the claim that the responsibility for the protection of refugees should be shared and thus major host countries should receive financial and physical assistance.[18] OIC countries were very supportive of each other, acting *en bloc* and constituting a rather homogeneous and stable coalition (each of them supporting the amendments of the other with a sense of loyalty towards the group and a certain social pressure to maintain good relation with other members). They would also quite often use obstruction strategies to block amendments proposed by other countries. Thanks to these strategies, they succeeded in having many of their amendments passed, including the deletion of any reference to homosexuality. Their positions seemed to be influenced at once by the political stance of their country vis-à-vis refugees,[19] different cultural representations of childhood and sexuality, but also by group dynamics during the negotiation. Some claims, such as burden-sharing, contraception or homosexuality, were not central themes to the Conclusion, but, because the group of 77 had made them into themes of controversy in other forums, they compelled the diplomats to react to them. A diplomat emphasised that: 'lots of people have had experience in New York before. So they come with their habits and just pick up the same themes of confrontation even though they may not have instructions'.[20] Yet diplomats from OIC countries justified their position with legal arguments (national legislation incompatible with principles such as homosexuality), and economic ones: 'How can we ensure the right to education for all refugees when we are not even able to ensure this right for our own children'.[21] To these official justifications, one could also add the fact, outlined by Barutciski, that poorer refugee-hosting states may be 'fed up with rich northern States pontificating about the importance of protection while avoiding contact with refugees thanks to their geographic position and their interdiction policies' (2010: 137).

Compared with the active presence of the OIC countries, the relative absence of the main donor countries (the USA in particular) was striking. They either did not have an interest in the thematic, did not attach too much importance and legitimacy to the process (see below) or favoured other channels to influence the UNHCR's policies, such as direct bilateral negotiations with the UNHCR's management. Furthermore, those who did participate on a regular basis were divided. Some of them, such as Scandinavian, European and North American countries (Canada), defended progressive issues such as contraception and homosexuality and were in favour of developing the international refugee regime beyond existing standards.[22] Others adopted a line characterised as 'harder' by some diplomats, because they were more keen to defend national sovereignty.[23] As with OIC countries, the latter renegotiated certain recommendations that they perceived as not being in line with their national legislation.

Although donor countries managed to have some of their amendments passed (on reproductive health and prevention of HIV/AIDS for instance), their weight in the negotiation was overall reduced by their divisions, or lack of involvement. Negotiation theories confirm that multilateral negotiations under the consensus rule tend to diffuse structural power inequalities by granting minor actors – here, non-donor countries – a greater share of influence than they would normally have because of the veto power they can use at any time (Lang 1994). This observation was confirmed in our case, but not all smaller countries had the same capacity to use their veto power. Countries from sub-Saharan Africa, for instance, were either absent or in compliance with the position of either South Africa or OIC leader countries. This was due to the absence of instructions from their capitals, or their lack of expertise, or the small size of their diplomatic missions.[24] Finally, out of the twenty diplomats who regularly participated in the negotiations, only seven were truly acting as leaders. If the consensus rule reduces structural inequalities, it does not stop other forms of differentiation between member states, linked to their capacity to build coalitions, their expertise and human resources.

The Experts

As holders of expert knowledge, the role of UNHCR staff members was not restricted to the drafting of the first draft of the Conclusion; they also were actors in their own right, 'teaching states their interests' (Park 2004: 80) during the negotiation phase. The legal experts regularly intervened in the debates from their podium, to defend what they considered as 'their text'. They countered attempts by state representatives to amend or to reduce the constraining dimensions of the Conclusion. Their strategy was to go back to the technical aspects of international law, by reminding states that some contested standards of the Conclusion had already been approved in other multilateral agreements and that 'agreed language' could not be renegotiated (as the UNHCR has been mandated precisely to uphold already existing norms). By shifting towards legalistic and formalistic discussions, they thereby contributed to the depoliticisation of some debates, which otherwise would have led to complex discussions over the political, economic or cultural constraints related to the development of refugee rights, and the articulation of international norms with national norms, economic constraints and cultural contexts. The capacity of experts to depoliticise debates is well known at both national and international levels. Barnett and Finnemore (2004: 24) made the point that: 'by emphasizing the objective nature of their knowledge, staff of IOs are able to present themselves as technocrats whose advice is unaffected by partisan squabbles'. Mandated to uphold refugee rights and to be the guardians of refugee law, experts also have the perception that they act for the sake of the public good and build their legitimacy on an objective which is difficult to contest: the protection of human rights. Based on the legitimacy of their knowledge but also of their moral cause, they position themselves as the defenders of refugee protection against member states perceived as the 'adversary'. One legal officer felt that 'his' text was thrown to a group of wild animals, which was trying to empty its very substance. On their side, the member states I had interviewed all perceived the UNHCR as having an 'arrogant' and 'dogmatic' attitude during the negotiations. 'The UNHCR should remember that the negotiation of ExCom Conclusions is a state process. Compared to other forums, they intervene too much in the negotiations and are too technical, there is too much ownership on their part.'[25] These criticisms reflect again the tension, which is generated when the UNHCR affirms its autonomy vis-à-vis its member states. Although the latter created the UNHCR to be the guardian of refugee rights, they do not easily accept the way in which it affirms its authority, and the way that it depoliticises, moralises and makes technical issues that are inherently political. Besides, 'there are clearly limits to how much States will allow themselves to be led by the legal services of a multilateral institution (i.e. UNHCR's Division of International Protection) in the implementation of important norms concerning refugees that seek access to their territories' (Barutciski 2010: 138). Yet, although each paragraph was amended by diplomats, the technical and moral authority of UNHCR experts still allowed them to maintain in the final version the principles that were most important for them: the 'child protection system' and the recognition of the UNHCR's authority with regard to the determination of the best interest of the child refugee.

Intermediaries and Lobbyists

Less visible and apparently at the periphery, two other actors contributed to the negotiation dynamics: the ExCom rapporteur on the one hand and international NGOs with an office in Geneva on the other. The rapporteur, from the Canadian diplomatic mission, could not be absolutely neutral and influenced the debates by giving the floor to one or other state representative, deciding to stop negotiating a paragraph or moving to the next one, organising breaks, etc. She decided on the rhythm of the debates, when to start and end them, and used strategies such as sequencing and postponement to overcome blockages. This influenced the mood of the stakeholders and played an important and unexpected part in the negotiations. More significant still was her role of mediation, as she took the initiative to convene informal working groups outside the official sessions dedicated to the negotiations. These working groups were held each time the formal negotiations were blocked after the second or third readings, and facilitated a compromise. When the chair or rapporteur convenes secret working groups to facilitate negotiations behind the scenes, it creates unequal opportunities to influence the negotiation process as not all stakeholders are invited to join them. This has been observed in many other multilateral forums (Barston 1997). Lastly, the rapporteur influenced the negotiations by systematically informing NGOs about the evolution of the debates, sending them the newly drafted version of the text after each round and thus bypassing the formal rule, which does not allow them to be involved.

NGOs could thus play an active role at the periphery of the main scene. The Quakers, for instance, hosted informal lunches inviting some member states to lobby them on a number of controversial issues and to break down the north/south divide. Their technique was based on sensitisation and not on confrontation or imposition of an authoritative knowledge: they explained the importance of some recommendations for the life of refugees, giving concrete examples taken from their field experience.[26] Even more than the UNHCR, they drew their legitimacy from their field experience and proximity with refugees. Their attitude was generally perceived as more 'pedagogic' and less 'arrogant' than that of the UNHCR. Some diplomats told me that they sometimes changed their position after these meetings. During the negotiation phase, NGOs also continued to meet with UNHCR staff members who encouraged them to lobby a number of diplomats on issues at stake.[27] Although keenly affirming the existence of boundaries between them, NGO and UNHCR members were in fact working towards the same goals, as many of them were part of the same networks of experts. Just as NGOs swayed the UNHCR to incorporate their ideas during the drafting process of the Conclusion, UNHCR experts induced NGOs to push governments to soften their positions. However, the capacity of NGOs to influence the process depended on the quality of their personal relationships with members of the UNHCR and with the rapporteur, linked also to the geographical proximity of their offices in Geneva. Far from representing the diversity of positions within the non-governmental world, they appeared instead as institution-alised counter-powers that were well versed in the mechanisms of Geneva diplomatic arenas thanks to their presence in the city. In addition, their suggestions or amendments could only be passed during the negotiation phase if a state was willing to 'sponsor' them and to inform them on the evolution of the negotiations.

BUILDING CONSENSUS

Overall, the negotiations over the Conclusion no. 107 were a fragmented process involving diplomats, international civil servants (UNHCR) and NGOs. Each of them tried to influence the process, be it through techniques of coalition-building and obstruction (OIC countries), technicisation and depoliticisation of debates (UNHCR), mediation (rapporteur) and lobbying (NGOs). If OIC countries and UNHCR experts appeared to have the greatest capacity to influence, power dynamics remained diffuse and spread through various scenes, visible and invisible. Various representations of childhood and sexuality confronted each other, as well as diverse legal frameworks. Refugee experts mobilised international refugee standards and human rights law. Diplomats took into account national legislations, geopolitical and economic interests, as well as a social pressure exerted by their peers on the diplomatic scene. How was it possible, within this tense and fragmented arena, to reach a consensus over a final text that was to become 'universal'?

Negotiation theorists have answered this question by focusing on bargaining strategies (inclusive vs. distributive), argument and persuasion (Putnam 1990), coalition strategies (Zartman 1994) and degree of homogeneity of coalitions. In our case study, haggling and alliances did, indeed, play a very important role: consensus on certain paragraphs was reached through implicit agreements between adversarial camps installed outside the main negotiation room, far from peers' social pressure. Yet, subtle reformulations and the use of reservations were also key to reaching a consensus. Many issues of disagreement were indeed overcome by shifting debates from the actual content of the Conclusions to their form. After the second reading, for instance, discussions were increasingly focused on the choice of different, though apparently quite similar, verbs. The OIC but also certain western countries would, for instance, stop blocking the process if constraining verbs such as 'ensure' were substituted by weaker ones such as 'make all efforts to'. As time pressure increased, the rapporteur herself proposed alternative language that decreased the strength of the sentence in order to facilitate a compromise. Likewise, discussions focused on reservations such as 'where feasible', 'as appropriate', 'as necessary' or 'in accordance with national laws'. Discreet and not so visible to external readers, these reservations were actually a way for states to incorporate their case for not following the recommendations of the Conclusion. In order to reach consensus on different conceptions of childhood, another technique was to simply include both liberal and non-liberal views in the final text – one asserting the need to consider the best interest of the child and the other reaffirming the importance of taking into account the interest of the family as a whole. Furthermore, broad notions that were ambiguous enough to be interpreted in a variety of ways replaced precise formulations. By reformulating sentences at a higher level of generality or vagueness, contentious issues could be successfully avoided. This was the case for the controversy about the reference to homosexuality implicit in the expression 'the children who transgress social and gender roles', which was eventually reformulated into 'children who suffer from social discrimination'. These subtle reformulations were actually hiding fundamental oppositions between diplomats, or significant resistance to the recommendations proposed by the UNHCR. They were crucial in avoiding substantial discussions on the content that no one wanted to engage in, either because they were politically too sensitive or because they were impossible to resolve within a six-month negotiation framework. The ExCom members often described this focus on wording and formalistic issues in negative terms: 'There was huge discussions on small words like "recommend" and it became so technical that people just forgot the big picture of the text.'[28] Expressing tense power relations that sometimes had nothing to do with the theme discussed, the shift of debates from the content to the form was nevertheless crucial in order to depoliticise most of the controversies and to build a text which could be vague and contradictory enough to be agreed.

This last observation leads us to highlight the importance of the temporal dimension in the social construction of consensus. ExCom Conclusions have to be negotiated in a six-month timeframe to be officially adopted in October each year, during the plenary session of ExCom. This timeframe has been institutionalised and was perceived as non-negotiable by all stakeholders. Both member states and the UNHCR knew they had to reach a compromise at some point, and both wanted to avoid having to display their divisions and sometimes conservative attitudes in the public arena of the plenary session of the ExCom (to which other actors, including NGOs and media have access). Although none of the stakeholders mentioned this factor, I could clearly see that, as the deadline was approaching, the protagonists of the negotiations were more open to compromise. Stakeholders therefore also acted under a certain social pressure, the pressure of having to display, at least publicly (during the plenary), their commitment to developing the refugee regime in a spirit of consensus. Formally adopted in October 2007, the Conclusion no. 107 appeared in its final version as a long and weak text, written in watered-down language. Yet it included at least three new notions which were extremely important for both UNHCR experts and NGOs: the construction of the new category of 'children at risk' in the realm of asylum; the formulation of a new systemic approach with regard to child protection (child protection system); and the recognition that the UNHCR had authority to determine the best interest of the child refugee.

THE SOCIAL ROLE OF EXCOM CONCLUSIONS

Between 2005 and 2008, a group of UNHCR's donor countries began increasingly to question both the process and the usefulness of ExCom Conclusions, and required that UNHCR conduct an evaluation. Their main frustration was that ExCom Conclusions were not meeting their official objectives any more, as they were not necessarily addressing gaps in the international regime of refugee protection, nor helping to develop it in a progressive manner. The Conclusions were said to be systematically 'politicised' and weakened by what was described as a 'social dumping' of the text undertaken by states belonging to the UN group of 77 (including OIC countries), especially those that were not signatories to the 1951 Convention on Refugee Status and other major international conventions.[29] The characterisation of a number of countries as being 'conservative' produced a boundary between newcomers and older members of ExCom, while eliding the fact that some donor countries were also trying to limit the development of new standards in the realm of asylum or had de facto restrictive asylum policies on their own territories. Other diplomats also felt that the adoption of a Conclusion on an annual basis responded to an institutional imperative which had nothing to do with the 'reality of the field': 'Conclusions seem to be a holy cow for the UNHCR: they do it because they have always done it.'[30]

The UNHCR responded to these criticisms by hiring a consultant, who was actually an ex-staff member of the UNHCR, to conduct an 'external' evaluation. The report reasserted the 'useful role of Conclusions with regards to the international refugee protection regime and that they should continue to play such a role in today's challenging environment' (UNHCR 2008: vi). Despite the positive outcome of the evaluation report, certain member states, this time led by non-donor countries, refused for the first time since the 1970s to negotiate a Conclusion in 2010 and 2011, arguing that the process of the negotiation should be once again discussed and reviewed. This historical paralysis of the ExCom Conclusions process actually crystallised wider tensions, which were not only related to the Conclusions per se. On the one hand, it reflected the challenges raised by the democratisation of the UNHCR's ExCom and, in particular, the resistance of some donor countries to seeing the ExCom open its doors to states that tend to contest the hegemonic discourse over human rights in UN forums. On the other hand, it revealed a growing mistrust between the UNHCR and its member states as both donor and non-donor countries seem to be willing to re-assert their state power over the UN agency whose growing autonomy is perceived as a threat to their national sovereignty. But above all, this movement of discontent shed light on the fact that the negotiation process of the Conclusions can be mobilised by stakeholders for other purposes than advancing the refugee regime and is influenced by wider political and social dynamics. During my fieldwork, I have indeed identified at least three ways in which social actors mobilised ExCom Conclusions.

First, non-donor countries hosting large number of refugees on their territories, mobilise ExCom Conclusions not so much to develop new refugee standards but rather as a means to assert their cultural, religious or legal differences; to contest certain standards perceived as too 'hegemonic and westernized'; to claim rights for financial assistance ('burden-sharing'); and eventually to assert their state power against donor countries and against the UNHCR's pressure to provide more protection to refugees. This unexpected appropriation of ExCom, which is negatively perceived by donor countries, has thereby provided an opportunity for countries that do not have the financial power to influence UNHCR policy to express their views, claim their rights and influence the Conclusions from their own perspective and interests. In certain cases, such as in 2010–2011, this counter-hegemonic dynamic has reached such a point that it paralysed the ExCom Conclusion process. The negotiation process over ExCom Conclusions can therefore be seen as contributing to the symbolic restoration of a certain balance in power relationships between the UNHCR's member states: it allows non-donor countries to perform power within the institution and be considered, in that space at least, as equal partners thanks to their veto power. In that respect, it can be seen as a space of *ritual of inversion* within UNHCR whereby powerless stakeholders act as if they have power by contesting hegemonic views on what global refugee norms should be. If global refugee norms have sometimes been described as the vehicle of western hegemony, they can therefore also be nourished with counter-hegemonic views and become challenging narratives right from the stage of their definition.

Second, UNHCR experts use ExCom Conclusions first and foremost to provide international legitimacy to what they have defined as problems to which they can offer solutions. They are thus used to oblige member states to recognise the UNHCR's authority over new areas (such as child protection) or new categories of population (such as children at risk). UNHCR experts can refer to ExCom Conclusions to legitimise new appeals for funding in new areas and thus new bureaucratic interventions, while its NGO partners can mobilise them as lobbying instruments to remind states of their political and financial commitments in the realm of asylum (UNHCR 2008: iv–v). ExCom Conclusions are also mobilised to maintain the reputation and credibility of the institution of asylum that the UNHCR has been mandated to guarantee and to develop.[31] In a context of 'crisis' of the institution of asylum, characterised by increasingly restrictive asylum policies worldwide and, in a number of cases, the unwillingness of states to respect some of the minimum standards of protection such as the principle of non-*refoulement* or of fair asylum procedures (Loescher et al. 2008), the annual negotiation of ExCom Conclusions contributes to perpetuating the narrative that the international regime of protection continues to improve, and that new standards are being developed. Conclusions act as a universal and authoritative discourse and convey what refugee rights and standards should be in the ideal world, as well as what states and other stakeholders should do to guarantee them. A European diplomat confirms this observation quite cynically: 'One has the impression of being in an ivory tower where one discusses an ideal world while certain countries are incapable of applying the most basic standards.'[32] However, for UNHCR legal experts, the annual production of Conclusions is all the more important in that context of restrictive asylum policies as it helps them to maintain the issue of asylum on the international agenda and to mobilise people and institutions around it (Mosse 2007: 24). Rather than a tool for normalising the attitude of states or providing operational guidance, Conclusions are perceived as a 'semantic resource' with a strong legitimising force that can help sustain the mobilisation of a large number of institutional actors around refugee rights – an achievement per se.

Finally, ExCom Conclusions maintain a certain form of social prestige: by adopting a Conclusion on an annual basis by consensus, member states, and especially donor countries, publicly display their official commitment to improving standards in the area of refugee protection, although they actually practise increasingly restrictive asylum policies. Perpetuating this myth is fundamental for their international reputation. As Barutciski rightly notes: 'Self-promotion, whether by states or organisations, is a key part of the international refugee regime. Indeed, it should not be surprising that states often have an interest in appearing humanitarian while not necessarily committing themselves to significant obligations' (2010: 135). Indeed, states often commit themselves to international law by reciprocity, conformity, and the desire to be part of the international community or to appear 'civilised' (Merry 2003). Furthermore, they also care about international legitimacy, which has become an important influence on perceptions of domestic legitimacy held by their own citizens (Finnemore and Sikkink 1998: 903). This important political function may suggest that, although some delegates have recently contested the operational (problem-solving) function of ExCom Conclusions or tried to obstruct the negotiation process, the UNHCR and its member states will do everything possible to restart the annual negotiation of ExCom Conclusions as putting an end to the process would be too costly politically.

In the end, ExCom Conclusions may not only be about improving refugee standards and providing concrete guidance to states and the UNHCR. They may also be about perpetuating narratives, performing power and making claims, maintaining the social and political reputation of institutional actors, as well as mobilisation and dialogue around political agendas at the global level (Van Gastel and Nuijten 2005: 101). The process of their adoption may also crystallise a number of wider issues and tensions, which are both internal to UNHCR (such as the structural tension between UNHCR and its member states) and external to it (such as larger North–South power dynamics taking place in other UN forums).

THE MAKING OF UNIVERSALITY

The ethnographic approach can help us understand the social processes that govern the fabric of global norms. Our case study suggests that international organisations – which are key actors in international governance – formulate and implement norms and policies that cannot be described in a realist and instrumentalist way as the simple product of interstate bargaining or of western imperialism (Park 2004: 80). Nor do they appear as the mere expression of the institutional interests of international experts or international organisations. Their social fabric involves a wide variety of actors, powers and counter-powers whose boundaries and influence are not clear cut. Among these actors, trans-institutional epistemic communities play a key role as entrepreneurs of norm making with a specific vision of the world based on human rights, compassion and interventionism. But state actors also redefine the content and the scope of these norms, be it by choosing the very topic of the negotiation, restricting their (moral) constraining dimension, or nourishing them with counter-hegemonic views or claims. More importantly, it is the states, as the incarnations of the international community, which continue to confer their universal legitimacy on certain norms. This also shows that if international organisations mobilise their expertise and negotiate their autonomy vis-à-vis their member states, they also constantly need states to recognise their authority in the international arena. It is therefore the encounter between various legitimacies – state, moral and technical – that gives certain norms and models of action their 'universal' legitimacy.

Although nourished by various actors, our case study also outlines that the Conclusion no. 107 did not necessarily incorporate the diversity of positions and interests of all member states or international NGOs. It remained the expression of a compromise reached between a few persons only: a bunch of technical and legal experts from UNHCR headquarters, less than a dozen active member states (with unequal levels of expertise, support from their capitals, personal charisma, and opportunities to access private meetings and information), and a couple of institutionalised NGOs that had built close relationships with the UNHCR in Geneva. Some major donor countries did not even participate in the process, because they considered it illegitimate or because they lacked interest in the theme discussed. This situation is what Barston refers to as the paradox of the consensus rule, namely that 'multilateral negotiations appear to be based on widespread agreement, whereas the depth of support to a multilateral agreement is never really known' (Barston 1997). International norms adopted through consensus tend to obscure the presence of social actors and coalitions of states, with the divergent political interests, bureaucratic strategies and cultural views that influence them. In other words, just as with national norms, narratives about international norms tend to cover over 'how global politics actually results from village politics' (Mosse 2007: 6). Global norms may also not be as liberal as is often assumed: the veto power of the consensus rule tends to give the final say to conservative forces, leading stakeholders to agree on the lowest common denominator and contributing to the preservation of the status quo.

Lastly, our case study raises the issue of the practical uses of global norms beyond their official objectives, questioning more broadly their mobilisation in multilateral forums. Institutional actors perceive ExCom Conclusions not so much as a means to normalise the attitudes of states but rather as a legitimising instrument, allowing them to perpetuate the narrative that the international refugee law continues to develop itself in a progressive manner. It keeps refugee issues on the international agenda but also upholds claims to financial assistance, cultural differences and political consideration. Yet, far from being a rhetorical tool only, ExCom Conclusions legitimise interventions into social reality, whether in terms of domination – over new categories of population on whom to intervene – or in terms of contestation.

NOTES

1. Assistant Professor, Institute of Anthropology, Neuchâtel. The author would like to thank Birgit Müller, Kristin Sandvik, Kim Eling, Bertrand Biju-Duval, Christine Bloch, David Bozzini, Etienne Piguet and Michel Gaudé for their comments on this chapter, as well as all the people who have contributed to this research.
2. Apart from Palestinian refugees, whom the United Nations Relief and Works Agency for Palestine Refugees in the Near East (UNRWA) has the mandate to protect.
3. Interviews and informal conversations were held with the ExCom rapporteur, NGOs, UNHCR legal experts and seven ExCom member states. I have not, however, been able to interview delegates from Organisation of the Islamic Conference (OIC) and southern countries, which may have influenced some of my interpretations.
4. I will use fictive names and will not directly mention the countries represented by delegates but their geographical area of belonging.
5. NGOs can only make one joint NGOs statement on each agenda item.
6. Only the European Union has negotiated an access to informal consultative meetings as an observer.
7. It can however happen that member states themselves suggest some topics on which to develop a new Conclusion (UNHCR 2008).
8. Informal conversation with UNHCR legal experts.

9. Interview with Mark, diplomat representing a European member state, December 2007.

10. Interview with Scott, a diplomat representing a North American member state, November 2007.

11. On the appearance of this category on the international agenda, see Chelpi-den-Hamer et al. (2010).

12. A UNHCR report (2008) notes, however, that the form and length of ExCom Conclusions are different from one year to the next and depend on the team in charge of drafting it.

13. This contradiction has also been highlighted by Bolzman (2008) with regard to Save the Children's representations of the child. She shows how the child was all at once perceived as a victim (isolated and deprived of the support of a family or of a nation and thus unprotected) and a 'resource', or even a 'redemptor of the world'. Other research work has also shown that 'children' affected by war and conflict situations have their own agency and coping strategies, and can sometimes cope better than adults. Besides, the discursive victimisation of children had led to the progressive construction of 'children' as an international bureaucratic category legitimising an increasing number of interventions targeting and attempting to 'normalise' the life of young people (Chatty 2010).

14. Interview with the representative of the European Union, December 2007.

15. Interview with ExCom rapporteur, Geneva, November 2007. The possibility of extending access of NGOs to ExCom's meetings is still an issue of intense debates among delegates today.

16. OIC countries constitute a regional bloc of the G77 which has been very active in UN forums since the 1960s.

17. Lebanon, Pakistan and Bangladesh. Iran would sometimes play a significant role as well.

18. Physical assistance here refers to resettlement programmes of refugees to western countries.

19. Restrictive asylum policies related to economic constraints, but also structural geopolitical and diplomatic concerns vis-à-vis the state of origin or internal political pressure, such as Lebanon vis-à-vis Palestinian refugees for instance.

20. Conversation with the ExCom rapporteur, and Mark, a diplomat representing a European state, December 2007.

21. Statement of a diplomat from an OIC country during the negotiation, June 2007, Geneva.

22. Their position was however shaped by similar structural factors as the one of OIC countries (national legislation already in accordance with international standards; fewer arrivals of refugees and economical situation more favourable to support them.

23. Such as Australia for instance.

24. Yet it is worth noting that, according to other research work, representations of African states' interests may also take place through NGO channels.

25. Interview with the ExCom rapporteur, Geneva, December 2007.

26. These meetings were held in Quaker House in Geneva, run by the Society of Friends, a Christian organisation which offers the possibility of organising lunch-time seminars and off the record meetings, thus providing a space for diplomats to meet and discuss issues.

27. Informal conversation with an NGO member of ICVA.

28. Interview with Heinz, diplomat representing a European member state, Geneva, November 2007.
29. Synthesis of various statements made by European and North American member States as well as the ExCom Rapporteur, November-December 2007.
30. Interview with Heinz, diplomat representing a European member state, Geneva, November 2007.
31. UNHCR Statute, 1951, paragraph 8 (a).
32. Interview with Heinz, diplomat representing a European member state, Geneva, November 2007.

BIBLIOGRAPHY

Abelès, Marc (2011) *Des anthropologues à l'OMC: Scènes de la gouvernance mondiale* (Paris: Ed. CNRS).

Agier, Michel (2008) *Gérer les indésirables: Des camps de réfugiés au gouvernement humanitaire* (Paris: Ed. Flammarion).

Ambrosetti, David (2009) *Normes et rivalités diplomatiques à l'ONU: le Conseil de sécurité en audience* (Bruxelles: PIE/Peter Lang).

Atlani-Duault, Laetitia (2005) *Au bonheur des autres: Anthropologie de l'aide humanitaire* (Paris: Société d'Ethnologie).

Backewell, Oliver (2007) 'Researching refugees: Lessons from the past, current challenges and future directions', *Refugee Quarterly Survey* 26(3): 6–14.

Barnett, Michael and Martha Finnemore (2004) *Rules of the World: International Organisations in Global Politics* (Ithaca, NY: Cornell University Press).

Barutciski, Michael (2010) 'Observations on ExCom's 60th session (2009): Does UNHCR need (more) ExCom conclusions?', *Refuge* 27(2): 133–141.

Barston, Ronald Peter (1997) *Modern Diplomacy* (London: Longman).

Bolzman, Lara (2008) 'The advent of child rights on the international scene and the role of the Save the Children International Union 1920–45', *Refugee Survey Quarterly* 27(4): 26–36.

Buchet de Neuilly, Yves (2009) 'Devenir diplomate multilatéral: Le sens pratique des calculs appropriés', *Cultures & Conflits* 75: 75–98.

Chatty, Dawn (ed.) (2010) *Deterritorialized Youth: Sahrawi and Afghan Refugees at the Margin of the Middle East* (Oxford: Berghahn).

Chelpi-denn-Hamer, Magali, Marion Fresia and Eric Lanoue (2010) 'Introduction: Éducation et conflits – les enjeux de l'offre éducative en situation de crise', *Autrepart* 54: 3–22.

Finnemore, Martha and Kathryn Sikkink (1998) 'International norm dynamics and political change', *International organisation* 52(4): 887–917.

Fresia, Marion (2009) 'Une élite transnationale: La fabrique d'une identité professionnelle chez les fonctionnaires du Haut commissariat aux réfugiés', *Revue européenne des migrations internationales* 25(3): 167–190.

Haas, Peter M. (1992) 'Epistemic communities and international policy coordination', *International Organisation* 46(1): 1–35.

Harrel-Bond, Barbara (1986) *Imposing Aid: Emergency Assistance to Refugees.* Oxford: Oxford University Press.

Lang, Winfried (1994) 'Lessons drawn from practice: Open covenants, openly arrived at', in William I. Zartman (ed.) *International Multilateral Negotiation: Approaches to the Management of Complexity*, pp. 201–212 (San Francisco: Jossey-Bass).

Loescher, Gil (2001) *The UNHCR and World Politics: A Perilous Path* (Oxford: Oxford University Press).

Loescher, Gil, Alexander Betts and James Milner (2008) *The United Nations High Commissioner for Refugees (UNHCR): The Politics and Practice of Refugee Protection into the Twenty-first Century* (London: Routledge).

Merry, Sally Engle (2003) 'Human rights law and the demonization of culture (and anthropology along the way)', *Polar: Political and Legal Anthropology Review* 26(1): 55–77.

Mosse, David (2007) 'Notes on the ethnography of expertise and professionals in international development: Ethnography and the public sphere', paper presented at Ethnografeast III, Lisbon, 20–23 June.

Mosse, David (ed.) (2011) *Adventures in Aidland: The Anthropology of Professionals in International Development* (Oxford: Berghahn).

Park, Susan (2004) 'The role of transnational advocacy networks in reconstituting international organisation identities', *Journal of Diplomacy and International Relations* 5(2): 79–93.

Pouwels, Ron (2008) 'UNHCR's Executive Committee Conclusion on Children at Risk', *Refugee Survey Quarterly* 27(4): 43–47.

Putnam, Linda L. (1990) 'Reframing integrative and distributive bargaining: A process perspective', in B.H. Sheppard, M.H. Bazerman and R.J. Lewicki (eds) *Research on Negotiation in Organizations*, vol. 2, pp. 3–30 (Beverly Hills, CA: JAI Press).

Sandvik, Kristin (2010) 'The physicality of legal consciousness: Suffering and the production of credibility in refugee resettlement', in R.A. Wilson and R.D. Brown (eds) *Humanitarianism and Suffering: The Mobilization of Empathy*, pp. 223–244. Cambridge: Cambridge University Press.

Snyder, Francis (1993) 'The effectiveness of European community law: Institutions, processes, tools and techniques', *Modern Law Review* 56(1): 19–54.

Sztucki, Jerzy (1989) 'The Conclusions on the International Protection of Refugees Adopted by the Executive Committee of the UNHCR Programme', *International Journal of Refugee Law* 1(3): 285–318.

Turner, Simon (2010) *The Politics of Innocence* (Oxford: Berghahn).

UNHCR (2005) Note on review of the process for drafting ExCom Conclusions on international protection, informal consultative meeting, 18 November.

UNHCR (2007) Conclusion on Children at Risk, 5 October 2007, No. 107 (LVIII).

UNHCR (2008) *Review of the Use of ExCom Conclusions on International Protection: Report of the Evaluation Team Led By Bryan Deschamps*. Geneva: UNHCR.

Wigley, Barbara (2005) *The State of UNHCR's Organizational Culture* (Geneva: UNHCR Evaluation and Policy Analysis Unit).

Valluy, Jérôme (2007) 'Contribution à une sociologie politique du HCR: Le cas des politiques européennes et du HCR au Maroc', *Asylon(s)* 2. Available online: http://terra. rezo. net/article667. html (consulted December 2010).

Van Gastel, Jilles and Monique Nuijten (2005) 'The genealogy of the good governance and ownership agenda at the Dutch Ministry of Development Cooperation', in David Mosse and David Lewis (eds) *The Aid Effect: Giving and Governing in International Development*, pp. 101–123 (London: Pluto Press).

Zartman, William I. (1994) *International Multilateral Negotiation: Approaches to the Management of Complexity* (San Francisco: Jossey-Bass).

Zerelli, Filippo M. (2010) 'The rule of soft law', *Focaal, Journal of Global and Historical Anthropology* 56: 3–18.

4

The Politics of Technicality

Guidance Culture in Environmental Governance and the International Sphere

Peter Bille Larsen

The production of guidelines and 'best practice' in virtually all fields of international action has mushroomed within the last four decades. On virtually every aspect of life, international organisations are not short of expert advice, best practice examples and 'how to do it' manuals and other forms of soft guidance. Guidelines, it seems, have become part of an international repertoire of cultural forms and devices exploding since the late twentieth century. From high-level negotiations to local-level applications, they take up a lot of time and energy of international organisations, civil servants and non-governmental organisations (NGOs). Nevertheless, they receive surprisingly little analytical attention compared to formal negotiations and hard conventions. This chapter[1] attempts to theorise the proliferation of such guidance and start filling the analytical gap. It seeks to present and theorise what we might tentatively label the emergence of an 'international guidance culture' explored here in, but not limited to, the context of the international environmental governance field. It argues that guidelines reflect a distinct and expanding field of international normativity with distinct characteristics as well as real social effects. Where much analysis of global environmental politics deals with 'hard' multilateral agreements, forums and organisations, the everyday technicalities manifest in reports, projects and guidelines have arguably received far less attention. How are we to understand and conceptualise the omnipresence of such prescriptive practice and devices manifest both in documents and 'capacity-building' activities of all forms? How are we to understand the ways in which guidelines appear, inform and affect the lives of our interlocutors, whether they be international civil servants, state agencies or local communities? The omnipresence, even transposability, of guidelines among neoliberal and socialist states as well as international organisations are among the elements making up the puzzle addressed here. Just as Marilyn Strathern argued in relation to 'audit culture' and accountability (Strathern 2000), guidelines phenomena are not restricted to one institutional setting or part of the world. In this chapter, the Palcazu valley in Peru appears as both a site of implementation and one of multiple sources of a broader guidelines culture in the making.

The approach tested here thus combines specific ethnographic insights with historical analysis of the environmental governance field to chart out a broader anthropology of guidance, allowing us to approach a heterogeneous bundle of phenomena and processes. The analysis follows a broader trend towards increasingly exploring the dynamics of international governance from the 'inside' in their own right (Bebbington et al. 2004; Müller 2012; Weaver 2007) rather than as mere epiphenomena or residues of interstate collaboration or conflict. In some cases, guidelines are lengthy negotiated processes bound by codified procedures and language harmonisation (Boyle 2010: 124), while the authorship of others is quietly left in the hands of technicians. Where some analyses may highlight the proliferation of guidelines as a sign of low-level agreements, apolitics and the technical insignificance of international environmental institutions, this analysis proposes an alternative anthropological reading, considering guidelines as a vibrant cultural field. Rather than assuming environmental politics as having been rendered technical and politically impotent by guidelines, the chapter suggests the idea of technicality displacing or requalifying power and politics.

The chapter proceeds in several steps, starting with a local case of guidelines and their effects in the Peruvian Amazon. Second, the 'non-definition' as a defining quality of guidelines is explored. Third, I track the emergence of guidance language in international environmental policy, followed by a discussion of common justifications and points of critique. The fourth section explores guidelines as a form of techno-politics. The fifth section suggests viewing guidelines as meta-communicative devices installing relations of symbolic authority, normative order and hierarchy. The chapter ends with a brief discussion about guidelines as a new field of normativity and its social effects.

GUIDELINES IN THE AMAZON

My interest in guidelines partly emerged from work as an applied anthropologist to facilitate the development of guidelines (Borrini-

Feyerabend et al. 2004; Carling et al. 2006; Larsen and Springer 2008; Maffi et al. 2000). Their significance later resurfaced during ethnographic fieldwork in the Central Peruvian Amazon, while following the interaction between state officials and indigenous communities.

Dry season 2008. Indigenous Yanesha representatives were seated in a small meeting room in the main district town of the Palcazu valley. Coming from different communities surrounding a protected area, the Yanesha Communal Reserve, they listened attentively as a consultant explained how a series of conservation 'objects' and priorities had been identified for a new management plan. It was the first time 'management' was being formalised after the reserve had been formally recognised and delineated some twenty years earlier. Back then, core objectives had been to 'avoid the total dispersion and weakening of the territorial stability of native communities' and secure traditional hunting grounds. The reserve was now part of a national protected area system. The consultant listed the new conservation priorities identified by the planning team: aquatic systems, bird and mammal salt licks along with high-profile species such as jaguars, giant otters and peccaries. Cedar trees and even traditional knowledge and use practices featured among the newly identified 'conservation objects'. The consultant coordinator noted in passing how 'international guidelines' were used to identify and prioritise these 'objects'. A specialist subsequently presented a map dividing the reserve into 'zones'. It followed national zonation guidance, he emphasised. Initially 69 percent of the reserve would be defined as forest zone, where only scientific activities and education was to be allowed, just as only some 26 percent would be considered for 'direct use'. Strict no-go zones were also identified. What seemed to be a technically neutral guideline to strengthen protected area management de facto represented a dramatic tenure transformation. Even where legislation in fact allowed for flexible zoning approaches, the rationality of guidelines was preferred by consultants. Customary hunting areas, indeed the initial raison d'être of the reserve had become habitat and feeding grounds of focal species. The biologist in the team had even suggested banning all hunting in *collpas*, favoured hunting spots, though this was eventually contested by other members familiar with local practices. Villagers' use of forest resources went from being everyday practice to a carefully circumscribed and zoned phenomenon. Protected area guidance reduced underlying ontological difference (Descola 2006) to questions of rational choice and progressive improvements. It situated local resource management decisions in a national systems context, where more zoning was the answer rather than different modalities altogether.

Far from being a trivial technicality, guidelines had structuring effects on questions of resource access and decision-making power. Not only were local forms of use and access restricted, customary hunting grounds, cultural practices and harvest areas had become anomalies, rather than defining features of the *reserva*. A reserve initially set up to protect hunting grounds was, for a technical reason, being guided to do the exact opposite. Such radical transformations were not immediately rejected by villagers, still uncertain about the implications, but formed part of multiple discursive projects reframing local resource realities and practices.

From one perspective, the ethnographic snapshot may seem far from the subject of global environmental governance regimes. Yet at stake were critical intersections between local forest politics and global regimes of guidance. The consultant team had elaborated a list of conservation priorities using technical criteria framed by guidelines and Latin nomenclature. Rather than being an isolated incident of unfortunate interpretation, at stake were broader qualities of international environmental governance and the common, yet ambiguous, position of guidance. The (social) impacts of protected area policy have been widely noted, yet the role played by soft guidance require far more explicit analytical attention. The Yanesha case illustrates the potentialities of seemingly insignificant technical guidance.

As contemporary world politics addresses environmental challenges and policy language in unprecedented ways, guidelines have become naturalised ingredients in technical repertoires. The Convention on Biological Diversity specifically, in Article 8, calls for parties to 'develop, where necessary, guidelines for the selection, establishment and management of protected areas or areas where special measures need to be taken to conserve biological diversity'. The International Union for Conservation of Nature (IUCN) publishes a series of 'Best Practice Guidelines' for protected areas, covering everything from staff training and evaluations to sacred sites. The guidelines used in the Palcazu had been developed by The Nature Conservancy (TNC), a US-based conservation NGO. Phrased in technical terms, often authored by specialist 'knowers', guidelines have become central governance vehicles for green practice. My point here is not so much to interrogate the local effects of such international guidelines proliferation, but more fundamentally to trace and qualify the emergence of guidelines culture and practices in the environmental governance field. This requires stepping back and exploring the definitions and global trajectories of guidelines production.

NON-DEFINITION AS A DEFINING QUALITY

> Guideline ... recommendation, instruction, direction, suggestion, advice; regulation, rule, requirement, specification, prescription, precept, principle, guiding principle; standard, criterion, measure, gauge, yardstick, benchmark, touchstone; procedure, parameter, constraint, limit. (Hanks, 2000)

Guidelines are all the above – and even more. Despite their omnipresence, guidelines are quite poorly defined as a non-legal category. Environmental governance literature tends to concentrate on formal intergovernmental policy agreements. Guidelines, at best, appear down the line in individual articles. In the architecture of international law, they are often lumped together with the rather amorphous body of 'soft law', defined negatively as non-binding or non-enforceable principles and statements prescribing action or bringing up a new topic for international normativity. Guidelines may expand upon an existing standard, as they may trail-blaze normativity in new areas. Their normative properties are unstable. They may, alternatively, be seen as in opposition to law and normativity altogether, relegated to (perceived secondary) operational and technical roles.

Despite the proliferation of guidelines within international organisations, the concept is virtually absent from core reference works in relation to international organisations. While this from a legal perspective reveals a normative grey zone, their popularity as a device makes anthropological sense. Their non-definition may in fact be seen as a defining quality or property allowing for their elasticity and perceived utility. It also explains the surprising variety of political contexts in which they appear. Consider, for example, their popularity among both state-centric and neoliberal regimes. In predominantly state-driven regimes, guidelines are favoured instruments to spell out in ever-increasing detail the realms of legally sanctioned action. Conversely, many neoliberal states equally embrace guidelines, limiting state intervention to the framing of voluntary action rather than direct state steering.

Saunier and Meganck, in their dictionary on environmental governance, define guidelines as 'a recommended method of working to accomplish an objective'. As they note 'a guideline is not enforced but is generally followed' (Saunier and Meganck 2007: 164). The eighteenth-century image of a guideline as the 'line marked on a surface before cutting'[2] captures the properties of description, precision and prescription. Whereas legal competence and jurisdiction may define the boundaries of law, guidelines evoke different boundaries, loci and agencies altogether. The following sections explore its confines in the context of environmental governance.

TRACKING THE EMERGENCE AND JUSTIFICATION OF GUIDELINES

The number of guidelines available in the United Nations (UN) library from the 1960s and 1970s is relatively limited, appearing with 'management language' (budgets, planning, personnel). Since then numbers have grown exponentially alongside technical cooperation activities.[3] The presence of guidelines-speak in major environmental agreements is evocative.

The Stockholm Declaration started with the 'need for a common outlook and for common principles to inspire and *guide* the peoples of the world in the preservation and enhancement of the human environment' (United Nations 1972b, italics added). Guidance from this perspective was a moral imperative, a raison d'être, indeed part of the global moral contract between the international environmental community and the peoples of the world. The Stockholm Action Plan for the Human Environment included seven references to guidelines, covering aspects ranging from pesticides, parks and fisheries to the environmental effects of hydro projects and work environments (United Nations 1972a). It suggested exchange of information on national parks and management techniques 'to serve as guidelines', rendering them the kinds of legitimacy which would materialise over the following decades in the Peruvian Amazon and elsewhere. Guidelines, from this perspective, reflect a core symbolic value of 'doing good' alongside other globally relevant technical repertoires such as reports, good practice case studies and project documents. A report about the Stockholm Conference outcomes spoke of a 'historical threshold', where 'the past may not be a reliable guide to what will be expected of public administration in the future' (IUCN 1974: 2). Instead there appeared the last four decades worth of managerial guidance and institutional proliferation projecting new futures and ways of doing things. Through its 109 recommendations, epitomizing modernistic optimism, it called for a public administration that is 'positive, future-oriented, experimental, innovative, integrative and holistic' (IUCN 1974: 10). By 1980, the 'World Conservation Strategy' (IUCN et al. 1980) emphasised ecology, life-support systems, genetic diversity and sustainable use. A year later the IUCN would note how the strategy was being well received and that many governments, NGOs and local groups were 'asking for guidance on the initiation, preparation for and content of such strategies and plans' (CEP 1981: 1). The IUCN Commission on Environmental Planning (CEP) made a 'first attempt to formulate a set of guidelines' (CEP 1981:3). Framed in systems, plans and phases, ten general guidelines involved identifying critical issues, spelling out conflicts and compatibilities. After the UN Conference on Environment and Development (UNCED) in 1992, the creation of guidelines (Carew-Reid et al. 1994) exploded, expanding from general strategies of national change, living and caring in the 1980s to more detailed micro-technicalities using domain-specific technical language. Guidelines would be mentioned seventy-eight times twenty years later in Agenda 21, the blueprint for achieving sustainable development referring both to existing guidelines and to new ones in the making (United Nations 1992). This can partly be explained by the shift towards implementing the Rio principles (Engfeldt 2009), but equally reflects the consolidation of a particular cultural form and language. As environmental degradation has intensified, guidelines have become part of a consensual standard inventory in global policy documents intended to communicate 'progress'. They respond to stated needs and calls for action which environmental organisations, of both multilateral and NGO nature, have since 1992 so masterfully exploited. The sheer number of reports and web-pages dedicated to guidance compared to 'hard' multilateral environmental agreements is illustrative. A search for 'guidelines' on the United Nations Environmental Programme[4] website led to 55,700 hits (compared to 8,080 for a search on MEAs (Multilateral Environmental Agreements). Guidelines on compliance, municipal wastewater management, information networks, consumer protection and monitoring of marine litter are among the first to appear.

A similar search on the IUCN website offers 7,760 hits for guidelines compared to 506 for MEAs.[5] Recent IUCN guidelines include protected area legislation, private sector engagement and reducing the impact of commercial logging on great apes. While guidelines may seem far away from the significance of overarching multilateral agreements, they figure naturally alongside the growing arsenal of conferences, standards, reports and procedures that make up the global environmental governance field. They represent contemporary forms of what the preamble of the UN Charter called employing the 'international machinery for the promotion of the economic and social advancement of all peoples' (United Nations 1945).

Where guidelines de jure 'rank' below harder instruments, the argument here is that they de facto occupy a significant governance space, both in terms of numbers and quality. Consider, for example, how guidelines become authoritative interpretations of harder instruments exemplified by the role of United Nations Environment Programme (UNEP) guidelines on 'compliance with and enforcement of multilateral environmental agreements' (UNEP 2006: 661) or IUCN guidelines on protected area legislation (Lausche 2011). Protected areas now cover some 13 percent of the globe's surface, not least due to intensive guidelines production to constantly expand protected area coverage. The expansion of protected areas and the attempt to treat them uniformly has long been criticised as the result of a 'blind' application of international protected area policy. Anthropologists have been in the forefront of documenting the social impacts of such work (West et al. 2006). Yet protected area policy and international agreements such as the Convention on Biological Diversity Programme of Work on Protected Areas are relatively recent, and only binding in a limited way. At stake, in fact, is rather the role and influence of guidance.

Where key conventions operate with distinct secretariats, procedures and responsibilities, guidelines appear as flexible and free-floating transposable devices whose authorship, ownership and practices need singular analysis to be adequately understood. Their formulation and implementation may be relatively formalised, or the very opposite. Whereas many of the protected area guidelines mentioned above have been written by technical specialists, others, such as the Food and Agriculture Organization (FAO) voluntary guidelines on 'Responsible Governance of Tenure of Land, Fisheries and Forests in the Context of National Food Security', are negotiated documents. To understand such differences requires stepping back and addressing a series of prototypical arguments and qualities linked to guidance.

The main, and generally explicit, justification of guidelines is of a functionalist kind. For technocrats, guidelines are necessary instruments of explanation and guidance in an ever more complex world 'despite politics'. Within such discursive jungles, guidelines offer walkable paths or layman's guides, enabling users to find their way. They also, alongside other soft-law siblings such as codes, principles, reports or declarations, offer vehicles of normativity, where treaty-making is either impossible or without effect (Birnie et al. 2009: 34). They are thus fundamentally, from the viewpoint of their institutional homes, about addressing commonly agreed upon challenges and normative complexity in practical ways under *competent* guidance. Environmental affairs, more than anything, epitomise such complexity, a characteristic per se presented as justifying guidance roughly since the establishment of global environmental governance processes. Guidance, in this functionalist vein, is part of the core business and mandate of international organisations promoting dialogue, facilitating technical cooperation and enhancing knowledge.

From early on, environmental politics remained largely a domain of expert dominance and administrative rationalism (Dryzek 2005: 95). In the environmental field, a managerial turn was particularly clear as conservation became a global issue. Take the 1968 UNESCO meeting on 'the scientific basis for the rational use and conservation of the resources of the biosphere' (UNESCO 1970). Recommendations urged developed countries to share their legislation with the rest of the world (UNESCO 1970: 250–251) and specifically called for making experienced *hommes* [sic] *de science* available to developing countries. The 1968 UNESCO conference involved recognising human impacts, deteriorating environments and the need for conservation and rational use of resources (1970: 217). It recommended UNESCO set up an international research programme on man and the biosphere, among other things, recognising the 'good start' made by NGOs (1970: 239). States were recommended to protect their genetic heritage, inventory resources and fix priorities for optimal use. International organisations, including NGOs, were requested to generate a 'scientific basis' for the rational use of resources (1970: 246). Processes to unify and coordinate management systems accelerated and international environmental guidance was born. Guidelines, on concerns like protected areas, became part and parcel of the technical repertoires used to work within the newly recognised global system of environmental cooperation and needy localities. They represented Weberian rational forms of organisation breaking down global problems into smaller sub-sets and devising ways forward.

Two decades prior to my fieldwork in Peru, the Palcazu valley had acted as a laboratory for the development of national, and even hemispheric guidelines (INADE APODESA 1990; OAS 1987). It was not simply a peripheral site where internationally authored guidelines were being rolled out, but the basis for abstracting broader principles of thought and action. Throughout the 1970s, the Yanesha had become increasingly organised and vocal on development planning issues. As a major frontier colonisation project for the jungle area was in the pipeline backed by funding from the United States Agency for International Development (USAID), public protest and lobbying by the Yanesha, NGOs and their supporters eventually transformed it into a more benign 'resource management' project (Smith 1982). The Organization of American States (OAS) would later use this very resource management experience to produce guidelines 'for Planning the Use of American Humid Tropic Environments' (OAS 1987). The project served as a template for technical potential. The authors recycled local experiences in the Peruvian jungle into broad principles, explicitly seeking to tone down contentious issues, while emphasising technical possibilities. As the OAS director of regional development noted at the time: 'we discuss the concepts and methods of environmental management, but the words "environment" and "environmental" are seldom used; and horror stories are conspicuously absent' (OAS 1987). Instead, they suggested acting upon a range of technical topics – ecosystem structures, colonisation matters and the understanding of conflicts. A recommendation to 'use an environmental management advisor' (OAS 1987: 161) cemented the managerial response without the 'hasty analyses and confrontational pronouncements' of the 'environmental movement' (OAS 1987: xii). As the preface optimistically concluded:

> The result is a set of guidelines to set the stage for a level of environmental management that could lead to full, long lasting and equitably distributed use of the nearly infinite resources of the American humid tropics. (OAS 1987: xiv)

The authors actively sought to promote the relevance of technical guidance in a contested political landscape, showing how environmental management and equity could be reached without the OAS becoming a cell of green activists. The case epitomised how technical guidelines were often contrasted with the radical (read: irrational) critique of environmental movements anticipating the depoliticised discourse dominant in the Rio outputs (Chatterjee and Finger 1994). No need for sticks and shaming in the face of such enlightened insight into efficient solutions. Such technical and diplomatic logics, retreating from the politics of ecology, underscore much guidance-speak, and underlie technical solutions when the limitations imposed by the internal affairs of sovereign states, and their critiques, have proved insuperable.

From this perspective, finding one's way in the convoluted jungles of governance and other impenetrable domains – almost inevitably – requires some kind of guidance, and international organisations are ready to provide it. Proponents emphasise the advantages of the non-obligatory nature of guidelines, offering reluctant state actors technical carrots and means to consider innovation without the force of binding obligations. Guidelines offer vehicles to bring 'new concerns' to international negotiating tables, or conclude negotiations through non-binding measures (thus taking on the meaning of 'soft law'). Guidelines, from this perspective, potentially pave the way for harder agreements and instruments. Examples include the UNEP guidelines preceding the 1989 Basel Convention on transboundary movement of waste and the UNEP and FAO guidelines preceding the Rotterdam Convention on the Prior Informed Consent Procedure for Certain Hazardous Chemicals and Pesticides in International trade (Redgwell 2010: 694). Other examples are the International Atomic Energy Agency guidelines appearing after Chernobyl, eventually leading to a Convention on the Early Notification of a Nuclear Accident as well as UNEP guidelines on environmental impact assessments and marine pollution (Boyle 2010: 127). Guidelines, in contrast to complexity of legal language and obligations, are promoted as flexible ways or recipes to cook up problem-solving without the constraints of international responsibility. Their crafting entails practical formats, accessibility and 'functional' simplicity. While the functionalist argument is clear, the OAS guidelines from the Palcazu also reveal the politics of guidance and the importance of analytically moving beyond a strictly utilitarian perspective in understanding their authorship and effects.

In contrast to the functionalist argument above, critiques take guidelines as signs of environmental governance failure to reach more binding agreements. They are seen as second-best residual outcomes to non-resolved, and often politically controversial, issues. The world faces daunting environmental challenges, yet global institutions put in place are born crippled and limited to voluntary guidance and other instruments as strategies and plans of action; for some authors such institutions seem designed to fail by diffusing or disabling any coherent response. The predominance of guidelines – on topics ranging from climate change mitigation and global forest (dis)agreements to transnational corporations – alongside other voluntary measures, from the governance failure perspective, offers only poor substitutes for solid conventions and standards. Here the idea of global processes such as the 1992 Earth Summit is constrained from the outset (Chatterjee and Finger 1994). From this commonly held realist perspective, guidelines reflect the weak or second-best result of global negotiations and individual states not interested in granting sufficient powers, instead leaving normative space to be addressed through residual voluntary guidelines. From this perspective, international organisations are left with impotent normative instruments and a 'technical slot', neutralising the politics at stake and offering little chance of influencing actual state behaviour. Such arguments also resonate with critical analysis of environment and development machineries as anti-politics (Ferguson 1994). Where optimists conceive voluntary guidance as a stepping stone to tougher obligations, pessimists see them as legal dead-ends.

Rational guidance on tropical forests in the Peruvian Amazon in the 1980s emerged in a context of not only a crumbling state but also deforestation, guerrilla activity and coca production. Equally illustrative of guidelines' limitations has been the emphasis on guidance and voluntary measures in relation to extractive industries and the recent oil concession bonanza. Flexible language in relation to environmental impact assessments and mitigation planning, for example, has been severely criticised by activists for lacking teeth and hence the ability to change corporate behaviour. Yet such critique may miss a series of key potentialities inherent in guidelines. Reducing guidelines to signs of dysfunctional global or national regimes leaves us poorly equipped to address and understand their wider social significance and proliferation. I would argue that more attention is needed to separate out their actual function and practice. In the following I explore different avenues for interpreting guidelines in practice, while moving beyond both their immediate functionalities and the dysfunction critique.

TECHNO-POLITICS: MANOEUVRING THE TECHNICAL SLOT

Some lay commentators make the error of giving less credit to such quiet, invisible and humble measures that are less prominent in comparison to highly publicised measures like sanctions. However the complex reality of international life rarely reflects this superficial view of things. (Kolb 2010: 143)

Technical guidelines are by definition part of the apolitical space allocated, indeed demarcated, for international secretariats and supportive NGOs. Consider, for example, how natural resources are enshrined as a fundamental national sovereignty issue in Article 1 of both the International Covenant on Economic, Social and Cultural Rights and the International Covenant on Civil and Political Rights. The global South has, since decolonisation days, rejected northern impositions, fundamentally framing the contours of global debates on the environment in a sovereignty context. Soft guidelines, in turn, have offered politically acceptable ways for northern donors and organisations to engage with southern resource realities and to some extent bypass traditional political boundaries.

Distinct from functionalism or the cul-de-sac critique of governance failure, the emphasis here is on the techno-politics of guidance. This implies avoiding taking technical functionalism at face value (Bebbington et al. 2004: 36). Among international civil servants, there is generally strong awareness of the political ramifications of their technical work. Nor does the 'governance failure' argument do full justice to the creativity of guidelines production, strategic use and influence. The apolitics of technicality is not a dominant ideology, but more like a discursive constraint. Safely located under the benevolent umbrella of 'technical assistance', guidelines form part of operations (vs. the normativity of established decision-making bodies). Guidelines do not depoliticise but form part of replaying politics in technical terms (for the World Bank context see Bebbington et al. 2004: 51). The OAS guidelines were entitled 'minimum conflict', the preface arguing that environmentalists and the development community were 'showing signs of coming together'.

Whereas such coming together locally in the Peruvian Amazon resulted from political struggle and arm-twisting (Smith 1982), techno-politics, through reformulated 'resource management' projects and guidelines, translated contentious Amazonian politics into Amazonian technicalities. Even the term 'environment' was considered political and was avoided except in the term 'environmental management' or where it was accompanied by a 'description of a specific environment'.

Political disagreement was reframed in the guidelines in neutral terms such as misguided policy, lack of coordination and scarce information. I label this 'techno-politics' – something quite distinct from the anti-politics machine. It allows us to refocus on the political cultures of influence through technical means. Techno-politics involves managerial interventions greasing the wheels of tired machineries and conflicting state positions. The argument here is that the global environmental governance field, from its origins, has been a highly contested arena, where outcomes are in part determined by the mastery of technicality and ability to 'win the argument'. 'If there is a will, there is a way', international organisations are fond of repeating at general assemblies. Yet guidelines also reveal that if there is a (technical) way, (political) will may be generated. As the OAS guidelines authors noted:

> It is incumbent upon the planner to design development efforts that minimize conflict taking neither one side nor the other but making sure that all sides understand and agree to what has been proposed. That is the real route of minimal conflict and, if offered, the decision maker will take it. (OAS 1987: 184)

The depoliticised language of guidance does not rule out politics, it merely displaces it to different arenas and forms of action. Depoliticised managerial action through capacity-building, expert dialogue and technological transfer, at least in some forums, has come to predominate over conventional political decision-making (Müller 2011). Guidelines may form part of transforming politically contentious issues such as indigenous rights or social contestation into technical and 'do-able' matters. On the one hand guidelines thus serve as a legitimate way of dealing with what has been described as the 'creative tension' encountered by UN officials (United Nations 2011: 19). On the other hand, they exemplify how international organisations may act politically through technical means, thus remaining within their statutory confines while prescribing and reproducing remedies reflecting dominant organisational paradigms (Wade 1996). Guidelines, from this perspective, may be conceived as techno-political devices combining legitimacy, representation and prescription. They allow international organisations to reconfigure themselves and their relationship with nation states. This, I have argued, prompts a need for analytical attention to guidelines as new sites and forms of normative ordering, often with different systems of authorship, accountability and priorities. This I believe can be more explicitly stated, by rehearsing Gregory Bateson's notion of meta-communication.

GUIDELINES AS PLAY AND META-COMMUNICATION

Guidelines fundamentally create a particular relationship between a guide, who guides, and a follower or user being guided. They thus allow, in meta-communicative terms, social relations of representation, hierarchy and symbolical authority to be set up. This is evident in cases where guidelines appear as authoritative statements on a given subject. They may entail 'playing' in new fields as well as (re)producing moral authority and legitimacy in highly moving fields. This was particularly clear in the case of the Yanesha. Whereas consultants and planners used guidelines to develop a management plan, they also implied technical specialists 'knowing better' than local communities and speaking with the voice of authority. Such use of guidelines reveals a distinctive set of (hoped-for) properties well beyond their immediate technical contents.

I suggest introducing Gregory Bateson's (1973) notions of play and meta-communication to capture this creative dimension of guidance politics at stake. I use his notion of 'play' here, to portray guidelines not merely as technical direction but as wider communicative acts. Environmentalists, following the managerial turn, moved away from societal change and politics; here Bateson's work on play, framing and meta-communication allows us to interpret guidelines as environmentalists returning to questions of societal change and transformation using a different script. Bateson's classic example is of observing two young monkeys 'playing' as if in combat, yet clearly signalling, 'not being in combat'. This was used to illustrate the concept of meta-communication, that is, how social practice carries another level of signals ('non-combat') beyond its immediate meaning ('combat'). We may, in turn, use the concept here for managerial manifestations of determining good conduct through guidelines.

Guidelines are not only about reaching specific finalities (such as clean environments), but meta-communicating 'convenience', in Foucault's sense of things disposed in ways that arrange a plurality of specific aims as part of the evolving 'art of government' (Foucault 1991 [1978]). Prescriptive guidelines not only communicate their specific 'how to' contents, but meta-communicate contextual significance. They may not actually inform activities, but nevertheless communicate or flag the technical authority and ability of organisations to respond to contemporary matters. They denote long lists of expected changes, but not real forced change. Guidelines have a forward-looking temporality and potentiality versus the hands-on 'bite' of critical analysis and political debate. They conveniently imply change without necessarily pointing fingers at current problems – merely suggesting other ways of doing things. They thus meta-communicate a distinct position of authority in the environmental governance field, proposing 'change without change' so to speak. They s(t)imulate change where organisations or a country are being criticised while respecting the confines of sovereignty. While critical analysis may list such 'non-bites' as governance failure or lip service, I would argue that such a critique reduces the wider importance and significance of guidelines proliferation as a locus of change and meta-communicating authority. Clearly, there are ample examples of both. Guidelines may represent the non-binding as equivalent to the non-implemented, just as they may reveal spheres of innovation, positioning and change in building new normative standards. Guidelines are used to perform, to communicate exploratory games of innovation and change just as they are used to resist, co-opt and contain change. Such games have their roots in guidelines as communicative acts reflecting a number of potentialities.

Environmental governance remains a field whose boundaries, architecture and destinations remain in motion. Boaventura de Sousa Santos (1987: 283) has made the point about law including a dialectic of both representation and orientation. This is even more evident in the case of guidelines. Guidelines are not merely the 'technical end-product' following up on negotiations in operational terms, but a constitutive element in the ongoing framing of international environmental regimes in the first place. Guidelines do not merely steer actors through an opaque field, but help define and represent the field as such. As representational instruments and scale-making projects (Tsing 2000), guidelines contribute towards discursively defining the contents and contours of the field. Guidelines on protected area processes are particularly illustrative of this link between mapping an area and prescribing use regulations. Developing guidelines allows for the mapping out and the technical incorporation of particular and new political concerns, even where formal politics and procedures are in a deadlock. The proliferation of guidance on a wide range of climate change mitigation and adaptation aspects is particularly illustrative of its potentiality as a new device of international normativity. Domain capture or coding issues in particular ways, through a dual process of representation and prescription, characterise how guidelines are integral to what Charles Goodwin (1994) has labelled the professional vision. Authoritative guidelines not only reveal how to move about within a given field but also, in meta-communicative terms, describe what the world looks like in the first place. Underneath the technical surface, they entail the creation of new fields and positioning within these (Bourdieu and Wacquant 1992). Technically neutral guidelines thus disguise major political battles over the nature of a problem field in the first place. David Mosse (2005) has made this point in his ethnography of development agencies, where guidelines become convincing arguments and tools of legitimacy and authority. Production of guidelines thus gains meaning, not from the direct sense of steering followers, but from the perspective of competing representations and ability to remain relevant in highly competitive international arenas. Guidelines involve similar representational authority to an atlas, maps or illustrations. Take for example *The Gaia Atlas of Planet Management* (Myers 1985), edited roughly in the same years as the OAS guidelines aiming to be '*the* definitive guide to the crisis of the planet and humanity'. Global interconnections, environmental crisis and chaos became favoured representations on the part of environmental organisations intimately tied to 'steering' the world in the right direction. It was a similar logic to the 'spaceship Earth' image put forward by Adlai Stevenson, speaking at the UN in 1965, of humanity travelling together 'dependent on its [the Earth's] vulnerable reserves of air and soil'. Guidelines play a constitutive role in the renewal and adaptation of managerial problem sites and new prescriptive recipes. The combination of the descriptive and the prescriptive allows for international organisations to stabilise particular forms of meaning and action in turbulent governance fields. The logic is not only one of having people do particular things but also, more subtly, about consolidating particular ways of thinking, framing and talking about problem fields.

Yet, as a former colleague once said: 'Nobody reads guidelines any more!' Whereas the world conservation strategy (IUCN et al. 1980) and its by-products led to national strategies in over 50 countries (Munro 1991), the fate of many contemporary guidelines is far less certain. Although protected area guidelines are still appreciated by professionals (Turner 2009), many remain in the databases of international organisations and the resumés of their authors. They may claim to define meanings and action, but what does it matter if no one reads them? This can be understood by interpreting guidelines through the lens of meta-communication, as part of a broader quest not only for representation of environmental concerns but also as a legitimacy- and hierarchy-producing exercise.

ON HIERARCHY AND LEGITIMISATION

By stating what should be done, guidelines are hierarchy-producing exercises confirming particular kinds of authorities, whether in legal or technical domains. Binding guidelines – delineating how to implement law – thus confirm a practical hierarchy of actions corresponding to codified law. Non-binding guidance, in contrast, mainly confirms hierarchies of knowledge, agency and practice. From one perspective, they illustrate what Hannah Arendt called the bureaucratic rule of nobody, 'an intricate system of bureaux in which no men, neither one nor the best, neither the few nor the many, can be held responsible' (1969: 10), yet nevertheless as offices upholding 'best' practice.

They build authority around environment practitioners, government officials and expert-scientists participating in their authorship and giving advice. They also implicitly devalue other forms of actions, knowledge and knowledge holders – those not listed or quoted, and obviously those in need of advisors in the first place. Gregory Bateson (1973) emphasised precisely how playing was fundamentally about confirming relationships. Note how one of the OAS guidelines on the topics under the heading of conflict identification encourages 'use [of] an environmental management advisor'. Not unlike the phrase 'Get a psychologist!', the guidelines assumed that humid tropic troubles were better resolved with expertise on board from the start. For the Yanesha in the Palcazu, state agents had required protected area planners to be *professionals*. The latter, in turn, referred to international guidance to establish authority. Guidelines represented language judged credible and hierarchically superior to the everyday speak of indigenous leaders. While indigenous leaders clearly knew the forest area much better, guidelines as a set of principles and activities cemented a hierarchical relationship between 'expert planners' guiding 'locals' – incidentally in need of conservation. Technical propositions and procedures, couched in guidelines language, situated their operators as glocally relevant, even if their knowledge of local socio-ecological realities was limited.

Guidelines thus simultaneously create hierarchies of knowledge (someone knows better), hierarchies of agency (someone acts better) and hierarchies outlining the contours of appropriate action (some things work better). For donors they imply direction and hierarchy in relation to unruly nation states or funded organisations. For organisations they imply a symbolic knowledge hierarchy in relation to needy governments and competing organisations. For governments, they imply hierarchies – however slippery – in relation to corporations and other social actors. For technocrats they represent order within confused politics. For consultants, way down the hierarchy, they offer sources of legitimacy and common language.

Guidelines are not merely about 'how to' implement a given decision, regulation or engage in problem-solving, but often accumulate and encapsulate a whole set of moralities and norms redefining the contours of the field. The moral lessons given by protected area planners to Yanesha were illustrative. Long-standing local relationships with forests were transformed into deficient versions of 'ideal' protected area practice. Guidelines form part of the work undertaken by those Strathern labelled 'moral fieldworkers' (2000: 2). They imply the need for more of their sort – say, for example, by channelling development finance to big international organisations, given their technical capabilities and the authorship behind guidance.

The Rio summit favoured the participation, language and style of mainstream environmental organisations that promoted politically acceptable forms of social change (Chatterjee and Finger 1994). As organisations made use of new international and national governance space offered, technical policy recommendations came to predominate over radical transformative ecologies. Guidance offered apolitical ways of promoting change as well as competing in the new marketplace depending on political acceptance, technical competence and authority. Whereas Agenda 21 was the 'soft' plan, guidelines involved the doing – and competition for the growing resources made available for – environmental action. In that sense, rather than simply guide action, say of their own officials to start with, guidelines are often used to mobilise further support and interest – much like project documents. They form part of the repertoires of technically contesting or reproducing hierarchies and scales that underlie global environmental governance. Guidelines become the contents of training courses, the basis for measuring 'local' implementation, national policy and technical know-how.

They represent forms of technical warfare within contested policy terrains. They serve to compete for donor funding as well as being polite ways of 'winning' discursive battles between competing departments, specialist groups and other organisations. Conservation organisations, for example, thus typically operate with different guidelines for setting conservation priorities, which scales to work at and what efforts to support on the ground.

The truth is of course, that guidelines are generally written, not from a position of, but rather an aspiration for, such power. Technical advisors rarely have the final word, although certain political regimes have been more inclined to listen to them than others (Scott 1998). In effect, while guidelines proliferate and keep experts busy, their actual social effects are another story.

THE POLITICS AND EFFECTS OF GUIDELINES

Where international organisations may appear weak, neutral and 'technical', ethnography reveals their profound presence, political nature and impacts on local socio-environmental realities. What appears as 'soft text' or technical detail from an international law perspective may become hard reality on the ground through international funding schemes, testing realities and social engineering. The protected area field is a case in point, of which there were 130,709 by 2011, covering more than 24 million square kilometres, or more than twice the size of Canada.[6] Such expansion was not the result of hard conventions, but involved complex interplays between soft commitments, global conservation finance and technical guidance. Just as Gerhard Anders (2005) showed how good governance principles became conditions rather than potential good ideas, we also saw how guidelines were employed and became hard realities affecting management approaches and local resource use among the Yanesha. In the early 1980s, as USAID withdrew funding for agricultural frontier projects, protected area creation became a donor condition for continued support to a reworked resource management project. Such funding was instrumental in setting up the three protected areas today neighbouring Yanesha communities. Twenty years later, NGO guidelines were employed to further managerialise the Yanesha resource space.

Whereas guidelines may be seen as technocratic power devices, they are equally devices of social critique, resistance and activism. Producing guidelines offers technical opportunities to reach and contest political hierarchies otherwise out of reach. They offer legitimate non-political ways of engaging political spheres, providing access to decision-makers, interest groups and local bureaucracies. While privileging managerial protagonists, they nevertheless offer Trojan horses and weapons of the weak to engage and contest on managerial terrains. Civil society guidelines to understand multilateral processes, agreements and global institutions are a case in point. Guidelines are not confined to global think tanks in the centre, but are authored, employed, used – and resisted – across a range of localities. Guideline-type documents by organisations that are technically 'savvy' about the international rights system are a case in point. As guidelines have proliferated, indigenous representatives have been particularly successful in employing international soft standards as strategic 'weapons' to question policies and project practice on the ground. World Bank guidelines ('operational directives'), for example, are continually evoked by indigenous peoples and their support organisations to challenge infrastructure projects and loans.

Contesting state and international standard-setting monopolies through technicality also comes from other circles. Consider the International Council on Mining and Metals (ICMM), a coalition of fifteen major mining companies, producing 'Good Practice Guidance' on mining and biodiversity (ICMM 2006). 'Practical' steps are offered which de facto establish normative benchmarks for corporate performance compared to some rather modest references to national legislation and international standards.[7] Where UN efforts failed in establishing a code of conduct for transnational corporations (Gorman 2001: 242), voluntary measures and guidelines produced by civil society and industry have appeared. In sum, guidelines are not merely techno-driven sites of normalisation by international organisations and state bureaucracies, but equally sites of normative positioning by businesses, NGOs and social movements. Decrypting the politics of guidelines is thus also about simultaneously expanding the horizontal and vertical gazes of actors and authorship.

CONCLUDING REMARKS: NEOLIBERAL GUIDELINES CULTURE?

As arguments rage on about whether or not guidelines offer effective instruments, this chapter suggests recasting the debate. While the history of guidance as non-coercive power is old, guidelines as a source of power, legitimacy and action for non-state actors is arguably a contemporary phenomenon.

The significance of guidelines, I have argued, relates less to their technical contents than to their systemic flexible properties within the realm of managerial logics and authority-building. Catherine Weaver, studying the World Bank, spoke of its 'intellectual culture' characterised by economism, apolitics and technical rationality (2007: 493). Similar practices or technical-political cultures, arguably prevail across a range of international governance fields. We might, analogically, speak of an international guidelines culture, a proposal I here put forward to dialogue with Marilyn Strathern's (2000) notion of audit cultures to portray it as a socio-cultural field worthy of ethnographic attention. It encompasses technical visions of the world and depoliticised ways of prescribing action. Whereas audit culture is about assessing or verifying social acts and practices, guidelines culture suggests social action is legitimate and renders it possible. Where auditing uses sticks, that is, monitoring practices and possibilities of sanction, guidelines represent carrots and point to the efficiency of good conduct. They have become vehicles for story-telling, practicality and appropriate performance, linking global flows of politics, finance and power to local issues, problems and dynamics. Thus, while the Palcazu valley became the site of oil exploration as part of a nation-wide oil concession spree (Finer et al. 2008), district and protected area planning processes paid only scant attention to such concerns, even when environmental legislation was bypassed (Larsen 2011). Guidelines reflect long-standing modern ideas of hierarchies of knowledge, and the long-established state practice of operating within what is possible, rather than what is to be punished. Gramsci, for example, spoke of states not only punishing, but also urging, inciting and soliciting – civilising activities (2007: 247).

This obviously resonates with the neoliberal idea of empowering individual choice and rationales within a deregulated state (Cheater 1999), where rules are not imposed but suggested. In the global architecture of weak international and state organisations, guidelines perhaps illustrate how international collaboration has been compartmentalised thereby, and specialised in micro-spheres of techno-normativity. Each organisation, in turn reflecting such values of choice and freedom, develops its own tools, reflecting its own values, focus areas and entrenched languages, often facing great difficulty in communicating across institutional boundaries. Within the last few decades, both corporate and NGO actors have appropriated new governance spaces and called for moral legitimacy where wider authority is absent. Managerialism and market-driven governance have become natural bedfellows as influence is linked to claiming and mastering domains and showing 'added value'. Guidelines thus reveal new legitimate ways of meandering and retracing acceptable paths within de- or unregulated institutional landscapes. They offer reference points, and legitimacy, for consultants, NGOs and corporate actors to de facto author prescriptions, claim authority and influence decision-making normally beyond their political reach and legal competence. In the same way as anthropologists have studied law, we need to study guidance as a contemporary locus of normative ordering, politics and power involving new agencies, arenas and playgrounds, as well as the recycling, containment and reproduction of old hierarchies and territory.

NOTES

1. Earlier versions of this chapter were presented and benefited from inputs at different meetings in Philadelphia, Paris, Lucerne and Geneva. I am particularly grateful to Birgit Müller for her careful reading and comments.
2. See: http://www.etymonline.com/ (consulted 21 November 2011).
3. Whereas a UN library search on guidelines published before 1978 shows 129 hits, an open search between 1978 and 2009 exceeds the maximum list of results (8287). See: unbisnet.un.org (consulted 23 November 2009).
4. Guidelines production appeared early in the definition of UNEP core functions. It was part of the foundational logic of an agency supposed to provide 'general policy guidance' on environmental programmes within the UN system.
5. Both searches were done on 6 June 2012.
6. See: http://www.wdpa.org/Statistics.aspx (consulted 2 April 2012).
7. The first time the word 'law' appears in the guidance document is in a sub-set concerned with mining site closure (ICMM 2006: 44). 'Legislation' appears in guidance encouraging companies to have biodiversity policy statements committing them to 'comply with applicable legislation and regulations' (2006: 65).

BIBLIOGRAPHY

Anders, Gerhard (2005) 'Good governance as technology: Towards an ethnography of the Bretton Woods institutions', in David Mosse and David Lewis (eds) *The Aid Effect* (London: Pluto).

Arendt, Hannah (1969) 'Reflections on violence', *New York Review of Books* (special supplement, February).

Bateson, Gregory (1973) *Steps to an Ecology of Mind: Collected Essays in Anthropology, Psychiatry, Evolution and Epistemology* (London: Paladin Granada Publishing).

Bebbington, Anthony, Scott Guggenheim, Elizabeth Olson and Michael Woolcock (2004) 'Exploring social capital debates at the World Bank', *Journal of Development Studies* 40(5): 33–64.

Birnie, Patricia, Alan Boyle and Catherine Redgwell (2009) *International Law and the Environment* (Oxford: Oxford University Press).

Borrini-Feyerabend, Grazia, Ashish Kothari and Gonzalo Oviedo (2004) *Indigenous and Local Communities and Protected Areas: Towards Equity and Enhanced Conservation Guidance on Policy and Practice for Co-managed Protected Areas and Community Conserved Areas* (Gland: World Commission on Protected Areas, IUCN).

Bourdieu, Pierre and Löic Wacquant (1992) *Réponses* (Paris: Seuil).

Boyle, Alan (2010) 'Soft law in international law-making', in Malcolm Evans (ed.) *International Law* (Oxford: Oxford University Press).

Carew-Reid, Jeremy, Robert Prescott-Allen, Stephen Bass and Barry Dalal-Clayton (1994) *Strategies for National Sustainable Development: A Handbook for their Planning and Implementation* (London: IIED, IUCN and Earthscan).

Carling, Joan, Johnson Ole Kaunga, Maria Tuyuc. Elizabeth Moreno, Peter Bille Larsen and Diane Vinding (2006) *Manual for Combating Child Labour among Indigenous and Tribal Peoples*, ILO/PRO 169 (Geneva: International Labour Office).

CEP (Commission on Environmental Planning) (1981) 'Environmental planning approaches to the preparation of conservation strategies and plans for sustainable development', publication based on a workshop on environmental planning guidelines for strategies and plans (Costa Rica: IUCN Commission on Environmental Planning).

Chatterjee, Pratap and Matthias Finger (1994) *The Earth Brokers: Power, Politics and World Development* (London: Routledge).

Cheater, Angela (ed.) (1999) *The Anthropology of Power* (London: Routledge).

Descola, Philippe (2006) *Par-delà nature et culture* (Paris: Gallimard).

Dryzek, John (2005) *The Politics of Earth: Environmental Discourses*, 2nd edn (Oxford: Oxford University Press).

Engfeldt, Lars-Göran (2009) *From Stockholm to Johannesburg and Beyond: The Evolution of the International System for Sustainable Development Governance and its Implications* (Stockholm: Swedish Ministry of Foreign Affairs).

Ferguson, James (1994) *The Anti-politics Machine: 'Development', Depoliticization and Bureaucratic Power in Lesotho* (Minneapolis: University of Minnesota Press).

Finer, Matt, Clinton Jenkins, Stuart Pimm, Brian Keane and Carl Ross (2008) 'Oil and gas projects in the western Amazon: Threats to wilderness, biodiversity, and indigenous peoples', *PLoS ONE* 3(8).

Foucault, Michel (1991 [1978]) 'Governmentality', in Graham Burchell, Colin Gordon and Peter Miller (eds) *The Foucault Effect: Studies in Governmentality* (Chicago: University of Chicago Press).

Goodwin, Charles (1994) 'Professional vision', *American Anthropologist* 96(3): 606–633.

Gorman, Robert (2001) *Great Debates at the United Nations: An Encyclopedia of Fifty Key Issues, 1945–2000* (Westport, CT: Greenwood Press).

Gramsci, Antonio (2007) *Selections From the Prison Notebooks* (London: Lawrence and Wishart).

Hanks, Patrick (2000) *The New Oxford Thesaurus of English* (Oxford: Oxford University Press).

ICMM (2006) *Good Practice Guidance for Mining and Biodiversity* (London: International Council on Mining and Metals).

INADE APODESA (1990) *Desarollo sostenido de la selva* (Lima: USAID and Ronco Consulting Corporation).

IUCN (1974) 'Implications for the public administration of the United Nations conference on the Human Environment', in United Nations (ed.) *Organization and Administration of Environmental Programmes* (Geneva: Department of Economic and Social Affairs).

IUCN et al. (1980) 'The world conservation strategy: living resource conservation for sustainable development', (Gland).

Kolb, Robert (2010) *An Introduction to the Law of the United Nations* (Oxford: Hart Publishing).

Larsen, Peter Bille (2011) 'Municipal environmental governance in the Peruvian Amazon: A case study in local matters of (in)significance', *Management of Environmental Quality* 22(3): 374–385.

Larsen, Peter Bille and Jenny Springer (2008) *Mainstreaming WWF Principles on Indigenous Peoples and Conservation in Project and Programme Management* (Gland, CH: WWF).

Lausche, Barbara (2011) *Guidelines for Protected Areas Legislation*, IUCN Environmental Policy and Law Papers (Gland: World Conservation Union).

Maffi, Luisa, Gonzalo Oviedo and Peter Bille Larsen (2000) *Indigenous and Traditional Peoples of the World and Ecoregion Conservation: An Integrated Approach to Conserving the World's Biological and Cultural Diversity* (Gland, CH: Terra Lingua and WWF).

Mosse, David (2005) *Cultivating Development: An Ethnography of Aid Policy and Practice* (London: Pluto).

Müller, Birgit (2011) 'The elephant in the room: Multi-stakeholder dialogue on agricultural biotechnology in the FAO', in Cris Shore, Davide Però and Sue Wright (eds) *Policy Worlds: Anthropology and the Anatomy of Contemporary Power* (Oxford: Berghahn).

Müller, Birgit (2012) 'Comment rendre le monde gouvernable sans le gouverner: Les organisations internationales analysées par les anthropologues', *Critique internationale* 54.

Munro, David (1991) *Caring for the Earth: A Strategy for Sustainable Living* (Gland, CH: IUCN).

Myers, Norman (1985) *The Gaia Atlas of Planet Management*, revised and extended edn (London: Gaia Books).

OAS (1987) *Minimum Conflict: Guidelines for Planning the Use of American Humid Tropic Environments. Case Studies of Environmental Management: Integrated Development of an Area in the Humid Tropics – The Selva Central of Peru Project* (Washington, DC: OAS and UNEP).

Redgwell, Catherine (2010) 'International environmental law', in Malcolm Evans (ed.) *International Law* (Oxford: Oxford University Press).

Santos, Boaventura de Sousa (1987) 'Law: A map of misreading toward a postmodern conception of law', *Journal of Law and Society* 14(3): 279–302.

Saunier, Richard E. and Richard Albert Meganck (2007) *Dictionary and Introduction to Global Environmental Governance* (London: Earthscan).

Scott, James (1998) *Seeing Like a State: How Certain Schemes to Improve the Human Condition Have Failed* (New Haven, CT: Yale University Press).

Smith, Richard C. (1982) *Dialectics of Domination in Perú – Native Communities and the Myth of the Vast Amazonian Emptiness: An Analysis of Development*

Planning in the Pichis Palcazu Special Project. Cultural Survival Occasional Paper 8 (Cambridge, MA: Cultural Survival Institute).

Strathern, Marilyn (2000) 'New accountabilities: Anthropological studies in audit, ethics and the academy', in Marilyin Strathern (ed.) *Audit Cultures: Anthropological Studies in Accountability, Ethics and the Academy* (New York: Routledge).

Tsing, Anna Lowenhaupt (2000) 'Inside the economy of appearances', *Public Culture* 12(1).

Turner, Stephen (2009) *Strategic Review of the IUCN Programme on Protected Areas*. Available at: http://cmsdata.iucn.org/downloads/ppa_review_report_28_nov_09.pdf (consulted February 2012).

UNEP (2006) *Manual on Compliance with and Enforcement of Multilateral Environmental Agreements (MEAs)*. Nairobi: UNEP Division of Environmental Conventions.

UNESCO (1970) *Utilisation et conservation de la biosphère: Actes de la conférence intergouvernementale d'experts sur les bases scientifiques de l'utilisation rationelle et de la conservation des ressources de la biosphère, 4–13 septembre 1968* (Paris: UNESCO).

United Nations (1945) Charter of the United Nations, 24 October 1945, 1 UNTS XVI, available at: http://www.unhcr.org/refworld/docid/3ae6b3930.html (consulted March 2013).

United Nations (1972a) United Nations Conference on the Human Environment Action Plan for the Human Environment. New York: UN.

United Nations (1972b) Declaration of the United Nations Conference on the Human Environment, 21st plenary meeting, Stockholm, 16 June.

United Nations (1992) Agenda 21, United Nations Conference on Environment and Development, Rio de Janeiro, Brazil, June.

United Nations (2011) *Basic Facts about the United Nations* (New York: United Nations).

Wade, Robert (1996) 'Japan, the World Bank, and the Art of Paradigm Maintenance: The East Asian Miracle in Political Perspective', *New Left Review* I(217): 3–36.

Weaver, Catherine (2007) 'The World's Bank and the Bank's World', *Global Governance* 13: 493–512.

West, Paige, James Igoe and Dan Brockington (2006) 'Parks and Peoples: The Social Impact of Protected Areas', *Annual Review of Anthropology* 35.

Part II
Diluting Conflict – Creating Harmony

5
Before Audit Culture
A Genealogy of International Oversight of Rights

Jane K. Cowan

The key problem of global governance might be phrased: How do you get global outcomes when you don't have a global government? How do you nudge countries to do something in the 'global interest' in a context of nation state sovereignty? Attempts to resolve this problem have resulted in the emergence of a variety of global governance practices which range from sanctions and conditionality at the 'hard' end to peer review and voluntary compliance to codes of practice at the 'soft' end.

Whereas global governance tends to be examined in presentist terms, with exclusive reference to the neoliberal contemporary moment, in this chapter I introduce a longer-term perspective on the international nudging of states in relation to their agreements regarding rights and protections of their citizens. Rather than attempting a full historical account, I focus on two moments which exemplify different logics. I describe, first, some aspects of the interwar League of Nations minority treaty supervision.[1] I follow this with a description of a new human rights monitoring mechanism, Universal Periodic Review (UPR), introduced in 2008 as part of the reform of the Geneva human rights system.[2] I thus compare an interwar mechanism – involving some states and some citizens only – in which the international community scrutinised a state's treatment of its citizens, with a new mechanism, in which the international community reviews how, and how well, each and every United Nations (UN) member state is protecting and promoting the human rights of all of its citizens.

Broadly speaking, I conceptualise the movement from the first to the second to mark a shift from external supervision to what Strathern (2000) has described as audit culture. By external supervision, I mean a process centred on the practices of actors external to an entity – here, a state – to elicit compliance. Supervision in the case I examine refers to the diverse set of practices by which agents of the League of Nations, charged by its Covenant to guarantee the minorities treaties, tracked a state's treatment of its so-called minorities and, in response to complaints, tried to hold states to their treaty agreements. Acknowledging that audit takes a variety of forms in different institutional spaces and locations (see Kipnis 2008), I use the term 'audit culture' here to refer to practices of oversight that include an important element of critical self-accounting according to terms that are 'almost impossible to criticise in principle' (Strathern 2000: 3). UPR incorporates this critical self-accounting, along with numerous other elements of audit culture, although in a hybrid configuration with elements from other cultural practices, including cultures of diplomacy, peer review and of the UN system more generally.

Both processes invite a Foucauldian reading as disciplinary regimes. Yet in my archival work on the League of Nations supervision, as well as in my ethnographic work on UPR, I quickly discovered – much as David Mosse (2005) did when investigating a development project – that a totalising approach to these disciplinary regimes as producers of practices and subjectivities would not do. I saw that Foucault's emphasis on power/knowledge regimes needs to be tempered with de Certeauian interest in 'devious, dispersed consumer practices' (Certeau 1984: xiii, cited in Mosse 2005: 7). My account of these two cases thus includes not only practices of oversight, but also resistances and open contestations as to how oversight should be carried out.

A key feature of both processes is that they have opened up a space for members of the wider public to make claims about a state's treatment of its citizens, creating a new political field, in the sense of 'a configuration of forces and a site of struggle to maintain and transform those forces' (Bourdieu and Wacquant 1992: 101). Within such a field, multiple actors engage in struggles over power, authority and meaning. In both cases, the political field intersects with the bureaucratic field (Bourdieu et al. 1994) of the international organisation; my historical work in the League of Nations archives, as well as anthropological fieldwork in Geneva, have enabled entry into the less accessible and relatively understudied worlds of the Secretariat where much of the everyday work of rights monitoring occurs.

Describing very specifically the concrete practices entailed by the two processes of international oversight, while also paying attention to the contestations that oversight generate, I hope to show the distinctive operations of power in these two institutional sites. I trace this by attending to a cluster of analytical elements: the role of the Secretariat and of non-governmental organisations (NGOs) as well as fellow states in oversight, and the variable significance and meanings of certain concepts, including sovereignty, universality, transparency or visibility, and the political. In each case, actors, norms and practices operate together in a distinctive configuration.

Placing a contemporary audit process within a deeper historical timeframe allows us to identify and explore both similarities and differences, continuities and transformations in the logics and techniques of one domain of international governance over the past century. It allows us to begin to construct a genealogy, a 'history of the present' that helps us to understand how today's oversight processes became thinkable.

PRACTICES OF LEAGUE OF NATIONS MINORITY TREATY SUPERVISION

In the aftermath of the First World War, the peacemakers at the Paris Peace Conference not only haggled over the boundaries of nation states that replaced the now disintegrated pre-war empires but also set out the distinctive terms on which many of these states would relate to a newly institutionalised international order. The Committee on New States demanded that a number of states allied to the losing side, plus new or significantly enlarged states – most of them on Europe's eastern periphery – sign, as the price of international recognition, minorities treaties or agreements, guaranteeing full civil and political rights to 'persons belonging to racial, religious and linguistic minorities' as well as certain special rights relating to language, education and associational life; they handed responsibility for guaranteeing the treaties to the still unborn League of Nations. The Committee on New States justified the minority obligations by citing the continuing danger that minorities within these nationalising states would face discrimination or mistreatment, and that this could become a cause of or pretext for interstate conflict, threatening the political order of the New Europe. Consequently, in a context where state sovereignty and equality among states was the explicit norm, certain states were asked to accept both additional obligations and the international supervision that guaranteed it. The founding moment of the world's first international organisation thus also saw the creation of a more heavily encumbered category, informally but revealingly referred to as the 'Minority State'.

The problem of how, exactly, the League's guarantee would be executed was handed over to the new organisation's Secretary General, Sir Eric Drummond. The Secretariat that he was, at the time, carefully recruiting would prove to be both idealistic and enterprising, inspired by 'a spirit of initiative, a feeling of dedicating ourselves to a task ... of pursuing an ideal by taking part in a really new enterprise whose truly formidable goal was to ensure the peace' (Azcárate in Codding 1966).[3] The details of international supervision were hammered out by the canny and creative Norwegian diplomat, Erik Colban, who headed a new section of the Secretariat dealing with minorities. A minority procedure, drafted primarily by Colban but presented to the League's Council, its highest body, in October 1920 by a committee led by Italian delegate Tommaso Tittoni, navigated a path between the League's newly enshrined responsibility for collective oversight of a state's treatment of its internal 'others' and the traditional prerogatives of nation state sovereignty. Naming the Council and the Permanent Court of International Justice as the two organs charged with the practical execution of the guarantee, it set up an innovative procedure inviting petitions. Whereas only a Council member could bring an alleged infraction by a state of its minorities treaty to the Council's attention, anyone – any individual, group or state – could submit a petition to the League of Nations. However, the petition was defined as 'information, pure and simple'; it did not constitute a judicial act which called upon the Council to intervene. Three days after the Tittoni Report was adopted, the Council agreed to set up 'Minorities Committees', later called 'Committees of Three', composed of the Council President, plus two non-interested states, to consider 'any petition or communication' that concerned an alleged infraction.

Although states had formal roles in the new process, the Minorities Section – a tiny unit of, initially, two and for most of its life rarely more than half a dozen staff, known as 'officials' (all men) – was responsible for the day-to-day working of minority supervision, particularly the controversial minority petition procedure at its centre. When a petition addressed to the League of Nations arrived, the Registry forwarded it to the Minorities Section. There, one or several Minorities Section officials examined it to determine whether it met the criteria of receivability. If it did not – as was the case for the majority of petitions relating to the region of Macedonia (that I studied in particular, see Cowan 2003, 2007a, 2007b) – the official sent the petition's authors a letter acknowledging receipt, and then filed it away.[4] If it was deemed receivable, that official forwarded it to the accused government for comment. Once the government submitted its comment, the official collated the original petition, the Section's assessments and the accused government's comments and drafted an analytical summary. The Secretary General created a Committee of Three charged to examine the case and decide whether to bring it to the Council's attention. In practice, the Director of the Minorities Section normally presented the case and its context and suggested a course of action. As the Committee of Three statesmen rarely knew much about the specific minority situation, they nearly always deferred to Section Director's greater expertise.

Petitions flowed into Geneva not only from individuals but from a wide variety of associations located within a state, such as organisations of women, students and youth, choral societies, refugee brotherhoods, and national branches of transnational organisations. Along with dealing with petitions as they arrived, the Minorities Section steadily gathered information in order to build up collective knowledge on minority situations under treaty jurisdiction. Each Member of Section was responsible for two to three countries; for reasons of 'impartiality', he never dealt with matters concerning his own country. The Section also read a range of newspapers, and kept its own press cuttings files. It met regularly with state diplomatic teams, minority representatives and individuals representing transnational organisations. According to a long-serving Minorities Section official, who joined in 1922 and took over as Director in 1930, the Spaniard Pablo de Azcárate, the most significant ways to gather information were through the regular visits by Members of the Section to countries with minority agreements, the four times yearly sessions of Council, which enabled innumerable informal meetings, and an 'open door policy' to minorities: 'We were extremely attentive and solicitous, we gave them the impression that there was no restriction, we never refused a representative of the minorities' (Azcárate in Siotis 1965).

A third major activity of the Section was the work of building and maintaining human relationships. Not only did this facilitate flows of information; good relationships with all the different parties were essential for all the work that the Minorities Section did. The files reveal frequent meetings and extensive written correspondence between Section officials and a host of interlocutors: statesmen, minorities (including elected or self-appointed community leaders, and minority intelligentsia such as professionals, intellectuals or politicians) and numerous 'concerned world citizens', as I call them, some of whom acted as western advocates of minorities.

Given that the Section was officially charged with maintaining 'informal and friendly communications with the Governments signatories to the Minorities Treaties' (Ranshofen-Wertheimer 1945: 110), relations between Minorities Section officials and political figures such as statesmen and ministers from Minority States were especially nurtured. Quite early on, the Minorities Section Director, or his delegate, began to visit these states, often spending six months a year travelling to capitals across eastern Europe. A visit followed an official invitation from the government; it was not an investigation. Although the Minorities Section official continued, discreetly, to keep his eyes and ears open, 'one ha[d] to do this [job] very carefully. One [had to] discover things, without seeming to want to discover them' (Azcárate in Siotis 1965). More than gathering information, the aim of the visit was to build trust between high-level government officials and these representatives of the League, while providing them an opportunity to discuss and study minority issues 'on the spot' without publicity (Azcárate 1945: 129). Colban believed that 'the most efficient manner to protect a minority against possible oppression by a government was through persuasion by personal and moral authority, rather than by the functioning of a formal and public system' (Azcárate in Codding 1966). Indeed, having no sanctions, the Minorities Section could achieve little without the cooperation of governments. Colban thus derided what would today be called the 'naming and shaming' tactics of those he dubbed 'zealous humanitarians'. Not only could such tactics cause a backlash for the vulnerable populations the League was charged to protect, but secrecy – and the threat to make a problematic minority situation public if a state was uncooperative – gave the League some leverage.

Through these activities, bureaucrats in the Minorities Section sought to establish themselves as unrivalled experts on minorities questions. Their extensive knowledge of specific minority situations, as well as their reputation for impartiality and tact, gave them both authority and autonomy: statesmen habitually relied on their well-informed advice. At the same time, the petition procedure created a political field where additional actors could get involved. A small but growing number of what the League called 'private organisations'[5] – nearly all of them transnational in scope and international in spirit – representing religious, internationalist, pacifist, feminist or other interests, along with a handful of concerned world citizens, debated 'the minority question' and attempted to influence both national and international policies. The Women's International League for Peace and Freedom, for instance, had a long-standing committee on 'Minorities and Nationality Questions', passed bi-annual Congress resolutions on 'Self Determination and the Protection of Minorities', and published analytical reports, pamphlets and articles on minority questions in their own newsletter and in the national and international press. This organisation developed a Janus-faced strategy that looked both towards Geneva and toward nationally based affiliates. Setting up their international headquarters in Geneva, they made contact with Secretariat staff and state delegates, lobbying both to alter and to expand the procedure and to make minority protection universal. They used the organisational knowledge they had gained to support their female colleagues in east Europe affected by the minorities treaties, for instance, by advising them how to write petitions so that they would be receivable.[6]

The efforts of these transnational organisations to influence minority supervision reveal a sense of entitlement with regard to meaningful participation in the international management of minority problems. The Minorities Section followed the activities of many of these activists, reading their publications and attending some of their meetings in a private capacity; they worked informally, but extremely discreetly, with those that they trusted while keeping others at a polite distance (Dyroff 2011; Fink 2004: 282; Granick 2010). Although happy to accept information from such individuals, they tended to discourage them in their campaigns for procedural changes, arguing that Minority States would reject any innovations that went beyond the treaties. While the Minorities Section's efforts to limit and manage the concerned public's engagement were partially rooted in the extremely delicate nature of their role, and of the sensitive, often confidential, information to which they had access, they were, at the same time, an assertion of their claim to greater expertise. Within a few short years, Colban could assert with satisfaction that the League had, by 1923, become 'the only proper channel through which minority questions are handled' (Fink 2004: 277). Not only minority well-being, but their own professional status and the League's reputation were at stake.

ARENAS OF STRUGGLE IN MINORITY TREATY SUPERVISION

From the outset, minority treaty supervision was controversial and led to continuous struggles over how it was carried out. Three areas of struggle are pertinent here: whether it should be selective or universal, the extent to which its texts and procedures should be visible, and its political versus legal character. The first issue was the most fundamental. With the Entente Powers, the victors at Versailles, unwilling to place a minority clause in the League Covenant that would restrain every League member in its dealings with its citizens, including themselves, minority protection was devised for each new territorial settlement on a case-by-case basis (Fink 2004: 160). Poland's was the first minority treaty created, and became a model for the fourteen others that followed.' The Entente Powers insisted that the exceptional measure of creating minorities treaties was necessary: the new, or in some cases, massively enlarged (and therefore, effectively 'new') national states had been carved out of Europe's four multinational, multilingual, multi-religious empires, and none of them were homogenous. In the unsettled postwar conditions, the League collectively needed to ensure that these often aggressively nationalising states acted justly in their dealings with those citizens they considered as nationally other; a persecuted minority community had too often been the pretext for conflict between neighbouring states in the past. According to this rationale, protecting minorities and ensuring their well-being were not ends in themselves; rather, they were the means by which conflict between states could be avoided and peace maintained.

While the western European statesmen of the Entente constructed the 'minority question' as an eastern European problem, the leaders and many citizens of Minority States wondered why Britain, with its 'Irish problem', or Italy, with its multilingual South Tyrol, should be exempt from minority obligations. This inequality provoked a debate over whether minority obligations should remain selective or become 'generalised'. It was not only Minority States that objected to the minority regime's selectivity. A number of humanitarian and internationalist organisations, including the British-led League of Nations Union, the Inter-Parliamentary Union and the Women's International League of Peace and Freedom, actively and continuously called for generalising the minorities treaties. One internationalist supporter of generalisation, Gilbert Murray, who straddled the worlds of transnational humanitarian activism and British imperial politics, submitted in September 1922 as a member of the South African delegation a motion to the Assembly; it advocated that even those League states not bound by a formal international agreement would promise to observe in relation to their own racial, religious and linguistic minorities 'at least as high a standard of justice and tolerance' as the minorities treaties demanded. Had this motion gained unanimous support, it would have imposed a legal duty on states; the Assembly managed only to support the weaker 'wish' (*voeu*) that this would happen (Robinson et al. 1943: 131). Right up until the collapse of the League minority regime in 1938, most Minority States reiterated their demand for generalisation, but Britain and France always strongly resisted, anxious at its implications for their own relations with both domestic and colonial subjects. The fact of selective scrutiny (Cowan 2009) fuelled the anger and humiliation of Minority States at their second-class status.

Selective scrutiny also fuelled contestation over how publicly visible the practices of minority supervision should be. Minority States saw many petitions as tendentious propaganda, or at least as the unwelcome airing of internal problems. Whereas initially, all petitions received by the Secretary General were automatically circulated to all League members (42 in 1919, 51 in 1923), in 1923 the Polish government submitted a series of letters arguing that petitions should be circulated only to members of the much smaller Council (then, ten) and that Council Committee of Three investigations and findings should be treated as matters of internal League routine. Seconding the proposal, the Czech government called for the rejection of petitions by 'professional propagandists', those jeopardising the dignity of a state and those whose demands were outside the scope of the minorities treaties (Robinson et al. 1943: 91–94). As a result, the 'conditions for receivability' for petitions were formalised; they included a prohibition against the use of 'violent language' (Cowan 2003). These various efforts reduced the visibility of a petition and the evaluative commentary it generated within the walls of the League institution, though it did not stop petitioners from publishing their petition in the press. A counter-move in March 1929 by the delegates from Germany and Canada to make the process more visible was strongly resisted by the Minority States, supported by the Secretariat (Fink 2004: 308–314); although it involved a minor concession to greater publicity, dictating that the *Official Journal of the League of Nations* would publish annual statistics regarding the number of petitions received, the number found receivable and irreceivable, the number under examination by Committees of Three, and so forth, such statistics revealed almost nothing beyond the numbers.

A third area of contestation concerned the character of minority petition supervision: was it best conceived as legal or political? This contestation reflected, in part, the two divergent visions for the institution as a whole: whereas some saw the League of Nations as part of the project of situating interstate relations within an increasingly elaborate and consistent framework of international law (see Kennedy 2004; Koskenniemi 2001), others, like Raymond Fosdick and Jean Monnet, two key architects of the League institution, saw it as a context for states to 'establish the habit of teamwork' (Monnet 1978: 82).[8] Interestingly, a more legal approach to minority grievances – one which better matched a public imaginary of the League as adjudicator of justice, held by many petitioners and internationalist organisations – had its advocates: thus, in the negotiations by the Committee on New States over the Polish Treaty, Lord Robert Cecil in June 1919 had proposed an article giving individuals the right of appeal to the Permanent Court of International Justice in the Hague if the state failed to carry out the promised minority provisions. The notion was clearly ahead of its time: Cecil's French and British colleagues vetoed his proposal, with stupendous consequences: minorities were 'deprived ... of the status of parties before the Court and reduced ... to "objects of protection"' (Robinson et al. 1943: 137–138). Instead, the committee supported the alternative proposal, that 'both individuals and communities shall have the right to bring the matter to the notice of a Member of the Council of the League of Nations', which became the foundation for the minority petition procedure.

In fact, the minority system was hybrid: the minorities treaties were legal agreements, but supervision, the mechanism devised to guarantee them and to deal with infractions, had both legal and political elements. The Tittoni Committee in 1920 had identified both the Court and the Council as appropriate spheres for minority supervision. Yet as supervision actually unfolded, few cases were sent to the Court: almost never for judgments, and only very rarely for advisory opinions. Access to the Court was restricted to League Council members (i.e. the permanent members, UK, France, Japan, Italy and, later, Germany and Russia, plus elected members), and while those states had the right to bring a case for adjudication on behalf of third parties (i.e. minorities of another state whose rights had been violated), in practice, they rarely did so. Parties that would have liked to appeal to the Court – Minority States, individual members of a minority or a minority group – were barred from it (Robinson et al. 1943: 136). These restrictions reinforced the message that petitioners were objects, rather than subjects, of international law, lacking a right to 'speak' in that domain and that their petitions were being treated as information only, rather than a legal claim. Yet they also reflected a preference among states to negotiate, rather than appeal to the law. Consequently, supervision emerged as a 'political' process, under the formal responsibility of the Council, a political body. As Azcárate explained in an interview in 1965, the Minorities Section adapted their practices to this reality, recognising minority supervision as primarily a space for negotiation:

> I myself, and I think Colban, too, were a little afraid to leave too much room for jurists to intervene in minorities questions because the intervention of jurists constituted a danger of rendering the question too rigid rather than keeping it, as we tended to do, as fluid and malleable as possible, in order to be able to push the maximum and arrive ... at a compromise.... I don't think one could envisage a case whose solution gave the petitioners 100% of what they asked for, or the reverse, which gave the government 100% of what it asked for. It was always a compromise ... (Azcárate in Siotis 1965)[9]

The Minorities Section, in its position as broker, had to facilitate finding solutions to minority issues in a system in which the world's most powerful nations were reluctant to set in motion a process that might impose sanctions on violating states. They frankly recognised the constrained character of supervision, in which solutions had to be crafted in a spirit of pragmatism and compromise within the shifting power relations among states. Indeed, the writings of Azcárate (1945: 134–135, 160 and passim) indicate that for him, at least, this was not just a second-best approach; rather, through his experience in the Minorities Section, he came to believe that a political approach involving compromise actually worked better for minorities than the zero-sum game of adversarial processes. He was critical of the Arbitral Tribunals set up for Upper Silesia, in which 'minority and government appeared before [the president of the mixed commission] on the basis of equality' (Simpson 2001: 139) and he was required to make a judgment, thus creating winners and losers. Azcárate thought that the humiliation inflicted on a state which lost a case within such a judicial process could make it uncooperative, and even possibly punitive toward those bringing the case. Sanctions could easily be counter-productive. Without the state's cooperation and goodwill, conditions for minorities had no chance of improving. Azcárate was thus convinced that 'friendly' negotiations which made some concessions to a state's interests and allowed it to preserve its honour had better outcomes for minorities.

The League of Nations minority supervision created a new political field, one which had the Geneva institution spatially at its heart but which drew in the energies and activities of geographically scattered but transnationally connected civic associations, both national and international, and the press. For the Minorities Section in the Secretariat whose officials were responsible for supervision as an everyday practice, supervision was fundamentally political. They saw as their remit not a singular Problem of Minorities but rather, a series of small 'minority problems' that had to be addressed through negotiation with states, in a friendly spirit and behind closed doors. In their view, this opacity actually gave the League of Nations more leverage, allowing them to pressure for concessions and allowing states to make them without losing face in front of their own citizens. At the same time, the Minorities Section insisted that their brokerage – their ability to advise and put pressure on states – was only possible because they had cultivated a reputation for impartiality.

UNIVERSAL PERIODIC REVIEW – A NEW FORM OF INTERNATIONAL OVERSIGHT

By the 1930s, Nazi Germany's attempts to manipulate minority supervision for its national aims became increasingly overt. By 1938, minority treaty supervision effectively ceased. The new UN organisation created after the war established in 1946 a Commission on Human Rights, a political body with representatives appointed by governments. Human rights were now the birthright of all human beings, in principle, yet there was as much resistance as there had been in the League era on the part of the world's most powerful states to creating a UN system that would actually guarantee rights, and sanction those who violated them (Mazower 2004; Moyn 2010). Tensions between national sovereignty and international oversight remained as strong as ever. Although negotiations over the UN human rights regime also exposed sharp divisions *within* states – Simpson (2001) describes the wrangling between the Colonial Office, Foreign Office and the Cabinet over whether and how human rights obligations should apply to British colonial subjects – representatives of Britain and the United States were among those strongly in favour of keeping the Universal Declaration of Human Rights declaratory, rather than enforceable (see also Mazower 2004; Moyn 2010). When the Commission, even before it began to meet officially, was deluged with thousands of petitions from people all over the world claiming abuse by their own governments and asking the Commission for help, many governments reacted defensively, just as Minority States had in the interwar years, but this time they nipped this hopeful practice in the bud by simply deciding, collectively, that the Commission had no competence either to investigate or take action on individual petitions (Lauren 2007: 314–315; Moyn 2010: 68).

Almost immediately, too, the Commission became captured by Cold War polarisation. The western political camp hurled accusations of human rights violations at their counterparts in the eastern camp and vice versa. The anticolonial movements sweeping across Africa and Asia, although largely caught up in this polarisation, also fundamentally shifted the meanings of human rights at the UN. With the human rights of millions of colonial subjects worse than ignored, it is hardly surprising that their spokespeople and supporters consistently identified the 'right to self determination of peoples' as the prerequisite for all other human rights (Moyn 2010). In the midst of these multiple ideological struggles, the Commission laboured to construct an institutional architecture of human rights. The UN adopted in 1966 the core treaties, which had been under discussion since 1954, divided in two because of ideological conflicts that accompanied the declaration: the International Covenant on Civil and Political Rights and the International Convention on Economic, Social and Cultural Rights. As decolonisation of the Third World unfolded and newly independent countries became UN members, more specialised treaties were drafted. The Convention on the Elimination of All Forms of Racial Discrimination (CERD), adopted in 1965, was the first to establish a mechanism of supervision, here to be overseen by independent experts (Lauren 2007: 319). Over the next few decades, the Commission reopened the door to petitions in relation to 'gross violations' of human rights and invented a host of additional special procedures. As the Commission established itself as 'the most important global forum in the world for discussing human rights' (Lauren 2007: 325), countries increasingly sought to become members: sometimes to carry on the work, but increasingly often to use that position to shield themselves or their allies from human rights investigations.

By the beginning of the twenty-first century, the 'politicisation' of the Commission was perceived to have reached a crisis point. Critics meant different things by this word, but a prominent view was that the Commission investigated and responded to alleged human rights violations selectively. For some, it was a matter of 'the North wagging its finger at the South', whereas for others, the problem was disproportionate attention to Israel. There was also frustration at the use of procedure by notoriously abusive governments to avoid scrutiny, of 'bias' and 'double standards', of the trade-off between economics and human rights and of the 'I scratch your back, you scratch mine' mentality of states with common interests (Alston 2006; Lauren 2007). For many, politicisation had fatally compromised the Commission and addressing it was a key motive for the reform that culminated in the new Human Rights Council in 2006. Designed to avoid politicisation, UPR is seen by many as the flagship procedure of the reform. Its mission is to review as part of a regular cycle the human rights situation of all UN member states and to encourage states to fulfil their human rights obligations by asking them to describe their own human rights situation, and by supporting them through technical cooperation, constructive dialogue and examples of best practice.

The UPR is one element within a system of mechanisms and procedures that includes treaty bodies,[10] special procedures,[11] a complaints procedure, an advisory committee and the Human Rights Council. A social, political, legal and bureaucratic process, it involves myriad actors, including diplomatic delegations of 'Participating Governments' and of the 'State under Review', along with representatives of NGOs, national human rights institutions and multilateral organisations, and UN civil servants. The review is based on three reports, available for reading or downloading from the UN website – the National Report, drafted by the State under Review, ideally in consultation with its civil society; the Compilation of relevant observations of treaty body, special procedures and other UN documents, compiled by the Secretariat; and the Stakeholders Report, a summary of reports submitted by civil society organisations and other stakeholders, also compiled by the Secretariat. The three-hour review, known as the 'UPR Working Group', takes the form of an 'interactive dialogue' in which the State under Review presents its human rights successes and challenges, and Participating Governments, through 2-minute speaking slots in a set order determined by the speaker's list, make comments, ask questions and offer recommendations for improvement, which the State under Review is free to accept or reject. A period of consultation and preparation precedes the review, and after it, the state is expected to implement accepted recommendations and pledges.[12] At the next review, four to five years hence, the state is expected to report on its implementation.

Intended to complement, rather than duplicate, the other UN mechanisms and procedures of human rights protection, UPR is distinctive in a number of ways. Its principles, objectives, standards and modalities were the product of debate and compromise among the whole community of UN member states and are articulated in a General Assembly resolution. Rather than a scrutiny of a specific issue by a group of experts, it is a holistic review carried out by peers, that is, other states. Rather than being imposed on selected violators, it is universal, with all states agreeing to participate. Rather than involving naming and shaming, it is conceived as a cooperative mechanism which, according to the agreed wording of the Institution Building Package, 'should be conducted in an objective, transparent, non-selective, constructive, non-confrontational and non-politicised manner'.

The UPR Working Group is the most visible moment of the review process. It is held in 'public' session at the Geneva Palais des Nations in Room XX, la Salle des Droits de l'Homme et de l'Alliance des Civilisations, with its magnificent colour-splashed stalactite ceiling. Individual members of the public who have acquired a badge can peer through the windows of the public gallery to the conference floor below. Seated on the raised podium at the front of the room are individuals or small clusters grouped behind placards: including (the name of) the State Under Review, President, Secretariat. Below them are a series of semi-circled rows of tables, known as 'country desks': those closest to the podium are the desks of the forty-seven Human Rights Council Members, alphabetised by the French versions of their country names; behind them are rows of desks of Observer States. At the very back is the NGO section, where staff or activists from a hodgepodge of international and visiting domestic NGOs, national human rights institutions, other UN agencies like the United Nations High Commission for Refugees (UNHCR) or United Nations Development Programme (UNDP) and other multilateral organisations such as the European Union, compete for desk space. To the left is the press section, and to the right sit the Secretariat staff, when they are not traversing the floor distributing documents, or collecting copies of statements from country desks to transmit to the translators. Two or three security guards stroll around the edges. Against a foreground of constant movement and the low hum of greeting, chatting and consulting, the interactive dialogue unfolds.

The UPR is described as both a 'peer review' and a 'periodic review'. Although these terms are revealing as institutional self-descriptions, here I approach UPR theoretically as an example of audit culture, and of the UPR Working Group element as a public audit ritual. Why audit? Whereas 'review' conveys the idea of repeated surveillance, 'audit' as a process in which 'A can require B to give an account of compliance with a set of expectations or standards' (Beitz 2009: 34) captures better the nature of the mechanism as a combination of coercion and voluntary engagement, and of collective peer oversight combined with self-revelation and anticipatory self-regulation. The UPR Working Group involves the State under Review surveying itself, then giving an account of itself, under the gaze of others. Why ritual? Not only is the review highly ordered in terms of time, space and language, its repetitiveness being part of its power. It also transforms the subjects of ritual (here, officials of the State under Review), confirming them into the community of rights-respecting states. Finally, it is assertively 'public' and 'transparent': unfolding before its Geneva audience, it is simultaneously webcast, available for viewing in real time and from an online webcast archive.[13]

When the United States was reviewed on a crisp Friday morning in November 2010, the usually placid atmosphere in the Palais became electric. My two fellow researchers and I, correctly anticipating a rush by visiting NGOs for the forty-five seats in the normally almost empty public gallery, had arrived two hours early to take our place at the front of the queue. When the security guards finally let us file in, climbing the stairs, finding seats next to the window and putting on our headphones, we looked down into a room humming with activity, but still waiting for the US delegation to arrive. Eventually, a veritable rainbow delegation, led by Assistant Secretary of the Bureau of International Organisations at the State Department Esther Brimmer, Assistant Secretary of State for Democracy, Human Rights and Labor Michael Posner and State Department Legal Advisor and Yale law professor Harold Koh, took their seats. After the President opened the proceedings, the delegation introduced the National Report in a tone of earnest patriotism: Brimmer spoke with pride of '[making] the participation of citizens and civil society a centrepiece of our UPR process ...' while Posner, admitting his country's frequent failure to achieve its ideals, nonetheless insisted that 'the arc of our history has been toward justice'. Their speeches finished, the large screen to the podium's left displayed the Speakers List by country; each speaker had 2 minutes. Cuba was first: elegant and forceful, the Cuban Ambassador thanked the United States for its report and made seven elaborate recommendations:

> One: to end the blockade of Cuba, which is described as a crime of genocide ... Two: to release the five Cuban political prisoners ... Six: to halt the war crimes of their troops abroad and the killing of innocent victims ...

Venezuela followed, in even faster Spanish, the translator racing breathlessly to keep up:

> We welcome the delegation of the United States of America and would like to recommend that its government ratify without reservations the following conventions and protocols: CEDAW [Convention on the Elimination of All Forms of Discrimination against Women], the Covenant on Economic, Social and Cultural Rights, the Rights of the Child, Persons with Disabilities, Migrant Workers.... Abolish the death penalty.... End child slavery...

Iran, the Russian Federation and Nicaragua maintained the pressure, and only with the sixth speaker, Indonesia, did the tone begin to shift, becoming more conciliatory. After twenty speakers, the delegation replied, then returned to the Speakers List, taking another ten before replying again. Germany, forty-eighth to speak, 'noted with interest' that the first states to speak had spared no effort to participate in the review; 'its staff camped overnight in front of this building. I hope they will use the same level of commitment to extending human rights!' Two more states spoke, and then Posner wrapped up; he referred to internet freedom, to 'measures for equal opportunities in healthcare, housing, education', and to the seventy-five roundtable meetings of the '9/11 Backlash Task Force' set up by his government to address the post-9/11 anti-Islamic backlash and aiming, among other things, to 'protect the schoolgirl's right to wear hijab'. He finished, thanking states and 'our own civil society ... we recommend active engagement with civil society'. The President's gavel struck, cameras began flashing, ambassadors rose from their seats and crowded around the podium, smiling and shaking hands with the United States delegation.

As seen above, the mechanism elicits state performances. Each State under Review adopts a posture and tone and decides how to present the balance between achievements and challenges, often calibrating its performance for the domestic audience as much as for the community of states in Room XX. I asked a US diplomat how his delegation felt about the review: 'Pretty ecstatic, actually ... very proud that we did what we should in setting a good example.' Their performance would have gone down well with American viewers, but it was precisely this which irritated a Belgian diplomat: 'it was as if America were the source of human rights. "Now that we're here, and because we're here, the process will work."' In their reviews, other states, like Rwanda and Singapore, defiantly rejected criticism of their approach to human rights, or complained, like Myanmar, of being 'misunderstood'. Participating governments, too, may perform for both audiences when they speak, demonstrating their independence, integrity or reasonableness. The event regularly elicits collective performances of solidarity or challenge. Singapore was reported to have blitzed its allies with faxes and text messages, exhorting them to show up early in the Speakers List queue. In the United States review, Cuba organised its close allies to ensure that the review opened with an onslaught of recommendations aggressively pointing to the shortcomings and dark sides of that superpower's human rights record. Through these interventions, states express political stances and relationships, but it is significant that they do so through a diplomatically inflected language of human rights, asking the State under Review to account for itself in relation to internationally agreed human rights standards.

This sometimes exciting – yet more often, rather dull – political theatre is the front-stage of the Geneva element of the UPR. But it relies heavily on the less visible, back-stage work of the Secretariat. A tiny team of four or five staff plus an intern or two, many with experience 'on the ground' in UN field missions, work as 'UPR drafters', creating a summary of individual NGO submissions that will constitute the Stakeholders Report (ten pages maximum). Far from being a mechanical exercise, this requires meticulous checks of each NGO's ECOSOC status,[14] but also considerable institutional and country-specific knowledge, as well as judgment and diplomacy. The team must be ready to defend its decisions to meddling states, who may accuse them of including information provided by an NGO that is, in reality, a political party or even a 'terrorist organisation' and demand that its assertions be expunged. The team also undertakes the politically delicate task of extracting the opinions of independent experts from recent[15] UN reports of treaty bodies, special rapporteurs and so forth, for the Compilation. Here, too, the team, in consultation with other colleagues in the Secretariat, must select which observations to include, under which heading to position them within the ten-page document, and who or what to quote (the High Commissioner of Human Rights? the resolution of the Human Rights Council?) for the best strategic effect. Out of fierce arguments, staff find agreed phrasings. They struggle with – yet take pride in being able to find – the balance between preserving the institution's authority through respecting its language and codes and accurately conveying the human rights situation on the ground. During the review, Secretariat staff continue to produce documentation (e.g. of recommendations), often working through the night and sleeping in the office in order to meet tight deadlines.

Although a mechanism in which states are in the driver's seat, other collective actors participate under the category of stakeholders. The category includes national human rights institutions (NHRIs),[16] other agencies within the UN system and regional bodies like the European Union, but most numerous are bodies called either civil society organisations (CSOs) or NGOs. NGOs cannot take the microphone during the UPR Working Group; only at the very end of the review process, during the Human Rights Council plenary adoption of a country's UPR Working Group Report, can they express their views in the 20-minute slot allocated to stakeholders. But NGOs have found other ways to voice their demands: for instance, they formulate recommendations, then lobby states sympathetic to their issue – often successfully – to include one or more of these in their 2-minute statements. More concretely, after a state is reviewed, established NGOs may request, or be asked, to participate – frequently in collaboration with an NHRI, if it exists – in helping to set up an Action Plan for implementation, with targets and timetables. Organisations in both categories are also encouraged to raise awareness with the wider public about the government's UPR commitments. If audits are increasingly about 'the control of control', and thus about demonstrating that an institution has set up its own monitoring systems, we can understand the emphasis in the state recommendations on signing and ratifying treaties, establishing NHRIs and Ombudspersons and creating Action Plans. Through these practices, NGOs and NHRIs are explicitly enrolled into the job of monitoring the state's performance, and thus participating in a culture of continuous audit.

Many international and regional NGOs with offices in Geneva follow UPR, along with other human rights mechanisms. The larger, more established NGOs know their way around the Geneva system, actively lobby as well as influence the shape of larger debates, and are able to build relations of trust and friendship with particular state delegations and diplomats. Other NGOs work in their own country and come to Geneva for important human rights meetings and events. Within this heterogeneous NGO world, there are hierarchies of power and knowledge, and both competition and collaboration. Established NGOs may mentor in-country activists: Linda, an experienced Amnesty International staffer, described how she would take a national chapter step by step through the process of thinking what they wanted, devising recommendations that were 'very, very concrete' and identifying, using the database set up by upr-info.org, which states might want to support their recommendation. Saba, from an Arab world NGO, spoke of 'capacity-building' with local NGO partners so that they could 'engage independently and self-sufficiently with UN mechanisms on a long-term basis'. Rubbing shoulders with these organisations are others dubbed as GONGOs, 'government organised non-governmental organisations'. While these tend to be viewed by NGO activists as categorically different and morally tainted, GONGOs are better seen as the extreme end of a spectrum; in light of most states' regulation of their own NGOs, the funding by many states of NGOs beyond their national borders, and the alliances and collaborations between governments and NGOs, as well as frequent movement of personnel between NGOs, international agencies and diplomatic posts, NGOs are rarely free of government influence. Together, they constitute what Ferguson and Gupta (2002: 994) have called a 'transnational apparatus of governmentality' in relation to the UPR.

A COMPLICATED STORY OF CONTINUITIES AND DISCONTINUITIES

Although juxtaposing these two processes reveals, I argue, a shift from external supervision to audit culture, this shift is not absolute.[17] I therefore turn now to teasing out strands of an intriguingly complicated story of continuities as well as discontinuities, similarities as well as differences, in principles and practices between the two processes. To start with, I am struck by the fundamental continuity of engagement in international monitoring of the state, based on international law, regarding the state's obligations to its citizens and/or inhabitants, although in the League period the logic was protection and rights as means to secure peace, while today rights are a valued end in themselves. In the 1920s, as now, monitoring was framed by norms of state sovereignty and putative sovereign equality, while taking place in an international context of huge economic and political inequalities among sovereign states. In the 1920s, the view that the state's promises to ensure minorities' welfare were 'obligations of international concern' and that the newly formed League of Nations should guarantee them signified an innovative expansion of what had been understood to constitute a legitimate 'international' realm of action. The minorities treaties and the procedures set up to supervise them began to alter the meanings of state sovereignty. As international and supranational organisations have extended their reach, the meanings of sovereignty continue to evolve and to be contested.[18]

Within these continuities, there are shifts in emphasis. Then, as now, states were preoccupied with honour and reputation, but we find two very different stances in relation to this preoccupation in the two monitoring mechanisms. The emphasis at the League was on enabling states to present a dignified public face to the world. As a result of numerous struggles in the first decade of its operation, procedural concessions were made so that Minority States, which already felt 'humiliated' by the violation of their sovereignty that minorities treaties represented, were not further exposed to embarrassment by having to expose their 'internal' problems to the wider League community. By contrast, in the UPR, states are urged to 'take a self-critical look at their own human rights situation, to discuss challenges with peers, and to take steps to improve the human rights situation in their countries' (Sen 2009: 3). Yet in the UPR's first cycle, states worked hard at impression management, mobilising allies or even taking illicit control of the speaker's list of the interactive dialogue in order to ensure that 'friendly' states that could be counted on to offer praise and 'easy' recommendations spoke first.

In both moments, the Secretariat is at the centre of the field of activities associated with the review process. Under the League of Nations, the Secretariat played a determining role that was highly visible. Its Minorities Section acted as gatekeepers, deciding which petitions passed the crucial test of receivability. Collectively, its officials developed extensive expertise on regionally specific minority situations and were thus called upon to advise Council committees on how they might respond in their disciplinary encounter with the accused state. Although meticulously following procedure and proper etiquette, the Minorities Section emphasised the need for flexibility, malleability and compromise, which its expertise helped to facilitate. In contrast, in the UPR, the UN Secretariat has a quieter presence. Its role is crucial yet symbolically muted and largely unremarked. As well as coordinating the reviews overall, Secretariat staff produce nearly all of the institutional documentation, before and during the review. Producing documents in the flat 'objectivity' of UN-speak, often under extremely tight deadlines, demands not only familiarity with the connotations of words in the UN context, but also knowledge of the situation 'on the ground', political judgement and a keen sense of diplomacy. All of these skills and knowledge come into play when the Secretariat negotiate and position 'facts' within documents, and when they work at a personal level with diplomats; they are all the more efficacious for being hardly noticed by many of the more visible state and civil society actors.

In the 1920s, as today, NGOs were involved in the international surveillance of states. In the League period, many petitions submitted to the minority petition procedure emanated not from individuals but from a wide variety of associations located within a state. Simultaneously, transnational non-governmental organisations became involved in 'the minority question', actively lobbying statesmen and Secretariat in Geneva. In the UPR, NGOs, as they are now called, are recognised as 'stakeholders' and have a designated role in the process. They are expected to 'hold their government to account' as it implements (or not) the recommendations it has accepted. While their space for direct speech is diminished in the UPR compared to other human rights monitoring processes, NGOs increasingly lobby individual states to include recommendations that they have formulated in that state's own recommendations. Significantly, NGO numbers have swollen at the same time as, collectively speaking, their 'independent' and 'non-governmental' character looks less clear, since many are funded by donor states, entities like the European Union or private corporations.

What about the discontinuities between the two processes? Perhaps most importantly, the state has shifted from being the object of international supervision to being, also and primarily, a subject that self-reports. In the League system, the petition, if receivable, triggered an examination of alleged infractions and the accused state's response by a small committee. In the UPR, the state is self-accounting: it produces an account – comprising the

National Report, the government delegation's oral presentation and its answers to states' and stakeholders' questions – of its human rights situation and its actions. The UPR mechanism seeks an interiorisation whereby the subject gets used to surveying itself, even as it gets used to being surveyed by others.

The issues of temporality and of regularisation and repetition – a second discontinuity – are important here. Whereas the League supervision in relation to any specific alleged 'infraction' was set in motion by a petition, UPR calls itself 'periodic'. In the League system, states did not submit regular reports. Rather, Minorities Section officials, as well as Council members serving on the Committees of Three, primarily 'reacted' in a procedurally structured but nonetheless ad hoc manner to petitions or other external crises, although regular discussions and country visits might be ongoing. By contrast, in establishing UPR as a 'periodic' review, reviews are regularised and, in a sense, more continuous: reviews occur according to a set calendar so are anticipated and prepared for, while the interim period between reviews is the time for 'implementation' – itself, ideally, continuously monitored by civil society. On top of this, intermediary reports, like the mid-term reports which are often orally volunteered at intervening Human Rights Council sessions and sometimes backed up with a written document, are becoming increasingly expected, even if they remain formally optional. While UPR's 'periodicity' is similar to that of other human rights bodies, such as the treaty bodies, the much more 'public' character of the UPR disciplines the states that must perform on the day under the scrutiny not only of other states but also, potentially, of a world public.

A third discontinuity concerns the value placed upon 'transparency'. In the League process, non-transparency was an explicit value among most League bureaucrats and statesmen. It was argued that behind-closed-doors negotiations around minority problems allowed the Minority State to cooperate and to make concessions without losing face, as they would in a formal and public investigation and, moreover, that public shaming of Minority State authorities might not only be unproductive but could even lead to backlash against minorities (Azcárate 1945: 134–135). In UPR, transparency is an explicit value. The State under Review is encouraged to speak frankly and sincerely in the public sessions, while transparency is performed to the entire global public – and not just to the community of states – through the public's virtual accessibility to the UPR public sessions through webcam broadcasts and downloadable reports. At the same time, this performance of 'transparency' brings its own obfuscations. Proceedings and documents hide as well as reveal: reporting conventions, etiquettes of speaking, endless acronyms, use of summaries and aggregated data, and an intense politics around terminology and word choice lead to heavily coded and often opaque texts (Merry 2006; Riles 2006). Websites, similarly, require considerable literacy skills to decipher them and information technology skills to operate them technically.

A fourth 'discontinuity' is felt by many to vindicate the new system: whereas League of Nations minority supervision was selective in that only certain countries were compelled to accept minorities treaties, UPR aims and claims to be genuinely 'universal'. In a certain sense, it is: all UN member states are scrutinised and, after one cycle, not a single state has refused. The universality of the review is itself often cited as a key component of the 'real success story' of the mechanism. Nonetheless, by no means is there agreement that universality and equal treatment of states is genuinely possible. While some enthused at the 'level playing field' which UPR created, others cited the widely different resources – funds, knowledge, personnel – available to states to prepare their report and presentation, not to mention their different levels of power, prestige and ability to rally other states publicly to support them. For some engaged in the reviews, particularly NGOs, universality and equality of treatment were not even desirable; as one activist worried, 'Does it really make sense for Iran and Norway to have the same-sized slot?'

Finally, the concept of the 'political' as employed in both contexts reveals an especially complex array of continuities and discontinuities, similarities and differences. Despite the hopes of many, at the time of drafting the Universal Declaration of Human Rights, that human rights could be beyond politics, international oversight of rights has always been political. Yet this is true in several senses. First, both processes are 'political' in the somewhat formal and technical sense: when they examine a case – an alleged infraction by a state of its minorities treaty, or a state's human rights situation – this entails political deliberation and negotiation, rather than an investigative or adversarial procedure aiming to determine compliance with the law. In a second sense, 'political' overlaps considerably with 'politicised', connoting a selective rather than universal approach. League supervision was overtly – if controversially – political in this sense, whereas in UPR, this is more covert: state actors continue to manoeuvre, as well as to articulate alliance and enmity, within a field of geopolitical relations, but they are now compelled to do so with reference to human rights norms and using a friendly, constructive language.

The UPR is 'political' insofar as it is a site for 'dialogue' rather than an investigation of legal compliance. It is supposed to be conducted in a manner that is, among other things, 'non-politicised'. In contrast to other UN agencies, which emphasise the 'technical' character of their work, participants in UPR openly recognise its 'diplomatic' character as a state-run peer mechanism. 'Non-politicised' did not mean 'non-political', most stressed, since all states have legitimate political interests and act 'politically'. For one respondent, 'non-politicised' simply indicated that all states were subject to review: it was nothing more than a synonym for 'universality' and 'non-selectivity'. For others, UPR was 'less politicised' than, say, the Human Rights Council, because there was less scope for regional blocs to shape the proceedings. For still others, politicisation was the inverse of cooperation. When recommendations became too sharp or too critical, reaction within the UPR context was relatively muted; however, certain diplomats would use the General Debate on UPR under Item 6 in the subsequent Human Rights Council session to condemn the 'dangerous backsliding into politicisation', testily reminding their colleagues that the process was meant to be 'cooperative' and 'non-confrontational'. The ambiguity over what 'non-politicisation' actually means signals the hybrid character of UPR: conceived as a cooperative space for sharing best practice, it seems to exemplify what Chantal Mouffe calls 'post-political forms of regulation and governance' (Mouffe 2005; see also Garsten and Jacobsson 2011), in which antagonisms are difficult to articulate. Yet the 'old' geopolitics of nation state rivalries and alliances significantly shape the reviews and are, at times, openly expressed.

CONCLUSION: ARENAS OF STRUGGLE

Although many see UPR as a 'success story', there remain struggles over how it should be carried out. The three arenas of contestation that we examined for the League system – around universality, visibility and its political character – have not been entirely resolved with the UPR. Whereas review is now universal, states have vastly differing resources to devote to preparing for the review, and to carry out recommendations. They have differing capacities to mobilise allies and to resist pressure from other states when setting their human rights priorities and policies: poorer states, such as those in the Least Developed Countries group, are constrained by the conditionalities imposed by international financial institutions and donor states. More subtly, the emphasis on universality and equality does not necessarily challenge a hegemonic narrative of a hierarchy of human rights virtue among states. Whereas diplomats of certain western states explicitly talked about 'setting an example', individuals from the global South complained that the review's putative 'universality' is still largely defined by the West, against which their countries are judged and always found to be inadequate. Whether as 'poorer' countries, 'the South' or 'the Commonwealth', they find themselves structurally placed in the role of 'learning'.

As in the League era, the question looms of how much of the state's inner workings, as well as its dirty laundry, should be visible. Of course, in the early twenty-first century, when 'transparency' is widely seen as self-evidently essential for good governance, it has been almost impossible to challenge this value directly in the context of UPR. Indeed, it is performatively invoked on a regular basis: Participating Governments often applaud the State under Review for its 'frank' presentation of its human rights situation. Yet the balance between revealing and obscuring is always finely tuned. States being reviewed work hard to keep tricky issues off the agenda and to discredit or manage critical voices, whereas others push for these same issues and voices to be made visible and audible. This leads to constant negotiations over how information about a state appears in public UN documents: how a problematic issue is phrased, where it is positioned in the text, what is highlighted and what discreetly excluded from summaries. Beyond this, 'UN-speak' in both its spoken and written form is itself frequently opaque to the general public, who get lost in the maze of acronyms, who struggle to understand the flat, grammatically correct yet somehow unfathomable prose, and who rarely know the institutional etiquettes or the histories, and thus special nuances, of ordinary words and phrases (see Merry 2006; Riles 2006).

A dynamic, still evolving mechanism, UPR involves a very different logic of oversight from that of the League of Nations minority treaty supervision. One analytical account has presented it as a 'soft governance accountability mechanism ... [that] uses peer pressure to influence members to adjust their national practices to conform with shared ideas as to how best to manage human rights in today's society' (Vega and Lewis 2011: 363). Whether such ideas are actually shared or not, the modalities of participation themselves tend to elicit state performances that express commitment to human rights obligations. The state publicly offers an account of itself and, through the recommendations it accepts, commits itself to improving. The intention is that, over time, the State under Review will become accustomed to surveying itself, as it is surveyed by others. As in many audits, UPR articulates values that are impossible to argue with (including human rights, objectivity, transparency, cooperation, sharing of best practice). Those audited cannot object to it directly without being seen as having something to hide. Above and beyond the explicit discourse and practice of politics, then, UPR works as an operation of power by enlisting a wide array of actors in myriad micropractices of auditing the state's human rights performance, compelling all parties to speak the language of human rights and enjoining them to coax, support, observe and monitor each state's journey to self-improvement. Its friendly language is double-edged: while softening criticism, it also firmly positions state actors within a project of self-management.

ACKNOWLEDGEMENTS

I am grateful to Marie-Bénédicte Dembour, Adil Hassan Khan, Toby Kelly, Birgit Müller and especially Charles Gore for very helpful suggestions and discussions. My analysis draws on many hours of conversation with Julie Billaud, who collaborated in the research; the discussion of the UN Secretariat, in particular, draws on her experience as an intern and her many insights. Finally, I thank Basak Cali not only for comments on this chapter but for being a stimulating interlocutor over the course of the research.

NOTES

1. The League of Nations minorities system has been extensively studied: major works include Azcárate (1945), Claude (1955), Fink (2004), Mair (1928), Mazower (1997), Robinson et al. (1943). Pedersen (2007) reviews a 'return to the League of Nations', including of the minorities system, in recent historiography. In my research over the past decade, I have been exploring aspects of minority treaty supervision through the case of the populations in the Macedonian regions of Greece and Yugoslavia that were categorised by the League as 'Bulgarian minorities' but whose actual identity, national or otherwise, was widely contested (see Cowan 2003, 2007a, 2007b, 2008, 2009, 2010). My description of the everyday workings of minority treaty supervision draws on both published and archival materials.
2. I undertook ethnographic research on UPR from November 2010 to July 2011, assisted by Dr Julie Billaud and Dr Basak Cali, and funded by the British Academy.

3. Codding (1966) and Siotis (1965) conducted interviews with former League of Nations civil servants in French. All translations of quoted material are mine.

4. Not infrequently, though, an irreceivable petition was forwarded as a 'private' communication to another League division or League-supervised activity, such as the Greco-Bulgarian Mixed Commission (see Cowan 2008).

5. The phrase 'non-governmental organisation' was coined in the UN in 1945 and the abbreviation, 'NGO' came into wide usage from the 1970s onward. Until that time, there was no single term; entities might refer to themselves as an international association, international union, international institute or international organisation (Willetts 2001).

6. This summary is based on my perusal of the Women's International League for Peace and Freedom archives, their publications (*Pax et Libertas*) and conference proceedings, and on Bussey and Tims (1965).

7. Minorities treaties or agreements were signed by the following countries, mostly between 1919 and 1924: Albania, Austria, Bulgaria, Czechoslovakia, Estonia, Finland, Greece, Hungary, Iraq, Latvia, Lithuania, Poland, Roumania, Turkey and Yugoslavia.

8. An American, Raymond Fosdick, served as Under Secretary General at the League of Nations from 1919 to 1920, and the French political economist and diplomat Jean Monnet was named as Deputy Secretary General at its founding (see Monnet 1978).

9. Interestingly, although clearly rejecting the rigidities of a legal approach, Azcárate is not totally rejecting the petitioner as claimant; his last words indicate that, in his mind, the two relevant parties are 'government' and 'petitioner', rather than two states, one of whom makes claim on the minority's behalf. This is a startling slip of the tongue, suggesting a conceptual slippage anticipating a day when petitioners would, indeed, face their states more directly.

10. A mechanism in which committees of experts oversee how well states are honouring the nine core international human rights treaties or conventions pertaining to specific issues, such as the Convention on Elimination of Discrimination Against Women or the Convention Against Torture.

11. A mechanism comprising 'thematic mandates', in which expert individuals or groups are charged to investigate specific themes, such as the Special Rapporteur on the independence of judges and lawyers and the Working Group on People of African Descent; and 'country mandates' where they are charged to investigate the situation in countries with serious human rights issues, such as the Independent Expert on the situation of human rights in Haiti and the Special Rapporteur on the situation of human rights in Myanmar.

12. Sen (2009: 9) usefully distinguishes between the 'mechanism', the part that takes place in Geneva, and the 'process', a 'much larger and longer project that begins before the Geneva element and extends considerably beyond it', as I discuss below.

13. As of some time in spring 2012, the UN website was reorganised, and archived webcasts of UPR sessions, which previously were easily retrieved, have been merged with a wider pool of webcasts and can no longer be located. My search on 20 July 2012 using the phrase 'United States UPR' came up with 13,386 hits in seemingly random order. Super-transparency has ended up in invisibility.

14. In order to participate fully in UN processes, NGOs must apply for and be awarded 'accreditation' for their 'consultative status' with the Economic and Social Council (ECOSOC), a process that can take many years.

15. Within the previous four years.
16. A relatively recent genre of 'government agencies whose purported aim is to implement international norms domestically' (Cardenas 2003: 23; see also Shawki 2009).
17. Of course, it is important to remember that UPR is only one of a number of human rights monitoring mechanisms, each of which presents a unique combination of elements; looking at the treaty body monitoring system, for instance, where states produce periodic reports and are questioned by an international committee of experts in sessions that are not webcast, would give a different picture of continuities and discontinuities (see e.g. Kelly 2012; Merry 2006).
18. For instance, a post-Rwanda UN initiative established in 2005, 'The Responsibility to Protect', emphasises sovereignty as a 'responsibility', not a right; it also gives responsibility to the international community to intervene to halt certain crimes against populations.

BIBLIOGRAPHY

Alston, P. (2006) 'Reconceiving the UN human rights regime: Challenges confronting the new Human Rights Council', *Melbourne Journal of International Law* 7: 185–224.

Azcárate, P. (1945) *League of Nations and National Minorities: An Experiment* (Washington, DC: Carnegie Endowment for International Peace).

Beitz, C. (2009) *The Idea of Human Rights* (Oxford: Oxford University Press).

Bourdieu, P. and L. Wacquant (1992) *An Invitation to Reflexive Sociology* (Chicago: University of Chicago Press).

Bourdieu, P., L. Wacquant and S. Farage (1994) 'Rethinking the state: Genesis and structure of the bureaucratic field', *Sociological Theory* 12(1): 1–18.

Bussey, G. and M. Tims (1965) *Women's International League for Peace and Freedom, 1915-1965: A Record of Fifty Years' Work* (London: Allen and Unwin).

Cardenas, S. (2003) 'Emerging global actors: The United Nations and national human rights institutions', *Global Governance* 9: 23–42.

Claude, I. (1955) *National Minorities: An International Problem* (Cambridge, MA: Harvard University Press).

Codding, G. (1966) Interviews with Pablo de Azcárate, 22nd and 25th March 1966. League of Nations Archives, Private Papers, P273, Geneva.

Cowan, J. (2003) 'Who's afraid of violent language? Honour, sovereignty and claims-making in the League of Nations', *Anthropological Theory* 3(3): 271–291.

Cowan, J. (2007a) 'The supervised state', *Identities: Global Studies in Culture and Power* 14(5): 545–578.

Cowan, J. (2007b) 'The success of failure? Minority supervision at the League of Nations', in M. Dembour and T. Kelly (eds) *Paths to International Justice: Social and Legal Perspectives* (Cambridge: Cambridge University Press).

Cowan, J. (2008) 'Fixing national subjects in the 1920s southern Balkans: Also an international practice', *American Ethnologist* 35(2): 338–356.

Cowan, J. (2009) 'Selective scrutiny: Supranational engagement with minority protection and rights in Europe', in A. Griffiths, K. Benda-Beckmann and F. Benda-Beckmann (eds) *The Power of Law in a Transnational World: Anthropological Enquiries* (Oxford: Berghahn).

Cowan, J. (2010) 'Justice and the League of Nations minority regime', in K. Clarke and M. Goodale (eds) *Mirrors of Justice: Law and Power in the Post Cold War Era* (Cambridge: Cambridge University Press).

de Certeau, M. (1984) *The Practice of Everyday Life* (Berkeley: University of California Press).

De la Vega, C. and T. Lewis (2011) 'Peer review in the mix: How the UPR transforms human rights discourse', in M. Bassiouni and W. Schabas (2011) *New Challenges for the UN Human Rights Machinery: What Future for the UN Treaty Body System and the Human Rights Council Procedures?* (Cambridge: Intersentia).

Dyroff, S. (2011) 'Minority protection in theory and practice: The efforts of transnational associations and their interdependences with the League of Nations system', Tabled paper for conference 'Towards a New History of the League of Nations', Geneva, 25–26 August.

Ferguson, J. and A. Gupta (2002) 'Spatializing states: Toward an ethnography of neoliberal governmentality', *American Ethnologist* 29(4): 981–1002.

Fink, C. (2004) *Defending the Rights of Others: The Great Powers, the Jews, and International Minority Protection, 1878–1938* (Cambridge: Cambridge University Press).

Garsten, C. and K. Jacobsson (2011) 'Transparency and legibility in international institutions: The UN Global Compact and post-political global ethics', *Social Anthropology* 19(4): 378–393.

Granick, J. (2010) 'Jewish international associations at the League of Nations, 1919–1927: A historical study of an uneven relationship between private associations and an international organization', MA thesis, Graduate Institute of International and Development Studies, Geneva.

Kelly, T. (2012) *This Side of Silence: Human Rights, Torture, and the Recognition of Cruelty* (Philadelphia, PA: University of Pennsylvania Press).

Kennedy, D. (2004) 'Humanitarianism and force', in *The Dark Sides of Virtue: Reassessing International Humanitarianism* (Princeton, NJ: Princeton University Press).

Kipnis, A. (2008) 'Audit cultures: Neoliberal governmentality, socialist legacy, or technologies of governing?', *American Ethnologist* 35(2): 275–289.

Koskenniemi, M. (2001) *The Gentle Civilizer of Nations: The Rise and Fall of International Law 1870–1960* (Cambridge: Cambridge University Press).

Lauren, P. (2007) '"To preserve and build on its achievements and to redress its shortcomings": The journey from the Commission on Human Rights to the Human Rights Council', *Human Rights Quarterly* 29.

Mair, L. (1928) *The Protection of Minorities* (London: Christophers).

Mazower, M. (1997) 'Minorities and the League of Nations in interwar Europe', *Daedalus* 126(2).

Mazower, M. (2004) 'The strange triumph of human rights', *Historical Journal* 47(2): 379–398.

Merry, S.E. (2006) *Human Rights and Gender Violence: Translating International Law into Local Justice* (Chicago: University of Chicago Press).

Monnet, J. (1978) *Memoirs* (London: Collins).

Mosse, D. (2005) *Cultivating Development: An Ethnography of Aid Policy and Practice* (London: Pluto).

Mouffe, C. (2005) *On the Political: Thinking in Action* (London: Routledge).

Moyn, S. (2010) *The Last Utopia: Human Rights in History* (Cambridge, MA: Harvard University Press).

Pedersen, S. (2007) 'Back to the League of Nations (review essay)', *American Historical Review* 112(4): 1091–1117.

Ranshofen-Wertheimer, E.F. (1945) *The International Secretariat: A Great Experiment in International Administration* (Washington, DC: Carnegie Endowment for International Peace).

Riles, A. (2006) 'Deadlines: Removing the brackets on politics in bureaucratic and anthropological analysis', in A. Riles (ed.) *Documents: Artifacts of Modern Knowledge* (Ann Arbor, MI: University of Michigan Press).

Robinson, J., O. Karbach, M. Laserson, N. Robinson and M. Vichniak (1943) *Were the Minorities Treaties a Failure?* (New York: Institute of Jewish Affairs).

Sen, P. (ed.) (2009) *Universal Periodic Review of Human Rights: Toward Best Practice* (London: Commonwealth Secretariat).

Shawki, N. (2009) 'A new actor in human rights politics? Transgovernmental networks of national human rights institutions', in N. Shawki and M. Cox (eds) *Negotiating Sovereignty and Human Rights: Actors and Issues in Contemporary Human Rights Politics* (Farnham: Ashgate).

Simpson, A.W.B. (2001) *Human Rights and the End of Empire: Britain and the Genesis of the European Convention* (Oxford: Oxford University Press).

Siotis, J. (1965) Interviews with Pablo de Azcárate, Edouard de Haller and W. van Asch van Wijk, on 19th February, 9th March and 7th April 1965. League of Nations Archives, Personal Papers, P273, Geneva.

Strathern, M. (2000) *Audit Cultures: Anthropological Studies of Accountability, Ethics and the Academy* (London: Routledge).

Willetts, P. (2001) 'What is a non-governmental organization?' *UNESCO Encyclopedia of Life Support Systems*, Article 1.44. 3.7. Available at: www.staff. city.ac.uk/p.willetts/CS-NTWKS/NGO-ART.HTM (consulted 10 August 2012).

6
Politics of Shame
The Bureaucratisation of International Human Rights Monitoring

Tobias Kelly

This chapter is about the shame of torture produced by international human rights monitoring mechanisms. With some notable exceptions, torture appears to be one of the few things people will near universally say is wrong. The dishonour of exposure would therefore seem to be powerful. As Thomas Keenan has argued the concept of shame 'gathers together a set of powerful metaphors – the eyes of the world, the light of public scrutiny, the exposure of hypocrisy' (2004: 436). Although shame can lead to denial, it also carries a sense of the vulnerability of reputation to the gaze of others (Piers and Singer 1972). Institutions can of course not feel shame in an emotional sense, although people who act in their name might well do. However, as with guilt, shame can be understood as a political process, as much as a psychological one, concerned with organising responses to claims of wrongdoing. The impact of shame lies in the social implication of being caught, and is enforced through external censure, rather than remorse. Human rights organisations, of many different hues, seek to expose violations and bring about change through the use of shame. Without means of direct enforcement, human rights organisations rely on the persuasive power of ignominy. Such shaming has a distinctly international dimension. The threat to expose wrongdoing from outside narrow national boundaries is thought to be particularly powerful against states sensitive to their reputations on the world stage.

The central argument of this chapter is that the shame of torture produced by international human rights monitoring mechanisms easily dissipates within bureaucratic regimes. Human rights monitoring is not simply a transparent form of information-gathering, revealing information to the wider world, but can also hide as much as it reveals. As a result of the technical ways in which human rights obligations are interpreted, the shame of torture is dispersed into arguments about procedure. If shame relies on an audience as well as a sense of failure, the focus on broad policies means that it is never clear when failure takes place, or if anyone is watching. In this way, the inherently political and ethical desire to eradicate the needless infliction of pain and suffering is transformed into a technical issue of audit, documentation and statistical analysis.

This chapter focuses on one of the most prominent international human rights monitoring organisations that focus on torture and ill-treatment the United Nations (UN) Committee Against Torture (CAT/the Committee). More specifically it examines the experience of the British government before the Committee. Since the start of the 'war on terror' numerous allegations of British involvement in torture have been made (see, for more details Kelly, 2012). Non-governmental organisations (NGOs) have turned to international monitoring mechanisms in order to try to make these allegations stick and mobilise the persuasive power of shame. The UK also seems to be the ideal candidate for shaming strategies, given its self-image as a bastion of human rights and the rule of law on the international stage. The chapter is based on extensive participant observation at the Committee, which involved sitting in on sessions and interviewing members and delegates. It also involved following the recommendations of the Committee after they left Geneva, through the press, British parliamentary committees and court cases. This part of the fieldwork involved further interviews with civil servants, politicians and human rights activists, as well as the analysis of the large amount of documentary material produced as part of the monitoring process. The chapter starts by describing one of the most controversial of British security policies since the start of the 'war on terror', namely the detention without trial of foreign security suspects, and uses this as the thread through which shame is explored. The chapter then moves on to describe the institutional, political and legal history of the monitoring committee. Next, it describes the UK's appearance before the CAT in 2004, and concludes by examining the 'impact' of the CAT in the UK, and the nature of human rights shaming strategies around torture in general.

DETENTION WITHOUT TRIAL

In February 2002, four men sat inside Belmarsh high-security prison in south London. They had been picked up three months earlier under UK anti-terrorism legislation and were being detained indefinitely without charge. They included Mahmoud Abu-Rideh, a wheelchair-bound Palestinian refugee. Abu-Rideh was born in Jordan to Palestinian parents and spent five years as a teenager in an Israeli jail, where he claims he was tortured. He had then travelled to Pakistan and Afghanistan before being granted asylum in the UK in 1998. Three years later he was detained by the UK government and accused of being 'involved in fund raising and distribution of those funds for terrorist groups with links to Al Qa'eda'.[1] Abu-Rideh and the other security detainees at Belmarsh were being held under a system that had been developed by the British government due to the tensions between the international prohibition of torture and the security policies of the UK government.

In the atmosphere after the attacks of 11 September 2001, the British security services suspected the men of being involved in terrorism but lacked the evidence to convict them in a criminal court. The next step would have been to deport them. However, Abu-Rideh was a stateless Palestinian and therefore had no state to be deported to, and all the detainees faced the risk of torture if returned to their home country. The British government had therefore developed a system under the Anti-Terror, Crime and Security Act (ATCSA) 2001 whereby the Home Secretary could 'certify' someone he or she believed was a 'risk to national security'. Such people could be detained if their removal from the UK was impossible at a practical level, or prevented by law. Evidence against ATCSA detainees was heard by the Special Immigration Appeals Commission, much of it behind closed doors, with the defendants given no access to 'classified' information from the security service that was used against them.

The men would later be joined by a man, known to the courts as 'P'. P was an Algerian who had been refused asylum in the UK in the late 1990s. He wore prosthetic arms, as he had lost one arm entirely and had the other amputated above the elbow, following a bomb explosion. While in the UK he had been arrested in 2001 and charged with 'possession of articles for suspected terrorist purposes' and conspiracy to defraud, but the charges were eventually dropped. P was detained again in January 2003 and certified under ATCSA, accused of being an associate of Osama Bin Laden. In particular he was accused of being linked to the plan to bomb the Christmas market in Frankfurt, and of plotting to launch a number of biological and chemical weapons attacks in the UK.

Both Abu-Rideh's and P's mental health deteriorated considerably while they were in Belmarsh and they were moved to Broadmoor high-security psychiatric hospital, outside London. The psychiatric staff at Broadmoor had argued that a high-security hospital was not the most appropriate place for someone with Abu-Rideh's mental health needs, but this had been overruled by the Home Secretary.

INTERNATIONAL MONITORING

International human rights monitoring mechanisms are an attempt to shine light into the darkest recesses of places of detention. They try to hold states to account for their treatment of detainees through a careful combination of transparency and persuasion. In the mid 1970s, two Geneva-based NGOs, the International Commission of Jurists (ICJ) and the Swiss Committee Against Torture (SCAT) began lobbying for a UN-based system for monitoring places of detention in order to prohibit torture. The assumption was that only an international body would have the necessary moral and political authority to carry out the task. However, as in the rest of the UN human rights system, many states, and the US and the USSR in particular, were keen to avoid any restrictions on sovereignty (Normand and Zaidi 2008). Any monitoring mechanisms they agreed to had limited powers to investigate allegations or to issue binding decisions. As such, it soon became clear that it was going to be difficult, if not impossible, to get widespread agreement from UN members for a universal system of visits to places of detention.

The UN body that was eventually created had a very restricted mandate. Formally, the CAT monitors compliance with the UN Convention Against Torture and Other Cruel, Inhuman or Degrading Treatment or Punishment 1984. The aim of the Convention was to set out specific legal obligations for states. However, according to the Dutch chair of the drafting committee many states were concerned that specific obligations such as these should not be tied to vague concepts like 'cruel, inhuman or degrading treatment or punishment' (Burgers and Danelius 1988: 39). It is therefore only when we get to Article 16 that we hear mention of other forms of ill-treatment.

The Committee is made up of ten part-time members and is supported on a part-time basis by members of the Office of the High Commissioner for Human Rights (OHCHR). Members are elected every four years by the states that have ratified the Convention. Members are nominated by their states, but once they sit on the

Committee they are supposed to act independently. The practice has been to have two South American, two African, three European, one North American, one Eastern European, and one Chinese member. Of the ten members in 2008, two worked in NGOs, three were diplomats, three worked in law schools, and two as judges.

The Convention Against Torture contains perhaps the most detailed definition of torture in any international instrument. Article 1 defines torture as:

> any act by which severe pain or suffering, whether physical or mental, is intentionally inflicted on a person for such purposes as obtaining from him or a third person information or a confession, punishing him for an act he or a third person has committed or is suspected of having committed, or intimidating or coercing him or a third person, or for any reason based on discrimination of any kind, when such pain or suffering is inflicted by or at the instigation of or with the consent or acquiescence of a public official or other person acting in an official capacity. It does not include pain or suffering arising only from, inherent in or incidental to lawful sanctions.

However, despite the length of the Article, according to perhaps the two most influential people involved in the drafting the Convention this is not really a definition at all, merely a guide to implementation (Burgers and Danelius 1988, 122). It does not, for example, say how you might even begin to measure 'severe pain or suffering'.

There are few explicit statements by the CAT clarifying what this definition might mean in practice. In large measure, the lack of a precise jurisprudence on what is or is not torture is due to a deliberate constructive ambiguity. Members argue, for example, that they do not want to create a clear distinction between torture and cruel, inhuman, or degrading treatment or punishment, as this will create a line to which states will automatically move. By leaving the division between the two categories unclear the Committee has more room to operate when censuring states.

It is important to note several things at this stage. First, the CAT is a fundamentally future-oriented institution. It focuses on general principles and practices rather than individual culpability. Such human rights regimes can rely on what Kurasawa calls a form of 'preventive foresight' (2007: 97). They try to envision possible future abuses and introduce the relevant precautionary measures. Second, the recommendations issued by the CAT are advisory rather than binding. The routine business of the Committee does not give it the power to visit signatory states directly; instead it relies on written reports and oral presentations given in Geneva. The CAT has very limited resources, relying on a handful of civil servants at the OHCHR. Its ten members work five weeks a year on a voluntary basis.

The general consensus among commentators, activists and practitioners, is that the CAT is a generally weak, although improving body, both in terms of resources and expertise (Bank 2000; Crawford 2000). Most importantly, the CAT is the product of political compromises and has to operate in the space of diplomatic persuasion, rather than direct enforcement. Given the political spaces within which the CAT operates, its roles and processes are constantly changing. Its practices are fragmented and conflicted because they are produced through the interaction of international diplomats, civil servants and NGOs.

THE UN COMMITTEE AGAINST TORTURE

On an autumnal day in late 2004, a senior British civil servant from the Department of Constitutional Affairs, by the name of Jonathan Spencer, sat in a conference room overlooking the shores of Lake Geneva. With the hum of simultaneous translation in the background he began presenting the UK's report to the UN CAT. A written report had been submitted a year previously. Normally there is at least a two-year delay before the Committee gets round to scrutinising the reports. However, against the background of the UK's role in the invasion of Iraq, and its support for the US in the 'war on terror', the UN had decided to bring the UK report forward. Spencer began his presentation by stressing that: 'the United Kingdom regards torture as an affront to and a denial of the inherent dignity and right to respect which is an inalienable birthright of every human being'. The UK delegation, of almost thirty people, was one of the largest the Committee had ever seen. In the audience were also representatives of around a dozen British NGOs, as well as an American diplomat who was shadowing the UK delegation in preparation for the US report which was due to be submitted in the forthcoming year.

This was the fourth time since the early 1990s that the UK had appeared before the Committee as part of the routine reporting cycle. This time around, the report ran to over 100 pages. It covered the criminal offence of torture, the training of personnel, procedures of arrest, conditions in prison and domestic monitoring mechanisms, among other things. Despite being the focus of much activity and protest in the UK, the system by which foreign terror suspects could be detained without charge under the ATCSA 2001 was given just half a page. In the oral presentation, however, Spencer argued that there was 'an emergency that threatens the life of the nation', and that the provisions of the Act 'were a necessary and proportionate response to the emergency'. He then went on to set out developments in asylum procedure, and conditions in prison, among other things, before handing over to an official of the Ministry of Defence who dealt with the situation in Iraq.

The afternoon before the UK presentation, the Committee had met with a delegation of British human rights NGOs, including Amnesty International, Human Rights Watch, Liberty, Justice and Redress. The British NGO delegation was one of the biggest to appear before the Committee in several years. The NGOs had also submitted several 'shadow reports', outlining the key issues that they felt the Committee should focus on.

To a great extent the part-time Committee relies on information supplied by NGOs, as it has limited investigatory powers to supplement the information received from states. As such, NGOs can play a central role in setting the Committee's agenda, the questions they ask, and eventually the recommendations that they make. During state sessions members sometimes refer directly to information from human rights organisations. More often than not, however, members simply quote from the NGO reports, without indicating the source. There is also a great deal of informal lobbying that can go on in the corridors around the meeting room, as NGOs try and slip in last-minute questions.

Following the UK presentation, the ten Committee members took their turn to ask the delegation questions. Taking the lead was Felice Gaer, the American member of the Committee. Gaer was the Director of the American Jewish Committee's Jacob Blaustein Institute for the Advancement of Human Rights and a veteran of US human rights delegations. Among other things, she asked for clarification over whether evidence potentially obtained under torture was used in British courts. When she had finished, other Committee members asked whether it was right to 'leave someone in legal limbo' under the ATCSA and requested further information about investigation of deaths in custody in Iraq. Depending on how they are counted, over seventy questions were asked by the Committee. Following the Committee's questions, the UK was then given just over a day to go away and prepare their answers. In their replies the UK delegation denied that the ATCSA created a legal limbo, reiterated that evidence obtained through torture was not used, and argued that diplomatic assurances were in compliance with the UK's international obligations.

As the Committee has limited investigatory powers, it cannot and does not make factual determinations, or even firm allegations. Committee members therefore pose highly qualified questions. They ask states to comment on existing allegations, using phrasing such as: 'I have a feeling that …', 'there are strong allegations that …' or 'could you comment on …'. When disagreements over basic factual issues arise, the Committee is in no position to determine who or what is correct. In general, the questions concern either broad policies, institutional arrangements or statistical clarifications. The polite tone and broad nature of the questions makes them relatively easy for states to avoid answering. In this context, specific substantive issues almost always give way to issues of principle and procedure.

Two weeks after the Committee had heard the presentations, it issued its Conclusions and Recommendations. In these, the Committee expressed concern about the use of diplomatic assurances but said that the arrangements being used were 'not wholly clear' and therefore could not be assessed. The 'resort to potentially indefinite detention' under the ATCSA was also singled out, and it was recommended that the UK should 'review, as a matter of urgency, the alternatives'. The recommendations of the Committee also included a request for further 'reflection' on the government's intention not to rely on evidence obtained by torture. Finally, the UK was asked to consider developing a statistical database on issues relating to the Convention.

The language of the recommendations makes it clear that they are not obligatory, as the CAT must walk a narrow diplomatic tightrope. Andreas Mavromatis, the veteran former chair of CAT explained to me, 'we need to go softly. We cannot throw everything at them. The purpose is not to point fingers but to save lives.... We cannot demand too much as otherwise they will close the door on us.' As such, it is also very rare for the Committee to tell states that they are in direct contravention of the Convention. Although in 2007, for example, the Committee recommended that the US 'should rescind any interrogation technique, including methods involving sexual humiliation, "water boarding" and "short shackling"', the language is ambiguous as to whether the US has used these techniques, and whether they were in direct breach of the Convention.[2] In 2004, at no point was the UK government told its actions were in breach of the Convention Against Torture.

The UK responded over one year later to the Committee's recommendations. By this time, the ATCSA had already been superseded and replaced by a new regime. The UK response began by saying that it did not consider it necessary to review domestic law prohibiting torture. It ended by setting out more details about the diplomatic assurances which had been obtained from Libya, Jordan and Lebanon for the extradition of terror suspects.

HUMAN RIGHTS MONITORING AND THE CONSTRUCTION OF RISK

As a future-oriented institution, concerned with prevention rather than punishment, CAT understands torture through the lens of risk. Risk is a very specific way of trying to grapple with events that have not yet happened. To work on the basis of risk reduction is to try to make the future measurable, or at least monitorable, to pin it down to identifiable problems. Risk is not simply about the recognition of danger, but is an attempt to calculate its probability. To work on the basis of risk reduction is therefore to try to pin the future down to identifiable problems and work out their respective odds (Beck 2002). In this context, risk can be understood as a technique for taming the future, for making it calculable, visible and intelligible (Ewald 1991: 207).

What type of future can be imagined through risk? The risk of torture or ill-treatment is not self-evident, as risks do not exist independently out there in the world. Instead, any understanding of risk is a product of the devices we have for measuring it (Ewald 1991: 207; Power 2007). At first glance this may seem an absurd thing to say about torture and ill-treatment, as what could be more real than pain and suffering? However, torture and ill-treatment are not simply pain and suffering, but a very specific way of understanding the infliction of violence. Thinking about torture and ill-treatment in terms of risk therefore implies setting down markers that can be measured, of freezing the ebb and flow of violence, so that its likely occurrence can be calculated.

For human rights monitoring to take place, torture and ill-treatment has to be made 'monitorable' and amenable to particular forms of assessment. Having limited investigatory powers, monitoring mechanisms are forced to take their information from the sources that are available. Files are produced, statistics taken and policies written, from which information can then be read. In order to produce monitoring information, they cut through the complex processes which result in detention and ill-treatment, highlighting some and ignoring others. As Sally Merry has argued about human rights indicators, but in terms also applicable to human rights monitoring in general, the result is a 'world knowable without the detailed particulars of context and history', converting 'complicated contextually variable phenomena into unambiguous, clear and impersonal measures' (2011). As such, monitoring is not a transparent process of information-gathering, but one of abstraction and generalisation, and its procedures can obscure as much as they reveal. Such processes are not unique to human rights monitoring, and can be seen as part of a broader process of 'technical governance'. Only those issues through which a technical solution can be proposed are highlighted (Li 2007: 126). Broader goals on political and social transformation are rendered as technical questions of procedure, documentation and the adoption of the correct policies.

Risk does not arise from a precise and known danger. Indeed, if the exact nature and occurrence of the threat were known, it would not be a risk. Rather, risk is a generalisation, based on a distribution of factors across a wider population. Risk, therefore is not a quality that can belong to individuals alone, but to general categories (Castel 1991). The specifics of individual life trajectories are thus subsumed. In this case the specificity of torture and ill-treatment as distinct forms of violence is lost. Instead, there is an examination of the general procedures of a state and its relationships with its citizens, rather than of the complex dynamics, which can lead to acts of ill-treatment and create individualised vulnerabilities. The point is not that assigning individual guilt or innocence necessarily reflects the processes that lead to violence better than institutionalised and generalised risk prevention. As David Kennedy has argued, to sort and separate the tangle of administrative, political and individual responsibility for the abuse of detainees, is not a 'matter of "getting to the bottom of it" or "finding out what happened". It is a cultural and political project of interpretation ...' (2006: 143). He goes on to claim that:

> It may be possible to identify the bad act precisely – torture of this person here, in this prison – and to assign responsibility to

one administrative unit, perhaps to this guy.... But it may also be possible to set in motion a broad ethical and legal discourse about the legitimacy of everyone until nothing can be pinned on anyone. And it is not clear that justice will be done, or seen to be done, either way. (2006: 156)

The crucial point is that whichever way responsibility or lack of responsibility is distributed is an act of cultural interpretation, with distinct political implications for the ways in which we respond to violence.

It is important to note here that the blind spots of the CAT are not simply a problem of expertise or knowledge. Many of the members of the committee are well aware of these problems. Rather they are an issue of the political space within which committee operates, and their institutional limits. Given limited resources, sources have to be created from which information can be read at speed. Indeed, it would be a mistake to talk about the problems of the CAT in terms of 'failure'. In many ways the CAT does exactly what it was designed to do by the signatory states, who were reluctant to create an international monitoring organisation with the power to infringe on what they saw as their own sovereignty. In this context, the CAT has to refrain from making firm accusations about matters of fact, and to issue advisory rather than binding recommendations.

What types of knowledge, then, does the monitoring process produce? The theory of risk that the Committee works with is implicit rather than explicit. There is little analysis of causes of torture and ill-treatment, and the focus instead is on its visible, or at least monitorable manifestations. As it is procedures, policies and legislation which the Committee has easiest access to, it is precisely around policies, procedures and legislation that the understanding of torture is built up. There is therefore a concern with issues such as access to lawyers, rules of evidence and the criminal law on torture. The risk of torture is also linked to the cultural attitudes of officials. The Committee particularly emphasises the training of police officers, prison guards, soldiers, lawyers, judges and the general public. Training is seen as necessary for, in the words of one CAT member, a 'shift in mentalities' and as such the eradication of torture is seen as an issue of 'cultural change'. A concern with individuals and wider political causes can seep into the work of the CAT. However, because of their political and resource limitations the default position is always a concern for technocratic and managerial processes.

THE 'IMPACT' OF SHAME

Given the focus on policies in human rights monitoring, what role does shame have? Can a state be ashamed of its procedures? In truth, it is difficult to get a sense of the impact of the CAT recommendations, as they become part of the general stream of politics. The influence of human rights monitoring can be diffuse and indirect because their conclusions, recommendations, and communications can take on a life of their own (Merry 2006). NGOs, courts and even governments use the Committee's recommendations in their own political struggles. In this process, it is impossible to say whether something changed because of the CAT, or whether it is the result of other pressures. There is no obvious causal link. Political change does not happen simply for one reason, but rather because of an accumulation of factors. However, it is possible to look at the rhetorical approach to the recommendations, the ways in which they are formally integrated into the policy-making process, and the locations where references are made to them. By doing so, we can begin to understand the spaces that the recommendations open up for political debate and those they close down.

Under the government of Tony Blair the political rhetoric of the UK was that human rights had to be rebalanced in favour of protecting the general population and that those who argued for the rights of terror suspects were naive at best, and dangerous at worst. The UK government seemed to be saying that it had nothing to be ashamed of. While it did not make direct attacks on the CAT, maybe because they were too low profile to warrant the effort, successive ministers criticised the international human rights regime. In one famous incident, Professor Manfred Nowak, the UN Special Rapporteur on torture was reportedly harangued in a meeting with Charles Clarke, then British Home Secretary and the man who introduced the ATCSA. Clarke accused him of wasting his time, and told him he should concentrate on places with a real human rights problem.

It is of course important to attach a certain level of scepticism to political rhetoric, as there is a strong sense of playing to the crowd in many of the attacks on international human rights mechanisms. These public criticisms also seem to have died down after 2007 and the resignation of Tony Blair. However, at a practical level, the general sense is that the UK government and its civil servants treats liaising with the CAT as a bureaucratic task to be dealt with efficiently, rather than as a source of guidance, accountability and moral authority. As the civil servant who had been responsible for liaising with CAT put it to me, 'Other departments have other priorities.... It is not that there is malice, just people are busy, the reports are low down the list of things to do.' Similarly, as a Home Office legal advisor told me:

> the CAT process is merely about providing legal comment and explaining the position.... We do not really have an international law problem in this area. This is not the same as saying we have done everything the UN has asked.

Lord Carlile, the government's independent reviewer of anti-terror legislation told me that he had never once referred to the CAT in any discussion he had had with the government.

All the above does not mean that the recommendations are not taken seriously. After all, the UK government will devote thousands of man-hours to responding to them, and write some of the longest reports. When I showed a draft of a version of this chapter to the civil servant in charge of coordinating responses to the CAT recommendations, he bridled at the suggestion that the CAT was not dealt with adequately by the British government, pointing to the high-level ministerial involvement in signing off on any responses. However, it is to say that the recommendations do not have bite in and of themselves. The former Chief Executive of the National Offender Management Service, responsible for all England's prisons, told me, for example, that while human rights monitoring recommendations do not drive policy, the prison service will try to cooperate 'if it is reasonable'.

The feeling among many activists is that the UK works with the CAT primarily to show that it is engaging at a formal level, rather than to listen to what it is being told. As such, although the formal role of the Committee is to produce a dialogue, there is very little evidence that this ever actually takes place. Benjamin Ward, Deputy Director of Human Rights Watch's Europe and Central Asia Division, a qualified barrister and former UN employee, put it to me that:

> the UK generally tries to engage on soft issues, but when the push comes to shove they will not give in ... when it comes to the hard

edge, they will not listen.… The purpose of engaging is to assert that it is compliant, rather than to take part in a dialogue.… The UK thinks it really has nothing new to learn.

It can seem that way to members of the monitoring organisations as well. As Phil Wheatley, the most senior person in the English prison system, put it to me 'we engage because we have signed a treaty and it is important in broader foreign policy terms that we engage with them as we expect other states to do the same'.

Given the widespread feelings about the government's relatively relaxed responses to monitoring recommendations, many NGOs try to hold up the recommendations to 'public opinion' in the hope that wider exposure will bring about the desired changes in policy and practice. As Sally Merry argues, NGOs mobilise the monitoring committee recommendations 'to generate public support or governmental discomfort' (2006: 71). As such, NGOs attempt to use the recommendations in order to get press coverage, which in turn might lead to increased political scrutiny, which might lead to some type of policy or legal reform, which might lead to practical change (see also Keck and Sikkink 1998). However, although anything with the world 'torture' in it can get a certain amount of attention, it is often very difficult to get the TV and newspapers to pay attention to the CAT recommendations. In large part this is because of the equivocal way they are worded, which reduces their impact as a headline. A top line that says 'UN body recommends more training for prison officers' is not going to grab that much attention. At most, it is normally the legal correspondents who are interested, but their stories can be buried deep in the newspaper.

Perhaps the key way in which the recommendations of the CAT are kept alive, are the inquiries and reports of the UK parliament's Joint Committee of Human Rights (JCHR). The JCHR is an all-party committee from both Houses of Parliament. Since 2002 the JCHR has conducted follow-up inquiries looking at the ways in which the UK government has responded to the recommenda- tions of UN human rights committees. In the words of the JCHR's legal advisor: 'we decided we were going to take the concluding observations of UN human rights committees and give them life … we try to bridge the gap between diplomatic rhetoric and practice'. Following the release of the CAT's recommendations, the JCHR held a five-day inquiry and received written evidence from human rights organisations such as Justice, Human Rights Watch and Amnesty, as well as from government departments. Senior ministers, civil servants and police officers gave oral evidence as well as NGO activists. In many ways the inquiry was more thorough and systematic than the original CAT report. The report's conclusions were also relatively hard hitting (JCHR 2006). The experience of many NGOs is that the JCHR attracts more press coverage than international human rights monitoring mechanisms and is therefore taken more seriously by government. However, in many ways the JCHR is very similar to CAT. Like CAT, it does not look at individual cases, but rather at broader processes. It also hears only oral evidence and reads written reports, and does not have direct investigatory powers of its own. Perhaps most importantly, its recommendations are non-binding, and although they are responded to in detail, there is space for disagreement and they can, if need be, be ignored. It appears, for example, to be the only parliamentary committee, which ministers have refused to attend.

The final area where CAT recommendations can be invoked is court cases. However, in practice it is very hard to find mention of CAT recommendations in English case law. One decision of the House of Lords even goes so far as to describe a recommendation from CAT as 'having no value'.[3] In large part this relative lack of reference to the CAT recommendations is due to their very nature. They are not authoritative on facts, and make generally vague jurisprudential claims. More importantly, the language of the CAT, phrased in terms of diplomatic politeness, is often not hard-edged, and therefore not persuasive in a legal context.

Despite the lack of reference to the CAT, it was court cases that made the biggest difference in the areas on which CAT and the JCHR had expressed concern. Litigation rather than shame was most persuasive. In December 2005, the Law Lords ruled that the courts could not hear evidence that might have been obtained through torture by officials of a foreign state.[4] Much of the evidence used to certify people such as Abu-Rideh was obtained by security forces in places such as Pakistan, Afghanistan, Algeria or Syria. The Home Office argued that it would be practically impossible to prove that all evidence was untainted. However, the Law Lords ruled that if the courts are unable to conclude that there is not a real risk that the evidence has been obtained by torture, it should refuse to admit the evidence. Passing mention was made in the judgment to the concerns expressed by the CAT over the possibility that evidence obtained by torture was being used in British courts. However, the stress was not on human rights issue, but rather on the ban on torture as having its roots in over 400 years of English common law.

Prior to the ruling about evidence, the regime under which the ATCSA detainees were held was also declared unlawful by the House of Lords. The ruling argued that the detention of Abu-Rideh and others was a disproportionate deprivation of the right to liberty and was discriminatory on the grounds that it applied only to non-citizens in an arbitrary manner. This ruling came just weeks after the CAT recommendations were released, but they were not mentioned at all.

In response to the Lords' decision, a new regime was introduced by the Home Secretary that applied to non-citizens and citizens alike. The detainees remained 'certified' as suspected terrorists, but were released on bail and kept under effective house arrest in a system known as control orders. Abu-Rideh was released in March 2005, but had to wear an electronic tag, live at a designated address and observe a curfew from 7 p.m. to 7 a.m. If he wanted to meet with people outside his immediate family he had to get permission from the Home Office. He was also banned from having a mobile phone or computer. P was also released around the same time, and placed under similar bail conditions. However, after his initial release, he was re-arrested in the summer of 2005 and then placed once more under house arrest. Fed up with his living conditions P agreed to leave voluntarily to Algeria in early 2007. On arrival he was detained, but released after three days. Abu-Rideh tried to commit suicide several times while under house arrest. In the days after the House of Lords' ruling on the use of secret evidence, he was given a travel document by the British government, something he had been asking for years, and agreed to leave the UK voluntarily. The travel document had a 'right of return' clause written into it, but was cancelled as soon as he left the country. Abu-Rideh is now believed to be in either Syria or Jordan.

THE SHAME OF TORTURE?

Is there any evidence of anything resembling shame in the ways in which the UK government and its civil servants approaches human rights monitoring mechanisms? Critics might dismiss human rights shaming as an unenforceable irrelevance. From this perspective, strong states such as the UK will inevitably follow their own interests. Shame is far too soft an emotion for the hardball of international politics (Hathaway 2002). This critique would claim that, at best, state officials will respond to human rights recommendations in a cosmetic and instrumental way in order to gain access to international financial support, military assistance or diplomatic kudos, but will manifest little real commitment (Risse et al. 1999).

A perhaps less cynical view of international human rights monitoring would point to the vast resources that the UK puts into the reporting process, and the often high-level discussions that go on about how to respond to criticisms. From this perspective, the UK government is worried about being shamed by international human rights organisations and responds in order to limit the impact. Serious efforts are therefore put in to engaging with monitoring mechanisms because they have a persuasive normative force and cannot simply be ignored (cf. Franck 1998). A related line of argument is that the UK is rarely shamed by international human rights monitoring because a consciousness of human rights obligations is built deep into the domestic political fabric. States such as the UK are forced to take their obligation to prohibit torture seriously because of their own internal pressures to do so, from parliament and the courts as well as NGOs, activists and lawyers (Çalı and Wyss 2009). Even if the recommendations of the international human rights monitoring mechanism are not directly fed back into the system, the UK government is already working in the same general direction.

There is an obvious danger in asking whether or not and why the UK government experiences shame in the face of its international obligations, of treating the state as a unified entity. The UK government's interaction with the CAT is far from being a seamless web. The liaison with the Committee is coordinated by the Ministry of Justice, which needs to seek detailed information from other parts of government – a necessarily time-consuming task. Even if the Ministry of Justice moves quickly to meet the deadlines set by the committees, other parts of government have their own commitments and priorities to manage. This has important implications. Whereas people may be ashamed if they are exposed as torturing, the impact is diffused when the accusations are about rules of evidence, the monitoring of diplomatic agreements and procedures on arrest. Although individuals within government may be worried about many of the practices and policies of the UK government these are dispersed into bureaucratic chains. Many of the officials that I spoke to would privately admit to being worried about 'some of the things going on', largely the apparent complicity of the secret services in the ill-treatment of detainees elsewhere in the world, but these were always elsewhere and carried out by other people.

Shame implies a vulnerability to being exposed for failing to live up to professed ideals and goals. However, it is not clear what human rights monitoring exposes and precisely what ideals are not being reached. Little, if no, new information is provided by the monitoring organisations. Not only are officials rarely surprised by the information produced, but NGOs, parliamentary bodies and journalists nearly always already know the information the monitoring committees present to the world. UK government officials and NGO activists broadly agree that the CAT does not tell them anything they did not know already. Light is not shone into new corners. As an official at the Ministry of Justice, who liaises with the CAT put it to me: 'very rarely do any of the questions raise a new issue. In nearly all cases though we already have well established lines…'. Activists and lawyers have a similar response, saying that the reports and replies very seldom tell them anything new. What is more, it is not clear who the information is being exposed to. If shame requires an audience, it is not obvious that anyone is watching. Government officials largely know what is going on, and the press are rarely interested.

What, if anything, is specific to international shame? International monitoring organisations are not after all the only organisations that try to use shame to bring about change. Many domestic groups do something similar. Yet many of these same groups, such as Amnesty, also pushed for the creation of international monitoring organisations, arguing that only an international mechanism could hold states to account outside of the restrictions of domestic politics. Yet, in a double bind, entering into the realm of international politics also means facing up to the reluctance of governments to limit their sovereignty. The result is monitoring mechanisms that rely on the soft power of persuasion. However, as information travels backwards and forwards from London to Geneva, or between the UN and any other capital city, it becomes more and more abstract, losing real-time urgency, making it harder to pin down.

The shaming strategies of international human rights monitoring mechanisms can produce spaces for the deflection of responsibility. This is not simply due to the fact that denial can be an immediate response to shame (Cohen 2000). More importantly, it is because it is not always clear what there is to be ashamed about. If shame requires a sense of failing to meet standards or goals, what these standards or goals are is far from self-evident. When international human rights monitoring mechanisms talk about torture and other forms of ill-treatment they tend to talk about broad institutions and policies. As such, a concern with torture is often dispersed into procedural issues. In this context, the ambiguity in the ways in which torture is defined, and the technical ways in which its obligations are interpreted, give the UK plenty of wiggle room. There are always more policies and procedures that civil servants can refer to.

International human rights monitoring works to disperse shame into bureaucratic procedures. As Scott Veitch (2007) has argued, legal institutions can work so as to effectively facilitate disavowals of responsibility. From the ways in which they conceptualise harm in limited and particular ways, to the devices they have for allowing claims to be made and then allocating responses, legal institutions help disperse responsibility into bureaucratic chains. Human rights monitoring turns torture from an issue of political violence into one of audit and technique. Through the monitoring process, human rights indicators can become confused with human rights. There can be a slippage between the process of collecting information and the practices designed to prevent human rights violations (Power 2007). Measurement, monitoring and prevention become merged. Indeed, the very question of compliance with the international prohibition of torture immediately shifts attention away from the question as to whether states are complicit in torture. Showing that you are compliant with international obligations is not the same thing as showing that you are not complicit with torture. Whereas people may be ashamed if they are exposed as torturing, the impact is surely diffused if the accusations are about rules of evidence, the monitoring of diplomatic agreements and procedures on arrest.

NOTES

1. A. and Others v. The United Kingdom [2009] ECHR 301, 26 BHRC 1, (2009) 49 EHRR 29, 31.
2. CAT/C/USA/CO/2.
3. *Jones v Ministry of Interior for the Kingdom of Saudi Arabia & Ors* [2006] 2 WLR 1424, [2007] 1 All ER 113, [2007] 1 AC 270, [2006] UKHL 26 [5].
4. *A & Ors v Secretary of State for the Home Department* [2006] 1 All ER 575, 19 BHRC 441, [2006] UKHRR 225, [2006] HRLR 6, [2006] 2 AC 221, [2005] UKHL 71, [2005] 3 WLR 1249.

BIBLIOGRAPHY

Bank, R. (2000) 'Country-oriented procedures under the Convention Against Torture: Towards a new dynamism', in P. Alston and J. Crawford (ed.) *The Future of UN Human Rights Treaty Monitoring*, pp. 145–174 (Cambridge, Cambridge University Press).

Beck, U. (2002) 'The terrorist threat: World risk society revisited', *Theory, Culture & Society* 19(4): 39–55.

Burgers, J.H. and H. Danelius (1988) *The United Nations Convention Against Torture: A Handbook on the Convention Against Torture and Other Cruel, Inhuman or Degrading Treatment or Punishment* (The Hague: Martinus Nijhoff).

Çalı, B. and A. Wyss (2009) 'Why do democracies comply with human rights judgments? A comparative analysis of the UK, Ireland and Germany'. Unpublished Working Paper.

Castel, R. (1991) 'From dangerousness to risk', in G. Burchell, C. Gordon and P. Miller (eds) *The Foucault Effect: Studies in Governmentality*, pp. 281–198 (Chicago: University of Chicago Press).

Cohen, S. (2000) *States of Denial: Knowing about Atrocities and Suffering* (Cambridge: Polity).

Crawford, J. (2000) 'The UN human rights treaty system: A system in crisis?', in P. Alston and J. Crawford (ed.) *The Future of UN Human Rights Treaty Monitoring*, pp. 1–12 (Cambridge: Cambridge University Press).

Ewald, F. (1991) 'Insurance and Risk', in G. Burchell, C. Gordon and P. Miller (eds) *The Foucault Effect: Studies in Governmentality*, pp. 197–210 (London: Harvester Wheatsheaf).

Franck, T.M. (1998). *Fairness in International Law and Institutions* (Oxford: Oxford University Press).

Hathaway, O.A. (2002) 'Do human rights treaties make a difference?', *Yale Law Journal* 111: 1935–2042.

JCHR (Joint Committee of Human Rights) (2006) *The UN Convention against Torture (UNCAT). Nineteenth Report of the Session 2005–6, Joint Committee on Human Rights* (London: HMSO).

Keck, M. and K. Sikkink (1998) *Activists Beyond Borders: Advocacy Networks in International Politics* (Ithaca, NY: Cornell University Press).

Keenan, T. (2004) 'Mobilizing shame', *South Atlantic Quarterly* 103: 434–439.

Kelly, T. (2012) *This Side of Silence: Human Rights, Torture and the Recognition of Cruelty* (Philadelphia, PA: University of Pennsylvania Press).

Kennedy, D. (2006) *Of War and Law* (Princeton, NJ: Princeton University Press).

Kurasawa, F. (2007) *The Work of Global Justice: Human Rights as Practices* (Cambridge: Cambridge University Press).

Li, T.M. (2007) *The Will to Improve: Governmentality, Development and the Practice of Politics* (Durham, NC: Duke University Press).

Merry, S.E. (2006) *Human Rights and Gender Violence* (Chicago: University of Chicago Press).

Merry, S.E. (2011) 'Measuring the world: Indicators, human rights and global governance', *Current Anthropology* 52(S3): 83–95.

Normand, R. and S. Zaidi (2008) *Human Rights at the UN: The Political History of Universal Justice* (Bloomington, IN: Indiana University Press).

Piers, G. and M. Singer (1972) *Shame and Guilt: A Psychoanalytic and Cultural Study* (London: W.W. Norton & Co.).

Power, M. (2007) *Organized Uncertainty: Designing a World of Risk Management* (Oxford: Oxford University Press).

Risse, T., S. Ropp and K. Sikkink (1999) *The Power of Human Rights: International Norms and Domestic Change* (Cambridge: Cambridge University Press).

Veitch, S. (2007) *Law and Irresponsibility: On the Legitimation of Human Suffering* (London: Routledge-Cavendish).

7

Entangled in Artefacts

Governing Diverging Claims and Rights to Cultural Objects at UNESCO

Brigitta Hauser-Schäublin

This article is about the international governance of diverging claims, mostly by state parties, to be the rightful proprietor of material 'things'. These things – cultural artefacts – are highly valued and carefully preserved commodities, obtained lawfully for one party, while the other party argues that these are inalienable goods, people's cultural property or heritage, appropriated from them under doubtful conditions. Several of these claims are entrusted not to courts but to the UNESCO Intergovernmental Committee for Promoting the Return of Cultural Property to its Countries of Origin or its Restitution in Case of Illicit Appropriation (henceforth called the 'Committee for Return and Restitution'), and ICOM (International Council of Museums) (see also Prott 2009b; Skrydstrup 2009).[1] The reasons why such claims of restitution are by preference submitted to UNESCO are twofold. The disputes over such contested artefacts or collections no longer focus on mainly legal questions, such as investigating proofs about their legal or illegal removal or acquisition. The legal situation, such as in the case of the Hittite sphinx whose ownership was disputed between Turkey and Germany (see below), is often ambiguous, not least due to the existing legal pluralism (Zips and Weilenmann 2011) which allows different interpretations. However, an ambiguous legal situation is, as I suggest, only one reason for depositing such claims with UNESCO. The main reason lies in the nature of the values of the disputed artefacts and the relationship they embody. The argument of 'cultural property' or 'heritage' suggests an intrinsic value added to the artefacts as material 'things' and, therefore, an essential and basically 'inalienable' part of a nation's 'identity', as the case of 'Montezuma's feather crown' will show (see, for example Anico and Peralta 2009).[2] It is the symbolic or cultural capital, in the sense of

Bourdieu, as embodied in the artefacts on which the claimants base their demands. The claim to symbolic capital creates a tie between the artefact and the claimant which produces only one legitimate owner: the legitimate heir of the symbolic capital. At the same time, the reference to the symbolic value or capital which surmounts the 'secular' value of a 'museum artefact' creates an imbalance in the relationship between the two parties.

The UNESCO Committee for Return and Restitution cannot be considered independent from other UNESCO conventions, declarations and institutions; the most important of these is the 1970 Convention on the Means of Prohibiting and Preventing the Illicit Import, Export and Transfer of Ownership of Cultural Property, which has been adopted by 120 states (UNESCO 1970). Correspondingly, the Committee for Return and Restitution, which came into being in 1978, is an instrument that facilitates the implementation of the Convention in cases where its assistance is sought. The Committee is not, therefore, a 'neutral', but a committed actor. Its goals are described as follows:

this Committee seeks ways and means of facilitating bilateral negotiations, promoting multilateral and bilateral cooperation with a view to the restitution or return of cultural property as well as fostering a public information campaign on the issue, and promoting exchanges of cultural property. (UNESCO IGC 2012)

Moreover, the Committee states that those 'UNESCO Member States who have lost certain cultural objects of fundamental significance and who are calling for their restitution or return, in cases where international conventions cannot be applied, may call on the … Committee' (UNESCO IGC 2012). In other words, UNESCO performs advocacy on behalf of the deprived.

However, the 1970 UNESCO Convention is not the only international regulation that deals with issues of cultural property and its illicit appropriation, or rather the protection of national heritage. There are other organisations and regulations, such as the UNIDROIT Convention on Stolen or Illegally Exported Cultural Objects (1995; signed by forty-four states), the Interpol Database of stolen works of art, and several regulations by the European Union and the Council of Europe, as well as those of individual nation states. They all serve as guidelines and instruments for the international governance of diverging claims about contested artefacts and collections. These are complemented by a number of ethical codes, such as the International Council of Museums' (ICOM) *Ethical Code* (1986, revised 2004) and UNESCO's *International Code of Ethics for Dealers in Cultural Property* (1999), and their corresponding national ethical codes (as far as they exist). Taken together, they constitute an increasingly dense web of governance tools to fight violations of cultural property regulations.

In this article,[3] I discuss the governance of three different cases of claims for the return or restitution of artefacts. Two of them were reported to the UNESCO Committee for Return and Restitution and gained through the public discussions to which they are subjected during the (bi-)annual meetings considerable international attention. The third case is being directly negotiated between the two parties and their numerous actors behind the scenes.

Taking the contested artefacts and collections as a starting point, I analyse the different configurations of the claimants and their claims in relation to the holder, their positions and arguments on the one hand and the negotiations between both parties and the modalities under which a solution is finally reached on the other. Since I understand the objects as the prime mover around which such disputes evolve, it is necessary to briefly outline the specific perspective applied before I proceed by characterising the positions of the claimants and the holders.

ARTEFACTS PROVOKING CLAIMS AND VINDICATIONS

In all these disputes about the return and restitution of artefacts, it was first and foremost 'things' which stimulated people to develop ideas about the history, meaning, value, and rights they have in them. These 'things' appealed to people and activated different communities of actors and stakeholders, who performed in specific arenas, and every community had its specific interests and goals. 'Things' as actors (Gell 1998) bring people together across nations and continents, and they relate people to each other in changing ways: They create property relations according to the multiple and divergent claims people have in the contested artefacts for differing reasons (Benda-Beckmann et al. 2006; Hann 1998).

As Appadurai has stated: 'Things have no meanings apart from those that human transactions, attributions, and motivations endow them with' (1986: 5). This is true of the ethnographic artefacts and antiquities kept in museums: they were all once produced by artists or craftsmen and used for some particular reason by people. Through different ways of collecting them in specific historical and socio-political circumstances (mostly selecting them from a greater number of objects by buying, gift exchange or simply by removing them), they became 'disembedded' from their cultural context and began their life anew as a valuable commodity. They were transported to other countries and became integrated into new contexts, museums or private collections. There, such artefacts gained new functions and new meanings – and new values (monetary and others). The cultural biography of things (Kopytoff 1986) is about the trajectories of objects and their corresponding transformation within the social contexts they are passing through. Thus, the claims for return and restitution take place in a specific historical moment and consequently also in the life of the artefact or collection. 'The major art and archaeology collections of the Western world, whose formation represents extremely complex blends of plunder, sale, and inheritance, combined with the Western taste for things of the past of the other' (Appadurai 1986: 27) have created a complex arena in which source nations (cf. Merryman 1968: 832) nowadays claim the return and restitution of artefacts held in such museums (and private collections) in 'destination countries'. These negotiations are therefore located in a power context (Benda-Beckmann et al. 2009), namely that between countries of the South – mostly former colonies – and those of the North or former colonisers, or between wealthy and poor countries. The claims for the return or restitution of single artefacts or whole collections by formerly dominated countries or colonies have to be understood also as acts of ideological and emotional decolonisation. Accordingly, the claimants emphasise the importance of their cultural heritage for nation-building and national identity; that is, they appeal first and foremost to a sacred dimension of the artefact and to ethical obligations of the holders to return them.

Museums of destination countries always focus on the legality of their property and emphasise that, according to the law of their country, they are the rightful owners. They have acquired the objects 'in earlier times' when 'different sensitivities and values' existed which are not comparable with current ones. On the other hand, they emphasise their role as responsible custodians of the collections and their obligation to conserve them, to conduct research and to present them in exhibitions open to a world-wide public. These are the main arguments put forward by those nineteen major museums from Europe and North America who signed the 'Declaration on the importance and value of universal museums' (ICOM 2004: 4; see also Prott 2009c: 116–130).[4] The modes of governance developed by the state and non-state actors to settle such cases produced various modalities of returning objects and collections (see also Cornu and Renold 2010); they range from 'loans', replica and exchange – even of disparate items and services – to plain return or restitution.

Developments over the past few decades have shown that the cases officially submitted to UNESCO may take up to thirty years and more until they are solved. Only eight requests have been lodged with the Committee since its beginning (Prott 2009b: 16). Three cases have been resolved by mediation (Thailand and the United States, the Phra Narai Lintel; Jordan and the United States, the Panel of Tyche; and Turkey and Germany, the Bagozköy sphinx); two have been resolved by direct return (Turkey and the German Democratic Republic, the Bagozköy cuneiform tablets; Switzerland as the mediator between the private Barbier-Mueller Museum and Tanzania, the Makonde mask); one case by litigation (Ecuador and Italy, pre-Columbian gold); one case is still pending (Greece and the United Kingdom, the Parthenon marbles); and one case appears to have been suspended (Iran and Belgium, archaeological objects from the necropolis of Khurvin).

All the cases brought to the attention of this UNESCO Committee so far have ended with the return of the claimed artefacts or collections, and all cases involved a renowned holding institution, such as the Metropolitan Museum, the Getty Museum or the Pergamon Museum.

While a highly diplomatic language dominates the official discussions at the meetings of UNESCO, it is evident that the holders of such contested artefacts/collections are in a position of having to justify themselves, and are implicitly haunted by the fear of appearing as defenders of colonialism or imperialism, or as holders of stolen goods. Although this term is never used, the holders finds themselves in the position of the accused. As long as such a contested issue is on the agenda of the Committee, each party is asked by the chairperson to give an account of the progress achieved since the last meeting. The first word always comes from the claimant, who repeats the case from his/her perspective and describes the current state of affairs. The representative of the claimant party underlines the rightfulness of the claim and expresses his/her regret about the fact that the negotiations are only moving slowly. Then the chairperson asks if the representative of the state in which the holding institution is located wants to speak. Subsequently, this representative gives an official statement from his/her country. Such statements mostly have an undertone of apology, and reveal that the holding state – consistently the economically 'stronger' country – is in a rather uncomfortable and definitely weaker position than the claimant. The official reports of both parties are also subject to comments from member state representatives. These comments mostly put pressure on the representative of the holding institution and its corresponding country. In fact, the commentators constitute a pressure group, as the following example, the return of the Makonde mask, will show.

AN ACTION OF RESTITUTION TURNED INTO A DONATION

At the UNESCO Committee meeting in 2010, the representative of Tanzania officially gave a brief account of the successful return of the stolen Makonde mask to the National Museum of Tanzania in 2010 after almost twenty years of complicated negotiations, assisted both by ICOM and UNESCO, with the Barbier-Mueller Museum in Geneva.[5] He did not go into details about the conditions of the return. A representative of ICOM, under whose auspices the agreement between both parties about the return of the stolen mask[6] had been signed, took the floor and explained that the return of the mask was a 'donation' by the Barbier-Mueller Museum. This phrasing was a crucial issue for the holding institution, as will be shown below. 'Donation' is the term used because of the fact that the museum had unknowingly bought the stolen mask from an (anonymous) art dealer in Paris in 1985; that is, it had acquired the mask in good faith. Furthermore, according to Swiss law in force at that time, the museum had become the rightful owner of the mask after five years and no appeal had been made during this period.[7] Thus, no international legal instruments could have been applied to enforce or negotiate a return or restitution. Therefore, it was ICOM's *Code of Ethics* for museums that served as a guideline for the negotiations, and not hard law in the strict sense. The official press release from ICOM even calls it a 'misunderstanding' that the Makonde mask was brought to the attention of the UNESCO Committee (ICOM 2010).[8] The ICOM representative pointed out that the solution of such cases as the Makonde mask is 'generally based on the goodwill of the parties' (ICOM 2010).

After these formal statements by both parties,[9] several representatives of African states commented on this return. A delegate from Burundi said:

It's an example of the fruitful cooperation for the return [of cultural property].... It also shows the strategic role which can and indeed is played by ICOM and UNESCO in defending the heritage and cultural property.... In this context, Africa had its heritage looted and we need excellent cooperation with international organisations if we are to recover our cultural heritage and property.... I think we need to organize an approach for a policy ... [for] returning these goods [kept in museums by former colonisers] to countries of origin. We need a strategy. We need an educational approach on restitution to facilitate agreements between those who currently possess these cultural properties and the countries of origin.

A representative of Zimbabwe wanted to know more about the conditions of this return and the implications of 'donation':

I hope one is not looking at the situation where this object went back on what is called 'permanent loan', whatever this means....[10] If it goes under that, a 'donation', to the source nation, then I don't think this was a win-win situation.... Maybe there can be clarity on this issue. Has it been returned, or nearly returned, or is it restitution?

A lawyer from the Tanzanian delegation then explained, that the holding museum had argued:

We are not the one who stole this item and it is difficult for us to use the term return because we are not the ones who stole the item.... [S]o the ... museum was going to give us the mask as a present or as a donation. To us, that was not a very big issue, because what we wanted there was the return of the mask.

A delegate from Angola then added:

African countries, such as Angola, welcome the efforts made by countries like Tanzania to recover the Makonde mask because it is a mask that represents Tanzanian identity. But in the broader context of African culture, it's not just about Tanzania, it represents regional identity, Tanzania's and Mozambique's. So it is not just the mask, it's a broader issue going beyond the national borders. And this is an achievement that will be welcomed because property has just been recovered that represents the cultural identity of Africa.

These comments illustrate the way in which delegates of other African states strongly support the claim for the return of artefacts. It is their statements that create the symbolic value of this artefact, representing the 'cultural identity of Africa', which before had been 'only' an ethnographic (though important) object stolen from the National Museum in Tanzania. The statements illustrate how the delegates who perceive themselves in a similar situation – being 'looted' during the colonial era – create a kind of ideological social network among themselves. One delegate even suggests that ICOM and UNESCO are or should be part of this in order to get back their (African) property kept in collections in the northern hemisphere. It is evident that these delegates act by their joint efforts as a pressure group in this UNESCO forum. It is no surprise that the delegates of the predominant holding countries simply keep silent. A second issue concerns the modalities of the return. It is clear that the speakers argue against diplomatic solutions, such as 'on permanent loan' or 'donation': instead, they pleaded for plain return or restitution, without any prerequisites. These statements are not a debate simply about notions, but reveal a struggle for power and the reparation of colonial wrongdoing.

The outcome of these negotiations – the return of the mask – produced at first sight no losers. However, the conditions under which this agreement was reached speak another language: Tanzania had, among other things, to confirm in writing that the Barbier-Mueller Museum was the rightful and legitimate owner of the mask, acknowledging the absence of any illicit appropriation. Furthermore, Tanzania had to agree that the mask would be displayed with the legend 'Donated by the Barbier-Mueller Museum, Geneva, Switzerland'. It has to be added that the mask is not on display, but has been kept in a strongbox of the National Museum in Dar Es Salaam ever since. This case – the return of a stolen mask as a donation – has found a critical echo, especially in African countries (see, for example Opoku 2010); African voices complained about the patronising aspect of 'donation' which showed the Tanzanian museum as the humble recipient dependent on a gesture of 'generosity'. This case also shows how keen advisers/experts who act behind closed doors are able to turn the imbalanced relationship upside down: through the donation instead of a (humble) return, the holding institution pushes the recipient into an inferior position.[11]

HYBRID MOTIVES, COMPLEX NETWORKS AND SENSITIVITIES

The example of the Makonde mask illustrated that the return declared as 'donation' was not simply guided by ethical motives or unselfish generosity but was the result of keen bargaining. The conditions of return are not always released to the public as another case shows.

In its 2011 report, UNESCO listed a number of cases which had been solved without the interference of the international organisation, but which complied with its overall goals. The way the solutions of such issues are publicly presented seems to suggest that ethical considerations were pivotal. However, a closer examination reveals other dimensions, more tangible ones, as in the case of the seventy-five volumes of Korean manuscripts dating back as far as the 14th century. French soldiers had looted Korean royal archives in 1867 as part of an act of retaliation after Korea had prosecuted French missionaries. These manuscripts were transported to Paris, where they became part of the Bibliothèque Nationale de France, and there they remained until recently. The restitution in 2011 was implemented on the basis of a 'loan' for five years, which is renewable indefinitely. South Korean officials consider that these manuscripts are unlikely to be reclaimed by France (UNESCO IGC 2011b: 10). President Sarkozy of France had agreed to return these manuscripts at the G20 summit in Seoul in December 2010. Yet he came under heavy criticism in his own country. According to French law, public archive items are 'inalienable state property'. According to media reports, Sarkozy said that he was fulfilling a promise made by the late President François Mitterrand. Mitterrand allegedly 'promised the return of the archives in exchange for a French-backed, high-speed rail link which has since opened between Seoul and Pusan' (Harris 2010). This information on hybrid practices (Bevir 2011: 2) was not given in the UNESCO report. Thus the return was, among other things, a final step in a series of political promises and economic relations between the two states.

Political considerations prevailed in another case – the negotiations about the return of the Hittite sphinx kept and exhibited in the Pergamon Museum in Berlin to Turkey[12] – and involved a complex network of different actors who participated in the governance process. Turkey had already made the request to UNESCO in 1987.[13] The case had been repeatedly discussed at its meetings. At the 2010 meeting, Turkey once again deplored the fact – by using the phrasing 'unfortunately' several times – that the bilateral negotiations had taken place without reaching a solution. The Turkish statement also hinted that Turkey 'would not like this issue to cloud bilateral cultural cooperation in the future'. The German delegate responded by first pointing out that a meeting with the Turkish delegation had taken place right before the official meeting of the UNESCO Committee to promote a joint draft recommendation on the case of the sphinx. He referred to the fact that the 1970 UNESCO Convention had only entered into force for Germany in 2008. He then went on – apparently to show Germany's efforts to comply with requests of return – to list all the cultural property that had been returned to different countries since.

In 2011, the UNESCO Committee was able to announce the successful resolution of the negotiations after 24 years: The 'restitution' (!) of the sphinx to Turkey (UNESCO IGC 2011b: 1).[14] The composition of the actors in this governance network which finally achieved the solution can only be perceived in its outlines, though there are many indications that the case had reached the highest governmental level in both countries before the final decision was reached.[15] For example, in February 2010, Turkey's culture minister threatened to stop all German excavations at Hattusha, saying that Turkey disposed of enough skilled archaeologists and did not need German archaeologists any more. At the same time, Turkey had not yet consented to loans requested by the Pergamon Museum for an exhibition due to open in October 2011 (Güsten 2011). Hermann Parzinger, an archaeologist by profession and president of the Stiftung Preussischer Kulturbesitz, published a statement in reaction to the threat by Turkey. He emphasised that Turkey and Germany continued to interpret the legal situation differently. He pleaded for a search for 'new and constructive ways to solve this case'; with the help from experts ('Fachwissenschaftler') from both Berlin and Turkish museums.[16] However, he also conceded that decisions about return/restitution had political aspects (Parzinger 2011). On the same day that Parzinger's statement was published, the newspapers reported that Berlin's State Secretary of Culture, André Schmitz (Social Democratic Party), who was at the same time Parzinger's deputy at the Stiftung Preussischer Kulturbesitz, had surprisingly pleaded for a restitution of the statue. His approval has to be related also to the fact that Berlin houses a large community of Turkish immigrants. The Department of Foreign Affairs admitted in an interview that it had assumed so far 'that Germany was the legal owner' of the sphinx (*Spiegel online*, 2011). The German State Secretary of Culture, Bernd Neumann, who represented the

German government in these negotiations, emphasised, after having reached an agreement, that the return of the sphinx to Turkey was a 'voluntary gesture of German–Turkish friendship' ('freiwillige Geste der deutsch-türkischen Freundschaft'), adding that 'both sides agree that the sphinx is a singular case that cannot be compared with other cases' (meaning the Nefertiti bust kept in the New Museum in Berlin and requested by Egypt) (*Berliner Morgenpost*, 2011). The Pergamon Museum will replace this second sphinx with a replica in its exhibition hall, as had been done earlier when the first sphinx was returned to Turkey in 1924.

The negotiations involved different actors of both states in this matter: museum experts and representatives of the Stiftung Preussischer Kulturbesitz, ministers, civil servants and politicians at different levels. UNESCO did not intervene though. Perhaps it was perceived as an international authority with whom the case had been deposited, lingering somewhere in the background, ready to offer its good offices. Nevertheless, these negotiations, the governance of this case, needs to be set in a broader context of relationships, treaties and regulations. We first need to put this return in the context of the political German–Turkish relationship and Turkey's possible candidacy to become a member of the European Union. As is well known, Chancellor Angela Merkel is sceptical about Turkey becoming a member. Instead, she suggested a privileged partnership with Turkey. The EU Treaty on the Functioning of the European Union (TFEU 2009), however, contains an exception to the 'free movement of goods' within the EU. This exception – to briefly sum up the complex matter – is formulated in §36 of the treaty, and refers to the 'protection of national treasures possessing artistic, historic or archaeological value'. As Stamatoudi has recently shown, treasures in this context can be defined as 'objects which represent, or are in fact, elements essential and basic to a nation's heritage and history ...' (2011: 117). Although Turkey is not a member of the European Union, this European law probably had its impact on the German decision, especially with regard to the suggested 'privileged partnership' with Turkey.[17]

Apart from UNESCO, on whose agenda the Hittite sphinx had been for such a long time, other UNESCO sections had been indirectly involved in this matter as well: Hattusha, the ruins of the capital of the Hittite Empire, was inscribed on the UNESCO World Heritage List in 1986, and the cuneiform tablets were inscribed on the UNESCO Memory of the World Register in 2001. Thus, three different UNESCO sections were involved in one way or another in the case of the Hattusha excavations and the contested artefacts. These prestigious listings, as well as the mediation by UNESCO's return and restitution committee, interacted with each other, since all of them are concerned with the safeguarding of 'cultural property' and the 'universal value' it has for 'humanity'. Thus, these international listings augmented and highlighted the value the contested artefacts have for Turkey and supported, directly or indirectly, Turkey's claim to the sphinx.

As the UNESCO Committee of Return and Restitution noted in its 'Recommendation' no. 3 (UNESCO IGC 2011a: 1) of the last meeting in summer 2011: 'the sphinx will arrive in Turkey by 28 November 2011', 'at the latest'. This was the date when the twenty-fifth anniversary of Hattusha's addition to the World Heritage List was commemorated, and it was precisely this day which was chosen for the ultimate return of the Hittite sphinx. We can conclude that UNESCO's many committees' multi-sided activities had an impact on Germany's decision as well.

Looking at the complex picture that emerges from this analysis, we realise that the Bagozköy sphinx – the artefact in its present condition is the result of heavy restoration work carried out by specialists of the Pergamon Museum[18] – became enmeshed in a whole network of state and non-state actors, conventions and regulations – and values. However, the final agreement and its conditions reached by Turkey and Germany were determined by a wide range of political considerations and the relationship between the two countries.

NEGOTIATIONS OUTSIDE INTERNATIONAL FORA

The discussions at the meeting of UNESCO and the subsequent negotiations reveal that the prestige of all these renowned holding institutions (such as the British Museum, the Metropolitan Museum or the Pergamon Museum) and their policies were at stake. As a consequence, museums and states apparently try to avoid entering into such formalised processes. Instead, they prefer negotiations in which only the two parties are involved and which take place outside the spotlight of an international arena. These confidential circumstances seem to promote the reaching of an agreement on a bi-national level, especially since the claimant may still keep the possibility of lodging its request with UNESCO or even with the International Court of Justice in reserve. Thus, the governance of such claims is much less transparent since only few actors enter the official discourse and the negotiations take place off the record.

This is the case with the 'feather crown of Moctezuma' (Spanish: Montezuma), the 16th-century Aztec ruler. This 'feather crown' is kept in the Museum of Ethnology in Vienna. Mexico has not (yet) made an official request, and the conditions for the return of the 'feather crown' the two parties seem to have agreed upon will require a change in the Mexican legislation (pers. comm. Christian Feest, September 2011). The modalities of returning such a contested artefact may be substantially worked out by the cooperation of museum experts of both countries. However, the political pressure on returning the artefact is quite high, not least due to Mexican activists.

There have been many stories told about this artefact (called *penacho*). They show that competing interpretations of the artefact exist depending on the stakeholders, their cultural background, their interest and their specific knowledge (see Fliedl 2001). It is one of the interpretations inscribed in the artefact that provoked the claim for its return. The artefact was part of the famous Castle Ambras collection (in present-day Austria) in 1596, one of the largest cabinets of arts and curiosities at that time; it was then interpreted as a 'Moorish hat'. It was 'rediscovered' by the Vienna Museum of Natural History by its first director, Ferdinand von Hochstetter, in 1878. Hochstetter interpreted it as a 'standard' that probably originated from the possession of Moctezuma. According to him, this standard was probably a gift Moctezuma had sent to Hernando Cortés in 1519, who, so the story goes, gave it to Charles V, who was King of Spain and Archduke of Austria (Bussel 2012; Feest 2012). Others understood the headdress to be a fan-like device, an apron or a mantle. The American Mexicanist, Zelia Nuttall (1857–1933), who knew about Hochstetter's interpretation, suggested that this artefact was probably a headdress that could only have been worn by Moctezuma himself in one of the most important rituals (Nuttall 1886/87). This interpretation was readily taken up by different actors in post-revolutionary Mexico in the 1920s. The *penacho* became, as Feest (2011) writes, 'an indigenist symbol of the identity of the new Mexico with the Aztek Empire'.

The historical research carried out since the 1940s has refuted Hochstetter's and Nuttall's speculations. Yet, the *penacho* is, nevertheless, a singular piece, since the technique with which it was made is unique (Rivero Weber and Feest 2012). This new academic interpretation inscribes a different sort of value into the artefact which is, at least in a political context, weaker than the symbolic value many actors still recognise in it. Thus, the headdress continues to be attributed to Moctezuma, be it in Europe or in Mexico (Bussel 2012). Between 1992 and 2002, there were repeated demonstrations by activists led by an Aztec named Xokonoschtletl (with his Spanish name, Antonio Gomora; see Schlager 2010) in Vienna who clamoured for the return of 'Moctezuma's feather crown' to the point that the police had to secure the entrance of the Museum of Ethnology in 1992 (Federkrone Montezumas 2002; Uber 1992).[19] Xokonoschtletl had contacted parliamentarians in Mexico and Austria, and carried out media campaigns. He had allegedly also spoken to the United Nations and the Pope about this matter. According to Schlager, it was he who put the case in motion – and, over decades, never gave up (2010: 39–45).

Mexico had a replica made in 1940 when the artefact was still attributed to Moctezuma. This replica is on display in the Anthropological National Museum of Mexico City. The replica, and even more the original, are still associated with Mexico's roots in the pre-colonial Aztec past, its identity and cultural heritage. Therefore, as Diner (2007), among others, noted, the artefact serves as a means for the reconfiguration of a memory of the pre-colonial origin of Mexico. A representative of the Iberoamerican University in Mexico said: 'The day the headdress returns to our country will mark a milestone in re-encountering (Mexico's) identity' (Ethnology Network 2011). It therefore becomes understandable why Mexico wants to have exactly this exemplar returned, although seven such feather works (though not headdresses) from the same period still exist, two of which are already in Mexico.

The claim for the return of this headdress has a long story too. There have been several moves by Austria towards returning it. One of the official motives for returning it some time ago was the retrospective recognition of the fact that Mexico had protested against Hitler's invasion of Austria in 1938 (Entschliessungsantrag 2005).

In the current negotiations, an agreement has been reached that this feather headdress will be regarded as the cultural heritage of both Mexico and Austria. Thus, the artefact will represent a shared symbol. As can be read in a lot of press media, there will probably be an exchange based on the principle of the 'loan' of artefacts to which both countries attach an emotional value, namely the Aztec feather headdress against the golden coach of the Austrian emperor Maximilian I, who ruled over Mexico from 1864 to 1867; his coach is kept in Mexico (derStandard 2011). He was executed in 1867 following a death sentence from a court-martial. His mummy was transported to Vienna where he was buried in the imperial crypt in the Kapuzinerkirche in Vienna.

Thus both artefacts exchanged on the basis of loans, the golden coach and the feather headdress, are seen as shared symbols of Austria's and Mexico's history, and both are related to identity discourses, though probably to different degrees.

CONCLUSION

The analysis of the three cases of contested artefacts held in renowned museums and claimed by 'source nations' for return has shown that they were not solved by applying legal means in the strict sense, that is, by court decisions, but by 'soft law' as applied by UNESCO. At the core of most debates about the contested 'things' was the claimant's assertion of the symbolic capital – 'identity', 'heritage', 'belonging' – the artefact embodies. It is an added value – sacredness – to the material 'thing' which allows only one legitimate owner: the source nation. Thus, what the claimants are bringing to bear cannot easily be rebutted by the holder, since they are linked to emotions and national pride. UNESCO, and also ICOM on its behalf, act as cultural brokers who mediate between the two parties. They look for solutions acceptable to both which are presented at the meetings of the UNESCO Committee. It is important to note that UNESCO performs a kind of advocacy on behalf of the deprived, the source nations. This advocacy manifests itself also in the procedure. The regular 'summons' of the parties involved at the (bi-)annual meetings provoke critical comments mostly from those delegates who belong to the potential claimants. These conditions imply a stronger position of the claimant, at least at the beginning, while the holder (mostly famous institutions in highly industrialised countries and the state representing them) is pressed into the position of a culprit who is forced to defend himself. This ideologically imbalanced situation is intensified by the arguments of the claimants which draw on ethics and the suffering resulting from former colonial/imperial domination.

In these public representations of the negotiations between the two parties, prestige is at stake, especially of the holder, which is generally an economically and politically more powerful state, and correspondingly, loss of face and shame. With few exceptions, the cases submitted to UNESCO came from source nations. As the cases solved so far have shown, they always managed to have the artefacts requested returned. However, the majority of return and restitution cases are not handled by the UNESCO Committee but are negotiated between the nations concerned. This is certainly a side-effect and impact of the powerful position UNESCO has and the way the cases reported there gain world-wide attention. We may, therefore, draw the conclusion that destination countries nowadays – not least after having learned how embarrassing situations may become for holders at the public meetings of the Committee – prefer bi-national negotiations, since they are carried out under the cloak of discreetness – unless activists enter the scene and publicly advocate for the return/restitution of the disputed artefact.

Nevertheless, the examples discussed have shown that the relationship between superior claimant and defensive holder may finally be turned upside down with the help of keen experts dictating the terms of return. Accordingly, the return of the artefacts is based on different modes in each case, ranging from 'donation' to 'restitution' (by keeping a replica), and from the sharing of the 'heritage' to the exchange of objects through conditional 'loans'. The symbolic value added by both parties to the contested artefact makes such issues extremely sensitive. Each of these values is relational to the opponent's, though twisted by a complicated history between the two countries and the corresponding trafficking of goods and services through time. Thus, governance deals first and foremost with these relationships and the coming to terms with the past.

NOTES

1. For an overview of the definition and meaning of the terms 'return', 'restitution' and 'repatriation', see Prott (2009a). As Stamatoudi notes, the terms 'return' and 'restitution' are often used interchangeably in the area of cultural property law. Nevertheless, 'the term "restitution" refers to any sort of restitution in the case of illegally alienated cultural objects, in order for the "wrong" committed to be rectified' (2011: 227). The UNESCO makes a significant distinction between both terms.

2. The World Intellectual Property Organization (WIPO), for example, states: 'The cultural heritage of a community or nation lies at the heart of its identity ...' (2010: 56). And Jenkins (2004: 9–10) writes:

   In international politics ... identity seems to have become a symbolic public good, the defence of which asserts a legitimacy that is beyond criticism or opposition. Reified into a sacred and holy apotheosis 'identity' is something to which everyone has a right.

3. This article is the result of an ongoing research project, which is part of the inter-disciplinary research group on Cultural Property at Göttingen University and is funded by the German Research Association. I have been able to participate in

various UNESCO meetings dealing with the 1970 Convention and its impact. In 2010 I was allowed to attend the meeting of the UNESCO Committee for Return and Restitution in Paris (21–23 September), where I also carried out interviews with a number of state delegates. I am grateful to all these interview partners but also to Susanne K. Schlager and Christian Feest, who generously provided me with several texts about the feather headdress from Mexico, the third case to be discussed in this article. My thanks also go to my colleague Karl-Heinz Kohl, who organised a panel on the topic of 'repatriation' during the meeting of the Deutsche Gesellschaft für Völkerkunde in Vienna in 2011.

4. At the meeting of UNESCO in Paris in 2010, the UK representative took up this argument in justifying why the Parthenon marbles (claimed by Greece) are still in the British Museum: 'The British Museum is a world museum and currently some six million people visit it every year free of charge from all over the world.' The purpose of the museum is 'to tell the story of all humanity.... Ancient Greece is an important part of the story told by the British Museum.'

5. The museum is a private institution and therefore not a member of UNESCO. Switzerland had offered its good offices for negotiating this case. To avoid Greece's request for restitution of the Parthenon marbles, for example, the representative of the United Kingdom argued that the British Museum is not owned by the state and the government, therefore, is not able to interfere in this case (see O'Keefe 1998: 167).

6. The theft (together with sixteen further artefacts, of which only this Makonde mask surfaced although the case was reported to Interpol as well) occurred in 1984. In 1990, the mask was identified by an Italian anthropologist in the Barbier-Mueller Museum since he knew about the theft in Tanzania. It was the museum itself which took the first steps by reporting it to ICOM.

7. Switzerland ratified the 1970 UNESCO Convention and issued corresponding laws of heritage protection in 2003 (in force since 2005); the appropriate time-limit is now thirty years.

8. In 2006, after several years of negotiations that did not fulfil Tanzania's expectations, Tanzania filed a request for the return of the mask with the secretariat of the UNESCO Committee. The private museum then immediately stopped the negotiations with Tanzania and filed a formal and official complaint against the United Republic of Tanzania. Finally, in August 2009, the Ministry of Natural Resources and Tourism of Tanzania informed the Barbier-Mueller Museum of its intent to accept the conditions proposed by the Museum in 2002.

9. Switzerland, apparently, did not want to speak on behalf of the Barbier-Mueller Museum (see ftn. 7); therefore ICOM, as the official mediator, took over this part.

10. On 'permanent loan' would imply a separation of ownership from possession (Cornu and Renold 2010: 18).

11. Expert lawyers assisting the Barbier-Mueller Museum formulated further conditions in 2002 that were anything but a testimony of a 'win-win situation': Tanzania should pay compensation to the museum in Geneva for all their time and effort and grant the right to repurchase the mask within ten years if the National Museum of Tanzania did not respect certain conditions, among others.

12. The sphinx dates back to the 2nd millennium BC. The statue was heavily damaged when, together with another sphinx and a large number of cuneiform tablets, it was excavated by German archaeologists in Turkey and transported to Germany in 1915 for restoration and research purposes. The first sphinx was

returned in 1924. In 1987, the German Democratic Republic returned 7,400 cuneiform tablets. After German reunification, the Pergamon Museum, and with it the Hittite sphinx, became integrated into the (West-)Berlin Preussischer Kulturbesitz. My thanks go to Dorothea Kathmann, head of the presidential department, Stiftung Preussischer Kulturbesitz, Berlin, with whom I was able to discuss this case.

13. One of the reasons why Turkey argued so fervently can be attributed to the fact that Turkey since Atatürk had been searching for its own historical roots or ancestry. In their nationalist endeavour, the modern Turks were declared to be descendants of the ancient Anatolian Hittite civilisation (Wilson 2007: 83–84). Modern Turkey extends partly over former Hittite land, and therefore understands the sphinx as an important cultural property inherited from their ancestors.

14. The sphinx was returned to Turkey on 27 July 2011 (*Hürriyet Daily News*, 2011).

15. All participants were keen to act behind the scenes. We also realised that museums are extremely cautious with regard to our research. Some of the museum directors and heads of departments did not even respond to our cautious enquiries when they realised what the subject of our research topic was.

16. Such meetings took place and several modalities were discussed.

17. Though the range of 'national treasures', according to Stamatoudi, still needs to be defined (2011: 121), Turkey would certainly not have had any difficulties in substantiating this claim. Apart from the EU regulations, the Council of Europe, with its forty-seven member countries, has also developed a 'Framework Convention on the Value of Cultural Heritage for Society', the so-called Faro Convention of 2005. According to this Convention, the Hittite sphinx would be considered as 'cultural heritage' as well.

18. Four sphinxes were originally excavated. Only the two which were transported to Germany in 1915 and are now back in Turkey have survived, thanks to the restoration and preservation work carried out by the German experts. The third has only survived in fragments; of the fourth, not even the fragments have been preserved (*Hürriyet Daily News*, 2011).

19.

> Wenn die Federkrone nach Mexiko zurückkehrt, kehrt mit ihr auch unser Herr zurück, damit wäre auch der Geist des Herrn, der sie getragen hat, wieder bei uns. Wir wollen Gerechtigkeit für das, was man uns in den letzten 500 Jahren angetan hat. Wir sind überzeugt, dass mit der Rückführung der Federkrone, die für uns so viel symbolisiert, uns unsere Identität wiedergegeben werden könnte. (http: //www.museo-on.com/go/museoon/ home/db/archaeology/_page_id_550/_page_id_999.xhtml)

BIBLIOGRAPHY

Anico, Marta and Elsa Peralta (2009) 'Introduction', in Marta Anico and Elsa Peralta (eds) *Heritage and identity. Engagement and demission in the contemporary world*, pp. 1–11. London: Routledge.

Appadurai, Arjun (1986) 'Introduction. Commodities and the politics of value', in Arjun Appadurai (ed.) *The Social Life of Things: Commodities in Cultural Perspective*, pp. 3–63 (Cambridge: Cambridge University Press).

Benda-Beckmann, Franz, Keebet Benda-Beckmann and Melanie G. Wiber (2006) 'The properties of property', in Franz Benda-Beckmann, Keebet Benda-Beckmann and Melanie G. Wiber (eds) *Changing Properties of Property*, pp. 1–39 (New York: Berghahn).

Benda-Beckmann, Franz, Keebet Benda-Beckmann and Anne Griffiths (2009) 'The power of law', in Franz Benda-Beckmann, Keebet Benda-Beckmann and Anne Griffiths (eds) *The Power of Law in a Transnational World: Anthropological Enquiries*, pp. 1–29 (New York: Berghahn).

Berliner Morgenpost (2011) 'Pergamonmuseum. Berlin bekommt eine neue Sphinx', 30 July. Available at: www.morgenpost.de/kultur/article1716856/Berlin-bekommt-eine-neue-Sphinx.html (consulted 8 November 2011).

Bevir, Mark (2011) 'Governance as theory, practice, and dilemma', in Mark Bevir (ed.) *The Sage Handbook of Governance*, pp. 1–16 (London: Sage).

Bussel, Gerard W.v. (2012) 'Der altmexikanische Federkopfschmuck. Aspekte seiner Rezeptionsgeschichte', in Alfonso de María y Campos, Lilia Rivero Weber and Christian Feest (eds) *Der altmexikanische Federkopfschmuck*, pp. 115–133 (Altenstadt: ZKF Publishers).

Cornu, Marie and Marc-André Renold (2010) 'New developments in the restitution of cultural property: Alternative means of dispute resolution', *International Journal of Cultural Property* 17: 1–31.

derStandard (2011) '"Montezumas Federkrone". Leihgabe an Mexiko noch nicht gesichert', 17 January. Available at: http://derstandard.at/1293370805298/Montezumas-Federkrone-Leihgabe-an-Mexiko-noch-nicht-gesichert (consulted 14 November 2011.

Diner, Dan (2007) 'Memory and restitution: World War II as a foundational event in a uniting Europe', in Dan Dinern and Gotthard Wunberg (eds) *Restitution and Memory: Material Restoration in Europe*, pp. 9–23 (New York: Berghahn).

Entschliessungsantrag (2005) 'Rückgabe der Federkrone Montezumas an Mexiko'. Available at: www.parlament.gv.at/PAKT/VHG/XXII/A/A_00608/ (consulted 14 November 2011).

Ethnology Network (2011) News, 19 January. Available at: http://www.ethnologynetwork.com/news (consulted 14 November 2011).

'Federnkrone Montezumas. Azteken marschieren wieder' (2002) News, 6 September. Available at: http://religionv1.orf.at/projekt02/news/0209/ne020906_federnkrone_fr.htm (consulted 14 November 2011).

Feest, Christian (2011) 'The feather headdress from ancient Mexico in Vienna: A story to be told', *Tribal Art* 16(1): 112–115.

Feest, Christian (2012) 'Der altmexikanische Federkopfschmuck in Europa', in Alfonso de María y Campos, Lilia Rivero Weber and Christian Feest (eds) *Der altmexikanische Federkopfschmuck*, pp. 5–28 (Altenstadt: ZKF Publishers).

Fliedl, Gottfried (2001) '… *das Opfer von ein paar Federn.' Die sogenannte Federkrone Montezumas als Objekt nationaler und musealer Begehrlichkeiten* (Wien: Turia+Kant).

Gell, Alfred (1998) *Art and Agency: An Anthropological Theory* (Oxford: Clarendon Press).

Güsten, Suanne (2011) 'Hethiter-Schatz. Türkisches Ultimatum. Berlin soll Sphinx zurückgeben', *Der Tagesspiegel* 24 February. Available at: http://www.tagesspiegel.de/kultur/tuerkisches-ultimatum-berlin-soll-sphinx-zurueckgeben/3875702.html (consulted 4 August 2011).

Hann, Chris M. (1998) 'Introduction. The embeddedness of property', in Chris M. Hann (ed.) *Property Relations: Renewing the Anthropological Tradition*, pp. 1–47 (Cambridge: Cambridge University Press).

Harris, Gareth (2010) 'Sarkozy criticised for loaning French manuscripts to Korea', *The Art Newspaper online*, 23 December. Culture in Development. Available at: www.cultureindevelopment.nl/News/Heritage%20Asia/659/Sarkozy_criticised_for_loaning_French_manuscripts_to_Korea (consulted 12 August 2011).

Hürriyet Daily News (2011) 'Bagazköy sphinx finally returns to Turkey after decades in Germany', 28 July. Available at: www.hurriyetdailynews.com/n.php?n=bogazkoy-sphinx-finally-returns-to-turkey-after-decades-in-germany-2011-07-28 (consulted 14 November 2011).

ICOM (International Council of Museums) (1986) *Code of Ethics*. Available at: http: //icom.museum/who-we-are/the-vision/code-of-ethics.html (consulted 26 May 2012).

ICOM (International Council of Museums) (ed.) (2004) 'Declaration on the importance and value of universal museums', *ICOM NEWS* 1: 4. Available at: http: //icom.museum/fileadmin/user_upload/pdf/ICOM_News/2004-1/ENG/p4_2004-1.pdf (consulted 29 May 2012).

ICOM (International Council of Museums) (ICOM) (2010) 'Makonde mask. Signing of an agreement for the donation of the Makonde mask from the Barbier-Mueller Museum of Geneva to the National Museum of Tanzania'. Press file, Paris, 10 May. Available at: http: //archives.icom.museum/press/MM_PressFile_eng.pdf (consulted 6 November 2011).

Jenkins, Richard (2004) *Social Identity* (New York: Routledge).

Kopytoff, Igor (1986) 'The cultural biography of things', in Arjun Appadurai (ed.) *The Social Life of Things: Commodities in Cultural Perspective*, pp. 64–91 (Cambridge: Cambridge University Press).

Merryman, John Henry (1968) 'Two ways of thinking about cultural property', *American Journal of International Law* 80: 831–853.

Nuttall, Zelia (1886/87) *Das Prachtstück Altmexikanischer Federarbeit aus der Zeit Montezuma's im Wiener Museum*. Berichte des K. Zoologischen und Anthropologisch-Ethnographischen Museums zu Dresden.

O'Keefe, Patrick J. (1998) 'Incidental collections: Protection against dispersal', *Art Antiquity and Law* 3(2): 165–177.

Opoku, Kwame (2010) 'Barbier-Mueller Museum signs agreement with Tanzania to return stolen Makonde mask', *Modern Ghana*, 16 May. Available at: www.modernghana.com/news/275929/1/barbier-mueller-museum-signs-agreement-with-tanzan.html (consulted 6 November 2011).

Parzinger, Hermann (2011) Zur Rückgabeforderung der Türkei. Die Sphinx von Hattuscha. Press File, 25 February, Stiftung Preussischer Kulturbesitz, Berlin.

Prott, Lyndel V. (2009a) 'Note on terminology', in Lyndel V. Prott (ed.) *Witnesses to History: A Compendium of Documents and Writings on the Return of Cultural Objects*, pp. xxi–xxiv (Paris: UNESCO).

Prott, Lyndel V. (2009b) 'The history and development of processes for the recovery of cultural heritage', in Lyndel V. Prott (ed.) *Witnesses to History: A Compendium of Documents and Writings on the Return of Cultural Objects*, pp. 2–18 (Paris: UNESCO).

Prott, Lyndel V. (ed.) (2009c) *Witnesses to History: A Compendium of Documents and Writings on the Return of Cultural Objects* (Paris: UNESCO).

Rivero Weber, Lilia and Christian Feest (2012) 'Der Schatten der Götter. Mexikanische Federarbeiten des 16. Jahrhunderts', in Alfonso de María y Campos, Lilia Rivero

Weber and Christian Feest (eds) *Der altmexikanische Federkopfschmuck*, pp. 41–60 (Altenstadt: ZKF).

Schlager, Susanne Karoline (2010) '"El penacho de Moctezuma". Fremde Federn oder österreichisches Kulturerbe?', Universität Wien: Master's thesis in Latin American Studies.

Skrydstrup, Martin (2009) 'Theorizing repatriation', *Ethnologica Europaea* 39(2): 54–66.

Spiegel online (2011) 'Rückgabeforderung der Türkei: Wertvolle Sphinx könnte Berlin verlassen', 25 February. Available at: http://www.spiegel.de/wissenschaft/mensch/rueckgabeforderung-der-tuerkei-wertvolle-sphinx-koennte-berlin-verlassen-a-747838.html (consulted 4 August 2011).

Stamatoudi, Irina A. (2011) *Cultural Property and Restitution: A Commentary to International Conventions and European Union Laws* (Cheltenham: Edward Elgar).

TFEU (Treaty on the Functioning of the European Union) (2009) Available at: http://eur-lex.europa.eu/LexUriServ/LexUriServ.do?uri=OJ: C: 2010: 083: 0047: 0200: en: PDF (consulted 26 May 2012).

Uber, Heiner (1992) 'Azteken vor Wien', *Die Zeit* 21(15 May).

UNESCO (1970) Convention on the Means of Prohibiting and Preventing the Illicit Import, Export and Transfer of Ownership of Cultural Property. Available at: http://portal.unesco.org/en/ev.php-URL_ID=13039&URL_DO=DO_TOPIC&URL_SECTION=201.html (consulted 3 February 2012).

UNESCO (1999) *International Code of Ethics for Dealers in Cultural Property*. Available at: http://portal.unesco.org/culture/en/ev.php-URL_ID=13095&URL_DO=DO_TOPIC&URL_SECTION=201.html (consulted 30 May 2012).

UNESCO IGC (2011a) Recommendations, 17th session, 30 June–1 July, Paris. Available at: http://unesdoc.unesco.org/images/0019/001937/193720E.pdf (consulted 8 November 2011).

UNESCO IGC (2011b) Secretariat Report, 17th session, 30 June–1 July, Paris. Available at: http://unesdoc.unesco.org/images/0019/001927/192728e.pdf (consulted 8 November 2011).

UNESCO IGC (2012) Intergovernmental Committee for Promoting the Return of Cultural Property to its Countries of Origin or its Restitution in Case of Illicit Appropriation. Available at: http://portal.unesco.org/culture/en/ev.php-URL_ID=35283&URL_DO=DO_TOPIC&URL_SECTION=201.html (consulted 3 February 2012).

UNIDROIT (1995) Convention on Stolen or Illegally Exported Cultural Objects. Available at: www.unidroit.org/english/conventions/1995culturalproperty/main.htm (consulted 26 May 2012).

Wilson, Christopher (2007) 'The persistence of the Turkish nation in the mausoleum of Mustafa Kemal Atatürk', in Michael Young, Eric Zuelow and Andreas Sturm (eds) *Nationalism in a Global Era: The Persistence of Nations*, pp. 82–103 (London: Routledge).

World Intellectual Property Organization (WIPO) (2010) *Intellectual Property Handbook: Policy, Law and Use*. Available at: www.wipo.int/about-ip/en/iprm/ (consulted 27 January 2010).

Zips, Werner and Markus Weilenmann (2011) 'Introduction: Governance and legal pluralism – an emerging symbiotic relationship?', in Werner Zips and Markus Weilenmann (eds) *The Governance of Legal Pluralism: Empirical Studies from Africa and Beyond*, pp. 7–34 (Wien: LIT).

Part III
Participation and Actor Building Across Scales

8
'We Indigenous Peoples ...'
Global Activism and the Emergence of a New Collective Subject at the United Nations

Irène Bellier

International organisations, such as the United Nations (UN), have played an important role in making indigenous peoples visible and guaranteeing respect for their human rights. They are responsible for a change in attitude and for new ways of considering these groups of peoples, both globally and locally, inducing a legal turn whose temporality, political scope and content vary in the different regions and countries of the world.[1] The UN system is responsible for four important changes relating to indigenous peoples' position in the world today. One is the process of institutionalisation of indigenous issues: it set up working groups and later a permanent organ, which served to inform on indigenous issues and to produce norms and policy recommendations. Second, it developed knowledge on indigenous issues, by commissioning expert studies, thus stimulating reflection on categories, criteria, indicators and figures, which in turn both highlighted and quantified the problems indigenous peoples are confronted with, in order to elaborate concrete solutions. Third, it sponsored a series of mechanisms that helped to develop dialogue between states, indigenous peoples or communities and third parties, including transnational companies. Finally, the UN is the place, where the United Nations Declaration on the Rights of Indigenous Peoples (UNDRIP) has been adopted by the vast majority of states in the General Assembly on 13 September 2007. The UNDRIP recognises the right of indigenous peoples to self-determination (Article 3), a right that has been hotly debated and contested by member states of the UN to this day. The negotiation of the UNDRIP highlights both the special conditions of indigenous communities across the world, and the importance of being recognised as 'peoples' to gain a legal personality under international law.

Before the UN Economic and Social Council (ECOSOC) started to document the issue of discrimination against *indigenous populations*, in 1972, the concept of *'indigenous peoples'* was not invested with the political and legal meaning it acquired later. Their legal, political, economic and social situations were not targeted, as they now are, as deserving special attention from nation states. Assimilation policies were contemplated as a positive measure to force modernisation and not evaluated as destructive to cultural diversity. In the 1970s, with the support of western human rights non-governmental organisations (NGOs) denouncing massacres in the Americas[2] (Bonfil Batalla 1977; Varese 2006; World Council of Churches/Conseil Oecuménique des Eglises ... 1972) indigenous peoples started to form an international movement and pursue processes of institutionalisation at a broader level, namely at the UN, with the intention of transforming their subaltern conditions at the local level. They used the space of the UN to draw attention to the severe threats faced by indigenous societies of physically disappearing or of being forced to radically change their way of life.

According to the UN, there are 370 million individuals belonging to the category of indigenous peoples, living in 90 countries. In the absence of a global census, information from different research groups and international support organisations are consistent with these figures and illustrate them with maps and reports.[3] However, not all the institutions of the world accept or use the internationally agreed category of 'indigenous peoples'; some states have their own procedures for designating these groups, which are the objects of policies and regulations; indigenous peoples also use their own names, self-definitions and ethnonyms.

For a number of UN member states, one of the reasons for delaying the adoption of UNDRIP for twenty-five years was the uncertainty over the definition of 'indigenous peoples' under international law and, linked to it, the question of whether the right to self-determination belonged to the state or to the people. While international law does not define what a 'people' is, a few states insisted on a definition of 'indigenous peoples'. Eventually, in line with the demand of indigenous organisations and 'friendly states' (Bellier 2006), the UNDRIP was adopted with no definition and no list of the indigenous peoples concerned. This has been considered as both an achievement, because it showed the capacity of indigenous peoples to resist dominant systems of control, and as a source of worry, because it created uncertainties regarding which indigenous peoples the normative framework applied to.

What makes this debate fascinating is the emergence of indigenous leaders on a stage that is usually shaped by the meeting of diplomats. The human rights sectors of the UN, in particular, played an important role in facilitating the encounter between the representatives of the states, some of them representing extremely powerful and global players, and the representatives of First Nations and Aboriginal communities, who are usually perceived as powerless, from remote localities and often as menacing the sovereignty of states when they aim to find a place in the political scene. It gave them the possibility of voicing their concerns directly, clarifying their claims and views, and being part of the emerging consensus which led to the adoption of the UNDRIP. It also paved the way for the building of an international indigenous peoples movement, which, though loosely structured, has been very active in articulating local and global concerns. Indigenous peoples participated through two mechanisms: first, through the work of the UN and, second, through their capacity to mobilise international support to resist aggression and development policies that states implement in what they consider their territories.

This chapter will identify what made the construction of an international indigenous movement possible and describe how indigenous activists were able to make their way through the UN system. We will focus on the progressive incorporation of the indigenous subject into mainstream policies and identify the consequences.

Today indigenous leaders meet in New York and Geneva, at events where governments and social movements enter into formal dialogues, such as recently in Rio de Janeiro during the 2012 UN Conference on Sustainable Development. The profusion of images, discourses and techniques has made distant encounters possible and created a global imaginary. The debates in the international arena demonstrate that indigenous peoples are contemporaries, their struggles modern ones. Connections have been drawn between local, regional and global levels. These connections changed the formation of knowledge on indigenous issues and allowed for the construction of a global actor who articulates a discourse against marginalisation with innovative proposals.

BUILDING AN INDIGENOUS SECTOR AT THE UN

Since 1919 and the creation of International Labour Organization (ILO), the international community has known of the existence of an *indigenous worker* problem. Before that, Europe had a picture of so-called Indians on the American continent, but this knowledge was limited to the flow of images provided by mainstream media (of the exotic Indian or of the poor Savage), some historical narratives, iconic representations of the Incas, the Aztecs and their superior civilisations. Europe also created an ontological difference between colonisers and colonised people, as for instance France did with the enactment of an indigenous status in its former colonies.

In the last decades of the twentieth century, thanks to the mobilisation of NGOs such as the World Council of Indigenous Peoples (1974–1996), Cultural Survival, International Work Group for Indigenous Affairs (IWGIA), Survival International and of the UN human rights sector (Dahl 2009), indigenous peoples were identified in all parts of the world. The interest in indigenous peoples' issues in places other than those colonised by white settlers coincides with the emergence of planetary concerns, with reduced spatial and historical distances. In the 1980s, Amazonia (where I did my PhD research), for instance, was extremely distant, a *terra incognita*, known for its wild forests and its inhospitable climate, not as the 'lung of the planet' or the 'treasury of biodiversity', which were characteristics it acquired after the Earth Summit took place in 1992. Today remote places are incorporated into global circuits and their inhabitants have become the objects of particular consideration. The Convention on Biological Diversity (CBD), for instance, 'recognises' and claims to protect 'the dependency of *indigenous and local communities* on biological diversity and the unique role of indigenous and local communities in conserving life on Earth'.[4]

This drastic change can only be described as a paradigmatic shift. One aspect of that shift relates to the UN stage, where the formation of the concept and category 'indigenous peoples' took place; the second relates to the identification of 'indigenous issues' to which specialised UN organs continue to devote their work. What happened on the UN stage cannot be separated from the processes of globalisation, whose ambivalence regarding its impacts on indigenous people are described elsewhere (Bellier 2008; Muehlebach 2001). However it did not appear all of a sudden. Indigenous peoples and social groups, which have been relegated to a certain episteme by colonial powers and state building processes, have a long history of resistance. In Namibia, the history of apartheid has created resistance to the use of categories based on ethnicity, and the donor-driven development agenda responds to discourses of 'marginality' and 'vulnerability', leading to a strong preference for these terms over the term 'indigenous' (Hays 2011). Other governments consider indigenous groups through the 'minority' lens, focusing on *individual* rights, where the indigenous peoples framework emphasises the dimension of *collective* rights.

The formation of a new legal international framework impacts the discussion about indigenous peoples on at least two grounds: one is the recognition of collective rights that aim to protect their possibilities of reproducing their cultural specificities, their relations to their lands and livelihoods, their social organisations and institutions; the second is that it contributes to defining the condition for their representatives to be considered as legitimate actors both within their respective countries and the global system.

An Indigenous Presence in the World of States

The building of an indigenous presence at the international level grew slowly from the early twentieth century and accelerated in the 2000s. The story of Deskaheh, the Cayuga head of the Haudenesaunee (Iroquois Confederation of the Six Nations, in Canada) who unsuccessfully attempted to address the League of Nations in 1923 (Rostkwoski 1986) links the change that took place to the mobilisation of individuals who decided to bring their cause to the UN. The former UN Secretary-General, Kofi Annan, referred to that story at the opening session of the Permanent Forum on Indigenous Issues (UNPFII) in 2002 and emphasised that indigenous peoples 'have a home at the UN', celebrating their will to determine their own destiny. *Self-determination* includes their capacity to determine who is a member of an indigenous people, and how to refer to such people, hence invalidating the dominant categories and political practices used to control them.

Interestingly, the 'home of the UN' did not define who are indigenous peoples. Article 33 of the UNDRIP says:

1) Indigenous peoples have the right to determine their own identity or membership in accordance with their customs and traditions. This does not impair the right of indigenous individuals to obtain citizenship of the States in which they live. 2) Indigenous peoples have the right to determine the structures and to select the membership of their institutions in accordance with their own procedures.

The idea that no substantial definition can be provided on what indigenous peoples are emerged from the 1972 study of José

Martinez Cobo and Augusto Willemsen Diaz, who emphasised instead a series of six criteria that had to be considered to capture their specific condition. They are:

> Indigenous communities, peoples and nations are those which, having a historical continuity with pre-invasion and pre-colonial societies that developed on their territories, consider themselves distinct from other sectors of the societies now prevailing in those territories, or parts of them. They form at present non-dominant sectors of societies and are determined to preserve, protect and transmit to future generations their ancestral territories and their ethnic identity, as the basis of their continued existence as peoples, in accordance with their own cultural social institutions and legal systems. (Martinez Cobo 1987: 22, para. 379)

This multidimensional approach to indigeneity considered indigenous peoples in relation to and as distinct from others, emphasised their willingness and capacity to act to protect themselves and their identity, and their consciousness of being oppressed or marginalised.

The first world tribune for indigenous peoples, the Working Group on Indigenous Populations (WGIP) was set up in 1982, as one of the six working groups overseen by the Sub-Commission on the Promotion and Protection of Human Rights, the main subsidiary body of the UN Commission on Human Rights (replaced in 2006 by the Human Rights Council). It had the mandate to 'review developments pertaining to the promotion and protection of human rights and fundamental freedoms of indigenous peoples' and 'to give attention to the evolution of international standards concerning indigenous rights'. This working group was both a place for representing cultural diversity and a mechanism to foster indigenous issues within the UN headquarters. It contributed to solidarity between indigenous peoples (including more than a thousand representatives from all regions of the world) creating a group capable of overcoming linguistic and political divisions. They contributed to drafting the UNDRIP that was adopted by the Sub-Commission, in 1995 (Daes 2008).

At this stage another subsidiary body was formed, the Working Group on the Draft Declaration (WGDD), which had the mandate to achieve an agreement between the states and indigenous organisations. It took twenty-five years to achieve a consensus on the main parts of the negotiation (Bellier 2003, 2006; Charters and Stavenhagen 2009), during which period indigenous participants did a lot of work to clarify their perception of what constitutes a 'people' under international law, and what specific efforts were to be demanded from the states. As American indigenous leaders expressed it when promoting their views: 'We have waited for so long, our resistance started 500 years ago, we can wait until a solution is found that we can agree with' (author's fieldwork notes). State representatives also presented their views on the proposed universal declaration, with regard to their domestic policies, and eventually found a solution to accommodate the right of indigenous peoples to self-determination (acknowledged in Article 3) and the protection of state sovereignty and territorial integrity. The final text, adopted by the Human Rights Council in 2006, and by the General Assembly in 2007, details the principles, the objectives, and indigenous peoples' rights in a text that interestingly alternates the formulas 'Indigenous peoples have the right to ...' with 'States shall ...'.

By the end of that period, three other institutions had been created at the UN, while the two working groups disappeared: the WGIP because its role was taken on by another body, the WGDD because its existence was limited to the making of the UNDRIP. The working groups proved to be a laboratory for institutional innovation (Bellier 2007), making space for indigenous peoples' participation that we will describe later. The three new institutions now have a crucial role in articulating the human rights sector that historically has been a referential pillar for indigenous people, and the many sectors of policy-making and programmatic action that are considered to impact indigenous lives. These institutions are the UN Permanent Forum on Indigenous Issues (UNPFII, created in 2001), the Special Rapporteur on the rights and fundamental freedoms of indigenous peoples (also created in 2001), and the Expert Mechanism on the rights of indigenous peoples (EMRIP, created in 2008). They form central mechanisms for imparting information on indigenous issues within the UN system, and their discussions both encapsulate and impact the ways other international organisations, such as the Organization of American States (OAS), the African Commission on Human and Peoples' Rights, the European Union, the UN agencies and NGOs organise their activities in their own space. While their mandates are distinct, all these organisations have incorporated the concept of indigenous peoples in their respective programmes and activities.

Over the last thirty years, the 'indigenous subject' was constructed internationally with regard to international law according to two principles which progressively converged: the definition of a global identity and the protection of cultural diversity. While common ground was identified for defining the indigenous condition within the different states, the issue of diversity became an important matter at world level. UNESCO adopted the Declaration on Cultural Diversity (in 2001), the Convention for the Safeguarding of the Intangible Heritage (in 2003) and the Convention on the Protection and Promotion of the Diversity of Cultural Expressions (in 2005). Indigenous peoples were consulted in this forum but did not take part in the decisions. It is an example of their circulation within the UN circuits of power, which differentiate the places where they are fully consulted from those where they are partially accepted and those they cannot access, such as the Security Council. Indigenous people have progressively been involved with several working groups and committees, such as that established at the World Intellectual Property Organization (WIPO), namely the Intergovernmental Committee on Intellectual Property and Genetic Resources, Traditional Knowledge and Folklore (IGC). The World Bank and the regional banks, which define indigenous policies in their own terms, also consult with indigenous people on a more individual basis. The testimonies of indigenous leaders to the UN made differences in status, living conditions, cultural resistance and economic aggression visible, and showed similar patterns of political and social exclusion. They also identified *common values* that linked the diversity of their peoples and situations to the need to be protected or defended.

Three lines of a document, published on the UNPFII website, illustrate such ideological commonalities:

> They are the values of sustainability, collectivity, naturality, spirituality, process-orientation, domesticity and locality. These are contrasted with prevailing modern values – productivity, individualism, technology, rationality, efficiency, commercialism, and globalization – that have become predominant principles in present-day social and economic development that can undermine a balanced human–nature relationship. (UNPFII 2009: 15)

Such 'values' can be expressed in several ways but they converge to make evident a paradigmatic opposition between an indigenous model and a western one. The global imaginary is instantiated in the form of discursive references to common emblematic figures such as 'Mother Earth' or to common aggressors such as the extractive industries (mining, logging, agro-industry, etc.). Interestingly, while the figure of Mother Earth (*Pachamama* is the Kichwa name that is often used) served to establish a human relationship to nature, during the negotiation of UNDRIP the legal statements regarding the definition of rights to the land, to territories and natural resources came from all over the world. This combination of cultural representations and legal references showed the multifaceted relation to the Earth (and the land) beyond mere possession. Recently some indigenous delegates advanced the concept of 'the right of nature' and advocated the concept of 'good living', which has its roots in the Kichwa notion of *sumac kawsay* that has become part of the constitution of Ecuador (since 2008).

Indigenous Organisation and the Formation of a Collective Voice

Locally, during the same period, indigenous peoples adhered to new models of organisation that led them to raise their voice at the country level (Yashar 2005). They formed alliances among themselves and with non-indigenous sectors, such as human and civil right activists, in order to reach a larger audience. All regions of the world have been touched by similar mobilisations and organisational processes, which also reflect the 'road' that indigenous delegates have taken to the UN: first from the Americas, Oceania and Scandinavia, then from Asia, Africa and the former USSR (Morin 1992). What we observe currently results from the encounter between, on the one hand, the organisation of states groupings within the UN structure (for setting up commissions and distributing responsibilities) and, on the other hand, indigenous organisations which progressively set up their own assemblies (regional caucuses) to discuss the formation of a common position, and have also built transnational organisations to strengthen their positions in global negotiation.

The Role of Caucuses

Indigenous delegates who attended the WGIP, developed a practice of deliberation in caucuses, which proved to be extremely efficient for the exchange of experience, the formation of a common voice and the designation of spokespeople.

The model of the caucus, now a common one, was introduced by Amerindian organisations. The present form of indigenous organisation on the UN stage is linked to a first inter-ethnic meeting in a Sioux reserve in 1974, which brought together ninety-eight delegates from North and South American Indian Nations, which created the International Indian Treaty Council, the first indigenous organisation registered at the UN ECOSOC, in 1977. In 1975, another meeting took place, in British Colombia, with Sami, Inuit, Maori and Australian Aboriginal people, where the World Council of Indigenous Peoples was formed. With the support of international human rights organisations and the World Council of Churches, these early organisations convened the first meeting at Geneva, on 'discrimination against indigenous populations in the Americas'. They had two demands: the revision of ILO Convention 107[5] and the creation of a specific working group. The point here is not to recall the whole story of indigenous people catching up with the UN system but to emphasise the contribution of Amerindian organisations to the formation of the international indigenous peoples movement. They recognised the importance of debating across cultures to forge transnational political strategies and to adapt indigenous practices to international negotiations.[6] They also brought to the UN an indigenous spirituality, which may vary from saying inaugural prayers, to holding an eagle feather at speech time giving strength and legitimacy to the holder. They contributed to forging the perception that they were not a collection of selfish individuals, but representatives of their peoples to whom they are accountable.

Indigenous caucuses are organised in complete autonomy, within the UN premises. They can exist outside the UN, when a large event is organised where different indigenous peoples participate and where collective decisions are taken. The caucuses have no legal status but have acquired a specificity, manifest in two ways: the enactment of statements – hence, the recognition that they constitute the body in which collective positions are taken – and their capacity to freely invite state or UN representatives to speak and discuss with them. There are no consolidated reports of such meetings (hence no secretary) but our observations show that they feed a continuous process from draft statements to consolidated views, which will be pursued at other meetings. They legitimise the expression of an indigenous voice, beyond linguistic, geographic and political differences. It is beyond the scope of this chapter to describe how discussion takes place in these caucuses. Discussions take place in one of the six languages used at the UN (Arabic, Chinese, English, French, Russian and Spanish). Linguistic difference is not a small problem to overcome, especially since indigenous delegates express themselves in a language that is usually not their mother tongue, and lack the financial capacity to pay for interpreters and translators.[7]

The initial work devoted to drafting the Declaration led to the formation of a global indigenous caucus, which served informally, but efficiently, as the main body where newcomers could experience the circulation of discourses and learn how to address the states and the UN. Later on, the difficulties surrounding the negotiation of the UNDRIP (which lasted for more than twenty-five years) led the indigenous delegates to set up regional caucuses in order to identify common positions and overcome their linguistic, cultural or political differences and develop more efficient strategies to lobby their respective states and the UN sectors. In the final years of the negotiation, indigenous regional caucuses appeared: the African caucus, the Asian caucus, the Arctic caucus, the North American caucus, the South American Caucus, the Pacific caucus, the 'Russian' caucus, the Sami caucus, the francophone caucus. The work of the UNPFII and the thematic focus on indigenous women, youth or participation in decision-making stimulated the formation of thematic caucuses at a later date, such as the youth caucus, the women's caucus, the conflict caucus and so on.[8]

At the beginning of each UN session, a presidency of the caucus (be it global or regional) is elected, usually shared by two people, a man and a woman, speaking two languages, the most widely distributed languages among indigenous participants: English and Spanish in the global caucus (this explains, in the absence of interpreters, quite a low francophone and Russian participation); English and French in the African caucus. For the global indigenous caucus, representatives from the North and South Americas are often elected, for historical reasons and because of the high number of indigenous participants from these regions.

The caucuses became the source of strong collective statements. Each caucus, whether global, regional or thematic, elects a spokesperson to deliver the statement in the plenary session, and that position rotates within the group. The initial meeting of the global caucus identifies the priorities and the 'elders' train the newcomers, explaining how the UN works, how to write a statement and, more recently, how to focus on the recommendations for the states. The regional caucuses replicate the modalities but focus on more specific issues, and on the articulations between local situations and the positions to convey at the global caucus. At the global and regional caucus meetings, the presidency introduces the subjects, explaining the items on the agenda, and participants take the floor freely. Each one is listened to with great respect. The regional caucuses show a greater degree of familiarity. Throughout the UN session, the global caucus meets every morning and the regional caucuses during the lunch break. The importance of time constraints in the plenary room is underscored – two minutes for an individual statement (one organisation, one country), five minutes for a collective one (thematic and regional caucus statements, and ad hoc groupings of signatory organisations). Time pressure is very great. Many activities take place simultaneously during the ten days of the UN Permanent Forum on Indigenous Issues, and the five days of meetings of the Expert Mechanism on the rights of indigenous peoples. More than 1500 people participate in the UNPFII, hence the number of participants who wish to take the floor on an agenda item regularly increases; there are strict rules for respecting speaking time, and an obligation to be in the room when a name is called.

The Making of Indigenous Experts

The indigenous members of UNPFII are called 'experts'. This qualification stems from the mandate of this body, which is to 'provide expert advice and recommendations on indigenous issues to the Council, as well as to programs, funds and agencies of the United Nations, through the Council' (in this case the Social and Economic Council). Indigenous peoples' representatives were thus transformed from being witnesses of human right violations, economic exploitation, political marginalisation – a position they had had at the WGIP – to becoming 'global experts' 'to raise awareness and promote the integration and coordination of activities related to indigenous issues within the UN system' and 'to prepare and disseminate information on indigenous issues'.

All UN experts are 'independent and function in their own capacity', but the position of expert remains, nevertheless, a sensitive one for both the indigenous group and the states. Half the experts are nominated by the states according to the regional groupings (Africa, Asia, eastern Europe, Latin America and the Caribbean, western Europe and other states), and elected by the ECOSOC. The other half are nominated by indigenous organisations and appointed by the ECOSOC 'to represent the seven socio-cultural regions determined to give broad representation to the world's indigenous peoples': Africa; Asia; central and South America and the Caribbean; the Arctic; central and eastern Europe, the Russian Federation, Central Asia and Transcaucasia; North America; the Pacific. In addition a rotating seat is attributed to one of the first three regions, given their higher number of indigenous people (central and South America and the Caribbean during the 2011–2013 term).

The UNPFII adapted its procedures to make space for a different 'reality' than that defined by the states and designed seven socio-cultural regions to represent the indigenous world. The Arctic region, for instance, corresponds to an environment and a type of livelihood shared by Alaskan tribes, the Inuit and Sami peoples, but it does not coincide with the limits of the states governing these territories (the USA, Canada, Greenland, Nordic European states and Russia), nor to the grouping of these states in the UN system, which was inherited from other historic divisions, such as those which opposed western countries and the former Soviet Union. The identification of the Arctic as a 'socio-cultural region', and the organisation of its indigenous representation, results from the direct implication of indigenous delegates, who exposed the necessity of addressing regionally the issues they were confronted with.

Transnational indigenous organisations, with their own agenda and activities, define participation and representation and circulate information among local organisations. They brought together indigenous people from across borders to identify similar problems posed by nation state building and transnational capitalism, and also to respond to the problems posed by border controls and by the limited capacity of states to address global issues, such as environmental disorders and transnational industries.

Strong historical organisations emerged locally, during the 1960s and 1980s, and evolved in the 1990s to become more transnational. They include, for example, the International Indian Treaty Council (created in 1974), the Indian Council of South America (CISA) for the highlands, created in 1980, the Coordination of Indigenous Organizations of the Amazon Basin (COICA), which emerged in 1984 to deploy its activities in nine countries, and the Abya Yala Parliament (all America). In Scandinavia, the Sami organisation (Parliament and Council) – including Finland, Russia, Norway and Sweden – emerged. In Asia, similarly, national indigenous organisations have decided to reinforce their efforts at a regional level by setting up, in 1992, the Asian Indigenous Peoples Pact (AIPP), which incorporated local organisations from fourteen countries into advocacy and policy activities. In Africa, three organisational movements are also relevant, all due to the existence of the UN international forum to which it was necessary to present a more cohesive discourse. In northern Africa, the Tuareg, Berber and Kabyle people joined forces,[9] in central Africa the Pygmies formed a transnational network,[10] and, during a UN meeting in 1997, representatives of indigenous francophone and anglophone Africa formed the Indigenous Peoples of Africa Coordinating Committee (IPACC), which covers the whole continent and now includes 150 organisations in 20 countries. In the Pacific, we witness the formation of local organisations such as the Agence Kanak du Développement (in 1991) or Hiti Tau, which includes thirty associations of Polynesian islands, as much as the process of consolidating a national organisation in Australia with the creation of the National Congress of Australia's First People in 2011. French-speaking organisations have joined the anglophone group of the Pacific Islands Association of Non-Governmental Organisations (PIANGO). Finally, for the seventh region, the organisational process started with the grouping of indigenous peoples of the Russian Federation (RAIPON).

From each region of the world prominent male and female representatives emerged. They had *expertise* on legal subjects, development issues, environment, food security, cultural matters, intellectual property rights, and developed positions on common issues, across the regional divisions. As an example, seven prominent figures, from Asia, Africa, North and Central America, Oceania and the Arctic wrote the UN document *State of the World's Indigenous Peoples* (UNPFII 2010). This book describes how a collective voice emerged, through the juxtaposition of indigenous voices from different regions and it affirms that indigenous peoples can express themselves without non-indigenous spokespersons. It focuses on the core issues of an 'indigenous development', rethinking state policy-making and the challenges of poverty, well-being, culture, environment, contemporary education, health, human rights and 'emerging issues' (such as disaggregation of data, conflict resolution, forced displacement, migration and urbanisation, indigenous peoples in voluntary isolation).

New Profiles of Indigenous Participation

The hundreds of indigenous delegates who attend the UN working sessions every year progressively develop an expertise on indigenous issues and on the UN mechanisms. No sociological studies have been done on the profile of indigenous participants since 1982, therefore we depend on the information provided by the UN reports that give the names of the attending organisations, and on our own observations and the data we have collected since 2001. Indigenous participants can be 'ordinary people' or 'elected representatives' in their own communities or at a national level. They present the views of their communities, nations or peoples, or organisations, or both. Some of them show the profile of an educated elite, trained in universities (often in law and in anthropology) and providing consultancies. Others have received only primary education and did not know of the UN before they took the road to Geneva or New York; they met indigenous fellows who opened the way, while indigenous mobilisations developed regionally in response to particular public policies. They might decide to join the movement because a transnational company entered their territory and developed activities against their will. Professionally they can be full-time activists, but often they generate a living from the exercise of different professions (engineers, bureaucrats, lawyers, teachers, nurses or physicians), a few of them depend on traditional livelihoods (hunter gatherers, agriculture, fisheries).

The voice given to indigenous peoples has evolved over the last decade, and reflects their progressive inclusion into wider political systems. At the beginning indigenous delegates were representatives of their people, bearing the signs of their authority and mandated by their community. Then, a larger number of indigenous people came to attend the UN meetings mandated by an organisation to which they were accountable. Today indigenous parliamentarians form a newly admitted 'group' within the general participation in UNPFII and EMRIP. This category appeared a few years ago and it reflects the changes taking place in Latin America.

Indigenous participation at the UN is now made up of several components. First there are organisations and leaders who have been involved historically, and who promote the spirit of their elders and predecessors: for instance the International Indian Treaty Council whose representative has attended the UN meetings since 1977; South American and Oceanian organisations, or the organisations of the Sami people. Second, there are more recent organisations that became, at the turn of the millennium, as central as the previous ones in the development of indigenous issues, for example the African, Asian and Russian organisations, whose leaders have opened up the spectrum of indigenous issues. Out of these two groups there emerged the figures of experts we mentioned before. Indigenous experts became, in their own capacity, the 'right person' to be invited to one of the thousand events organised by the UN specialised agencies or headquarters. Third, there are the indigenous people who, in very small numbers, work for the UN secretariats at the Department of Social and Economic Affairs in charge of UNPFII, at the Office of the High Commissioner for Human Rights or in some division of the UN specialised agencies. These professionals usually work on short-term contracts and have not reached the secure position of international civil servants. They fill a space within the UN division of labour, sometimes at a very high level as is the case for the Special Rapporteur on the rights and fundamental freedoms of indigenous peoples, an American professor of law of Purepucha origin. An indigenous person in a UN position, brings programmes and the modus operandi closer to indigenous expectations or interests, and overcomes the distance between UN staff and indigenous local people that is often described.

The composition of the UN indigenous representation also reflects national evolution. Either the state limits their political expression and blocks indigenous organisations or representatives, or it makes room for the constitution of an indigenous subject both at the domestic and global level. In the first case, indigenous delegates are isolated, criticised by the state representative and sometimes punished when they return home. In the second case, indigenous people can be invited to take part in government delegations (as in Greenland, Bolivia, Guyana, Ecuador or Venezuela). In the latter case, state representatives and observers are hardly distinguishable and the potential for criticising state policies seems also to be controlled.

The massive participation of indigenous people in the work of the UN raises concerns at the country level about their representativeness. On the one hand, indigenous delegates at the UN are often perceived (outside the UN) as being absorbed by the machine (what Ferguson [1994] calls an anti-politics machine), too much attracted by international life and too loosely attached to indigenous localities to be considered 'true representatives'. On the other hand, they are efficient in forming an indigenous voice and in determining issues on the agenda of the international community and in multiplying the recommendations adopted by the Permanent Forum.[11]

A PROCESS OF NORMALISATION

Several UN initiatives have increased knowledge about the situations faced by indigenous communities and the limits of legal norms to protect them, which has made indigenous issues, and consequently indigenous peoples more visible. A series of expert studies clarified problematic issues such as: litigations (study on 'Treaties and other constructive arrangements', Martinez 1999); the relationship to land, territory and resources (with the invention of the concept of 'indigenous peoples' permanent sovereignty'; see Daes 2001, 2004); the impact of globalisation and the problems posed by extractive industries; the right to food, to water, to a clean environment; the right to participate in decision-making and the right to free prior and informed consent. The proliferation of studies led indigenous activists to take a human rights approach to influence different policy domains, and to affirm their competence on these subjects. The UN level where normative action takes place then has to be connected with the local level where national policies are enacted, UN programmes implemented and where a number of conflicts of variable intensity develop.

The two organs in charge of indigenous issues within the UN structure, namely the UNPFII and EMRIP, devote most of their time to following up, including carrying out studies on how to make provisions in UNDRIP a framework for national policies. One expression of coordination is the mechanism that has come to be known as 'mainstreaming'. Exploring how this same UN mechanism is applied for different categories of marginalised peoples illuminates some important aspects of the position of indigenous peoples within the UN system, and outside.

The concept of mainstreaming comes from the rhetoric of equal opportunity policies developed by European institutions during the 1990s. At the UN, it is a formulation used for dealing with women's issues (Merry 2005; UNESCO 2003). An ECOSOC report of 1997 details its meaning:

> Mainstreaming a gender perspective is the process of assessing the implications for women and men of any planned action, including legislation, policies or programs, in all areas and at all levels. It is a strategy for making women's as well as men's concerns and experiences an integral dimension of the design, implementation, monitoring and evaluation of policies and programs in all political, economic and societal spheres so that women and men benefit equally and inequality is not perpetuated. The ultimate goal is to achieve gender equality. (UN 1997)

In the matter of indigenous peoples, no such UN definition can be found, but the concept of 'mainstreaming' goes together with that of 'integration', a term that is used both to explain what 'mainstreaming' consists of, and to translate the concept into French. In 2007, a UN official from the Office of the High Commissioner for Human Rights said at a UNESCO conference in Paris: 'mainstreaming indigenous peoples' perspective means to define a mechanism of integration'.[12] Depending on the context, and on the scale where action is defined, it may refer either to the extension of mainstream services to indigenous people or to assessing the implications for indigenous people of a planned action.

A shift has occurred from the 'integrated approach' towards a particular social *issue* (gender imbalance) to the 'integration of a social *group*', in this case indigenous peoples. The perspective that indigenous peoples were not 'integrated' is central to the UN approach, which identified the failure of states' policies that aimed at assimilating them rather than respecting their cultural differences. A mechanism of integration (or mainstreaming) was demanded by indigenous organisations for situations where political decisions could be taken with regard to situations of discrimination and marginalisation in which particular indigenous groups are involved.

In response to the difficulty of facing the heterogeneity of indigenous demands and situations, the UN set up an Inter-Agency Support Group (IASG) in order to coordinate the work of administrators in different UN agencies. It now includes more than thirty members among UN agencies, programmes and funds and other intergovernmental organisations. It functions within the UN system with no participation of indigenous peoples. Thus it is a mechanism for 'rationalising' the treatment of indigenous matters. It operates with focal points in each organisation aimed at coordinating their work and possibly sharing resources and information. The IASG sends reports to the UNPFII and is responsible for a greater involvement of the UN specialised agencies, which now integrate indigenous peoples' concerns in their respective programmes of action.

The same IASG mechanism was exported, in 2008, to the Convention on the Rights of Persons with Disabilities. That draws our attention to the relation between institutional coordination and the normalisation of people. What women, persons with disabilities, and indigenous peoples have in common are patterns of domination and processes that have resulted in a 'negative characterisation': they are defined by an absence of something; 'women are not men', 'persons with disabilities are not normal', or 'indigenous peoples are not peoples'. International organisations may use mainstreaming as a mechanism for integrating distinct social categories into policy-making, but an interesting point to notice is that the sources of differentials in power, which are an important matter for indigenous peoples, are not addressed. The focus is on participation, inclusion, empowerment, management and processes of decision-making, as if these were politically neutral and simple tools to improve society, perceived as a global whole, with no tensions between economic groups and no impact of the economy on the social sphere.

International staff thus use a common frame of reference. This explains how the concept of mainstreaming has moved from the European institutions to the UN and to national governments, and back, from the domain of equal opportunities (in labour and social access) to that of human rights, indigenous issues and the environment. The ideas contained in the frame of reference expanded to articulate several mechanisms at UNPFII and EMRIP, the UNDP (UN Development Programme) and many other agencies and programmes. When we try to clarify the meaning of 'mainstreaming' in the field of indigenous policies from a French-language perspective, we observe two interesting shifts. On the one hand, the concept draws from an English general definition of 'mainstream', which refers to 'the ideas, attitudes, or activities that are regarded as normal or conventional'. Hence the grammatical form of 'mainstreaming' induces the idea that 'indigenous peoples' need to be brought to some normality. On the other hand, 'mainstreaming' opens another field of blurred concepts, such as 'integration' – a polysemic word that may serve to mean social inclusion, or as a substitute for 'assimilation'. Social inclusion, is an aspirational horizon that very few indigenous or human rights organisations really contest (except when they deal with the issue of peoples in voluntary isolation), but mainstreaming may have other consequences, which have been analysed in Latin America and in Australia. The two cases shed light on what we observe at the UN.

The first focuses on the emergence of a socio-political category of 'the Authorized Indian' (*el indio permitido*), an expression coined by Silvia Rivera, a Bolivian sociologist, and later used by Charles Hale (2004) to criticise neoliberal policies of multiculturalism and how governments are using cultural rights to divide and domesticate indigenous movements. The second suggests, after analysing the Australian government policy of mainstreaming in the environmental sector, that normalisation – in this case addressing the Aboriginal population – is biased by other processes that define what normality should be. As Altman says:

> To what extent might the Australian government political consensus encapsulated in policy and discursive framing of 'mainstreaming', 'normalization' and 'Closing the Gap' be challenged by the Caring for the Country movement? When considering remote Indigenous development, the dominant policy

view fixates just two possibilities; either mainstream commercial development, in situ, where you live; or migrate away from remote communities, move up the settlement hierarchy and then join the mainstream. (Altman and Kerins 2012: 6–7)[13]

In both cases, what is currently at stake is the control of an indigenous capacity to forge autonomous bodies and movements to resist the impact of neoliberal policies the world over.

There are at least two possibilities for understanding what the logic of mainstreaming does in the field of indigenous policies. For indigenous organisations, a reference to indigenous peoples rights is central in their contributions to normative frameworks at the global level. In that direction, mainstreaming means to define a single approach – a human rights based approach – and apply it to all structural policies. For international organisations, mainstreaming is a tool to include an indigenous section in a larger programme. One might think the objectives are the same, and we observe that UN agencies do refer to UNDRIP and make use of the expression 'indigenous peoples' without reserve. However the goal is extremely ambivalent. Mainstreaming causes indigenous issues to grow in generality and simultaneously has the capacity to dissolve the specificities it is supposed to address. The process of normalisation that we observe in the UN also has the effect of absorbing indigenous energies and transforming indigenous leaders into convenient interlocutors. That is both an expected and an unexpected effect of the UN adoption. The radicalism of the movement is de facto domesticated. Indeed, the indigenous organisations which attend the UN meetings and follow up the many international processes that impact their communities are those who believe in this way of problem solving. Yet decisions remain in the hands of the states, and indigenous leaders' influence is effective at the margins only.

CONCLUSION

On the basis of collective rights, indigenous peoples re-articulated their position to defend their cultural, social and economic interests against state policies and interests. On the UN stages, indigenous mobilisations and the people leading them showed that they have the capacity to impact legal constructions through making effective alliances. In the UN framework of combatting discrimination, their difficult situation was scrutinised. On this basis the UN bodies – with the participation of indigenous peoples – started to think about legal tools to combat socio-economic exclusion and political marginalisation. While indigenous peoples gained in visibility, locally and at world level, indigenous subaltern groups (defined by the rhetoric of vulnerability and victimhood) transformed into innovative actors capable of proposing new forms of legal arrangements. This created an aspirational movement on the wake of the 1960s movement for civil rights.

However, today it seems the Human Rights Decades (Badie 2002) have lost their momentum. Indigenous people continue to attend the UN platforms of dialogue, and access and participate in a number of UN processes, yet a backlash can be observed at the national level, particularly when indigenous peoples started to take action to fight against land expropriation, extractive industries and big development projects. In several parts of the world and under the neoliberal distribution of work, a series of governments have dismantled social policies, redefined their role around the concepts of 'law and order' and discredited indigenous mobilisations by characterising their leaders as terrorists, instead of opening negotiations to solve historical conflicts.

The right to self-determination, an important axis for redefining indigenous peoples' struggles at the end of the twentieth century became central in the *dispositif* of the UNDRIP. Struggling for collective human rights and forming transnational alliances in articulation with the UN has opened a space for indigenous peoples to have a say about their destiny. Its success may depend on educational and financial capacities. However, with the pragmatism that characterises their action at the UN levels, indigenous leaders use different mechanisms that derive from the UNDRIP as a means to resist and, in particular, to oppose development projects, land expropriation, health degradation. One of these mechanisms is the effective implementation of the right to consultation that is inscribed in ILO Convention No. 169 and therefore becomes an obligation for the states that ratified it. The other is the concept of free prior and informed consent, which acquired a prominence that was not central during the negotiation of the UNDRIP. Now that the right to self-determination has been recognised, the incorporation of a collective self (that gives birth to expressions of 'self-government' and 'self-governing institutions')[14] can be re-associated with the figure of 'development'. The articulation is done through both claiming the rights and legal personality of indigenous peoples, whose voice is to be taken into consideration, and formulating innovative concepts such as the notion of 'development with identity and culture', later called 'self-determined development'.

The participation of indigenous people in the UN circuits of dialogue is a good demonstration of epistemic and political co-production. In that sense, indigenous peoples are included in the world agenda. However, their marginal position remains – because they constitute a demographic minority in most of the countries that include them, because their patterns of leadership and decision-making differ from those of the dominant societies, and because new forms of capitalist exploitation that intensify the level of competition are also important sources of divisions among indigenous peoples.

NOTES

1. I would like to thank Jennifer Hays for her advice on English phrasing and suggestions for structuring the chapter. The ideas presented here are, of course, my own. The research leading to these results has received funding from the European Research Council under the European Community's Seventh Framework programme (FP7/2007–2013 Grant Agreement no. 249236 – SOGIP: 'Scales of Governance: the UN, the States and Indigenous Peoples; self-determination at the time of globalization' (see: www.sogip.ehess.fr).

2. In 1971, eleven anthropologists met at Barbados, at a symposium on 'Interethnic Frictions in South America', sponsored by the World Council of Churches. They wrote a declaration that had a strong impact, which denounces the colonial pattern of domination over indigenous lives, and states' policies. It pleads for recognition that indigenous rights existed prior to the formation of national society; demands recognition of the rights of indigenous people to organise themselves and that states recognise their responsibility to respect their civil and political rights. It calls on missionaries to end their efforts to eradicate indigenous spirituality and on corporations to end economic exploitation. It calls on anthropologists to refute scientism, hypocrisy and opportunism, and to engage the discipline in support of indigenous communities' liberation movement. It mentions indigenous people as the protagonists of their own destiny (The eleven anthropologists were M.A. Bartolomé, G. Bonfil Batalla, V. D. Bonilla, G. Castillo Cardenas, M. Chase-Sardi, G. Grünberg, N. Arvelo de Jimenez, E. E. Mosonyi, D. Ribeiro, S. Robinson, S. Varese). In 1974, during the 41st Congress of Americanists in Mexico, the same anthropologists wrote another declaration highlighting the issues of ethnic identity and indigenous liberation. A second meeting took place in Barbados, with the same participants as the first, plus a large group of indigenous leaders from twelve countries, ranging from intellectuals to forest dwellers. A Barbados Declaration II, addressing the 'Indian Brother', was written in 1977, to denounce the physical and cultural domination manifest in land expropriation and states' policies of acculturation of indigenous people, leading to the devaluation of indigenous education and their being treated poorly by the media. It claims the

right to autonomous political organisation, and also considers the situation of indigenous women. Considerable debate arose from these declarations.

3. See for instance, the websites www.iwgia.org, www.gitpa.org, www.sogip.ehess.fr

4. The identification of that role fostered the participation of indigenous people to a CBD working group on Article 8 (j) through which the participation in decision-making emerged as a key issue for indigenous leaders with regard to decisions taken by states. This is one example where the recognition as *indigenous peoples*, endowed with a legal personality and a high symbolic capital, becomes a powerful instrument of negotiation.

5. The Indigenous and Tribal Populations Convention, 1957 (No. 107) was a first attempt to codify international obligations of states in respect of indigenous and tribal populations. The first international convention on the subject, it was adopted by the ILO at the request of the UN system. Ratified by twenty-seven countries, it remains in force in eighteen of them, which did not sign the revised Convention No. 169.

6. See the historical narrative in the webdoc (GITPA-UNESCO) realised by I. Bellier, F. Morin and B. Saladin d'Anglure, available at: http://www.gitpa. org/Dvd/Caf_a_l_Onu.html

7. In this domain, they rely on the help of 'support organisations' such as doCip, which since 1978 has sought to build a technical secretariat for indigenous peoples at the UN, or the IWGIA, which is committed to several aspects of UN work, and has facilitated both the construction of regional organisations and the travel of selected leaders, such as benevolent individuals who help to introduce indigenous representatives to the UN formalities – writing statements, translating, serving as guides to the city and the UN buildings, etc.

8. The name 'caucus' can also be used as a designation for a grouping of people such as the Touareg caucus or the San caucus, to include people who are not part of a common transnational organisation and to give them greater visibility.

9. In Morocco, in 1978, the New Association for Popular Culture to promote the Amazigh people (otherwise known as Berbers – in the Rif, the Souss and the Atlas of southern Morocco) was founded. After adopting, in 1983, a more explicit Amazigh name, Tamaynut, it joined other Amazigh organisations from Algeria, Tunisia and Libya, to found the Amazigh World Congress in 1995 in Douarnenez (France). Its former president, a lawyer, has also been elected to the UN Permanent Forum. In Africa, a number of cross-border associations were set up later, such as the Tuareg Tin Hinan (1994) for the 'advancement of nomadic women' (Mali, Mauritania, Algeria).

10. The first Batwa organisations started with the creation in 1994 of the Aboriginal Community of Rwanda (CAURWA), which was obliged by the government to change its name – considered too ethnic and therefore unconstitutional – to adopt that of the Potter community of Rwanda. 'Pygmies' is a derogatory name that is used in Central Africa by some organisations only. Batwa, Bambuti, Baka and other organisations joined a larger network (LINAPYCO), which includes scattered and powerless communities from eight countries (Burundi, Cameroon, Gabon, Rwanda, DRC, Congo, Central African Republic, Uganda).

11. Such recommendations – which are written following strict rules – are proposed by the indigenous observers (individuals and caucus), adopted by the expert members of the Permanent Forum in plenary session, transmitted by the secretariat to the ECOSOC and followed up by a coordinating mechanism among the UN specialised agencies.

12. Author's field note.
13. This is illustrated by the inclusion of an Aboriginal programme, designed in 1995 by the Northern Land Council (an independent statutory authority of the Commonwealth) and called 'Caring for Country', in the Australian environment policy that has been called 'Caring for *Our* Country'. The use of '*our*' in the name of the government programme indicates a political will to resist divergent perspectives on what caring means and for whom, in the face of land claims and the mining industry.
14. The translation of such institutions in French covers the field of 'autonomy'.

BIBLIOGRAPHY

Altman, J. and S. Kerins (eds) (2012) *People on Country: Vital Landscapes – Indigenous Futures* (Annandale: The Federation Press).

Badie, B. (2002) *La Diplomatie des droits de l'homme. entre éthique et volonté de puissance* (Paris : Fayard).

Bellier, I. (2003) 'Dernières nouvelles du Groupe de travail sur le projet de déclaration des droits des peuples autochtones à l'ONU', *Recherches Amérindiennes au Québec* 33(3): 93–99.

Bellier, I. (2006) 'Le projet de déclaration des droits des peuples autochtones et les Etats américains: avancées et clivages', in C. Gros and M.C. Strigler (eds) *Etre indien dans les Amériques*, pp. 27–41 (Paris: Institut des Amériques).

Bellier, I. (2007) 'Partenariat et participation des peuples autochtones aux Nations Unies: intérêt et limites d'une présence institutionnelle', in C. Neveu (ed.) *Démocratie participative, cultures et pratiques*, pp. 175–192 (Paris: L'Harmattan).

Bellier, I. (2008) 'Le développement et les peuples autochtones: conflits de savoirs et enjeux de nouvelles pratiques politiques', in V. Geronimi, I. Bellier, J.-J. Gabas, M. Vernières and Y. Viltard (eds) *Savoirs et politiques de développement: Questions en débat à l'aube du XXIè siècle*, pp. 119–139 (Paris: Karthala).

Bellier, I. (2012) 'Les peuples autochtones aux Nations Unies: la construction d'un sujet de droits/acteur collectif et la fabrique de normes internationales', *Critique international* 54: 61–80.

Bonfil Batalla, G. (1977) 'Declaración de Barbados II', in *Utopía y revolución. El pensamiento contemporáneo de los Indios en América Latina*, pp. 413–416 (Mexico: Nueva image).

Charters, C. and R. Stavenhagen (2009) *Making the Declaration Work: The United Nations Declaration on the Rights of Indigenous Peoples* (Copenhagen: IWGIA).

Daes, E.-I. (2001) *Les Peuples autochtones et leur relation à la terre*, rapport final à la Sous-Commission de la Promotion et de la Protection des Droits de l'Homme. E/CN.4/Sub.2/2001/21.

Daes, E.-I. (2004) *La Souveraineté permanente des peuples autochtones sur les ressources naturelles*, rapport final à la Sous-Commission de la Promotion et de la Protection des Droits de l'Homme. E/CN.4/sub.2/2004.30.

Daes, E.-I. (2008) *Indigenous Peoples: Keepers of our Past – Custodians of our Future* (Copenhagen: IWGIA).

Dahl, J. (2009) *IWGIA: A History* (Copenhagen: IWGIA).

Hale, C. (2004) 'Rethinking indigenous politics in the era of "Indio permitido"', in *NACLA Report on the Americas*, pp. 16–22 (New York: North American Congress on Latin America).

Hays, J. (2011) 'Indigenous rights in southern Africa: International mechanisms and local contexts', *International Journal of Human Rights* 15(1): 1–10.

Martinez, M.-A. (1999) *Study on Treaties, Agreements and Other Constructive Arrangements between States and Indigenous Populations*, E/CN.4/sub.2/1999/20. Available at: http://www.unhchr.ch/Huridocda/Huridoca.nsf/0/696c51cf6f20b8b c802567c4003793ec (consulted 13 April 2013).

Martinez Cobo, J. (1987) *Study of the Problem of Discrimination against Indigenous Populations*, vol. 5: *Conclusions, Proposal and Recommendation*, New York: UN. Available at: http://www.docip.org/Online-Documentation.32.0.html (consulted 13 April 2013).

Merry, S. (2005) *Human Rights and Gender Violence* (Chicago: University of Chicago Press).

Morin, F. (1992) 'Vers une déclaration universelle des droits des peuples autochtones', in H. Giordan (ed.) *Les Minorités en Europe. Droits linguistiques et droits de l'homme*, pp. 493–507 (Paris: Kimé).

Muehlebach, A. (2001) '"Making place" at the UN : Indigenous cultural politics at the UN Working Group on Indigenous Populations', *Cultural Anthropology* 16(3): 415–448.

Rostkwoski, J. (1986) *Le Renouveau indien aux Etats Unis* (Paris: Albin Michel).

UN (1997) *Report of the Economic and Social Council for 1997*. A/52/3,18 September. Available at: http://www.un.org/documents/ga/docs/52/plenary/a52-3.htm (consulted 13 April 2013).

UNESCO (2003) *The UNESCO Gender Mainstreaming Implementation Framework*. Available at: http://portal.unesco.org/en/ev.php-URL_ID=11481&URL_DO=DO_ TOPIC&URL_SECTION=201.html (consulted 13 April 2013).

UNPFII (2009) *The State of the World's Indigenous Peoples*. Available at: http://social. un.org/index/IndigenousPeoples/Library/StateoftheWorldsIndigenousPeoples.aspx (consulted 13 April 2013).

Varese, S. (2006) *Witness to Sovereignty: Essays on the Indian Movement in Latin America* (Copenhagen: IWGIA).

Yashar, D. (2005) *Contesting Citizenship in Latin America: The Rise of Indigenous Movements and the Postliberal Challenge* (Cambridge: Cambridge University Press).

World Council of Churches/Conseil Oecuménique des Eglises et programme de lutte contre le racism (1972) 'La Declaration de la Barbade', in *de l'Ethnocide* (Paris: Union Générale des Editions).

9
The Loss of Harmony
FAO Guidance for Food Security in Nicaragua

Birgit Müller

On the international level, the Food and Agriculture Organization (FAO) of the United Nations (UN) provides technical guidance in the highly controversial debate about how to feed the undernourished 1 billion people in the world. It also aims to provide a neutral forum, where contrary opinions, interests and projections for the world in crisis can meet and develop common solutions. From its headquarters in Rome, it claims the role of an 'objective' broker whose strength is based on 'competence' and 'knowledge', on its capacity to achieve consensus thanks to its capacity as an expert organisation that can claim superior normative authority (Müller 2011). Looking at the FAO's actions and technical interventions on the ground in a poor agricultural country like Nicaragua, however, its tensions and contradictions come out in the open when it promotes diametrically opposed farming practices simultaneously. The FAO can be encountered everywhere in Nicaragua, from the farmers' fields to government ministries intervening in the name of FAO's mandate of assuring a sufficient and healthy diet to Nicaraguans suffering from chronic or temporary food shortages. The FAO advised the Nicaraguan parliament on its law about food sovereignty and food security. It administers donations of the World Food Programme. It carries out the European Food Facility Programme in Nicaragua, promoting the Green Revolution package of input-responsive plant varieties, chemical fertilisers and pesticides in the poorest parts of the country. It elaborates small pilot projects in the frame of the Special Programme for Food Security (SPFS) in chosen villages, encouraging seed saving, agro-forestry, endorsing composting and production without chemical fertilisers.

Although as a global development goal, feeding the world's hungry is relatively uncontentious, this has not prevented the FAO from becoming deeply enmeshed in the complex web of politics, interests and passions linked with agricultural practice. FAO publications, however, frame problems and conflicts in seemly neutral ways and create a fiction of coherence and harmony. Instead of asking what mechanisms are responsible for making people go hungry in spite of the fact that a sufficient amount of food is produced in the world, or through what practices one social group makes another go hungry (Li 2007: 7), the FAO's approach focuses on how the poor could be empowered to become actors in the market in order to help themselves out of poverty and protect their own health and the environment. Yet the technical and policy recommendations that the FAO makes have an effect on substantial economic interests and have a direct impact on the livelihoods of people and on their environment. The FAO's mechanisms of governance not only govern people, but interact with things, particularly living things such as seeds, plants and soils.

In this chapter I examine how global guidelines, programmes and projects affect local and national actors following their own agendas. How do agricultural practices promoted by the FAO on the local level interrelate with global policy models? How is lived experience formulated, stylised, filmed, put on websites and presented as 'best practice'? How can the FAO stay credible and thrive in Nicaragua while promoting mutually exclusive agricultural practices? What effects does its governance have on Nicaraguan agro-biodiversity and soils? An anthropological look at these processes reveals the intricacies of practice that are left out of the models. When I wrote about the FAO as seen from headquarters (Müller 2011), I analysed it in terms of a *dispositif* (Foucault 1994), a term frequently translated into English as 'assemblage' or 'apparatus'. For Foucault, the general objective of a *dispositif* is not socialisation, structural stability, equilibrium or the reduction of complexity, but 'the ordering of human multiplicities' (Foucault 1975: 218). The *dispositif* of the FAO continually draws in new actors as experts, interlocutors and opinion-givers, engaging them with forms of calculation, technical reasoning, human 'capacity-building' and with non-human objects and devices such as agricultural technologies. I argued that to make a critical impact on what is going on in the FAO civil society actors had to constantly fight for 'a place of their own' (de Certeau 1990) outside the *dispositif*.

At the national level, the FAO still attempts to draw as many actors as possible into its realm, but it also becomes a development actor among others, competing with other organisations, including national political organisations, for precedence. An anthropological approach to development allows us to look beyond the smooth surface of a global governance 'without sovereign authority'. It shows the conflicted nature of interactions, as local actors, unimpressed by the gloss of harmony, reinterpret global policy models of good governance (Mosse 2005: 13). In this chapter I will analyse how the FAO's 'technical interventions' on the national level have political and material effects in a small, largely agricultural country that experiences in a particularly intense fashion most of the big problems that world agriculture faces today: rapid population growth, accelerated erosion of its fertile topsoil, extreme climatic variation and volatile prices for agricultural commodities. Since 1980 the Nicaraguan population has doubled and so has the amount of land put to agricultural use. The productivity per acre has thus not increased and the agricultural frontier is pushing into increasingly marginal lands while the population continues to grow rapidly. The problem is thus that production methods need to change to increase the output per acre and at the same time they need to avoid further environmental degradation. The question of how Nicaraguans are going to grow their food in the future, and with which techniques, is thus a central one. Also, Nicaragua is in the zone of hurricanes, which periodically devastate entire harvests and lead to periods of acute food shortage; indeed, global climate change has rendered agricultural cycles more unpredictable than ever. The problems have been exacerbated by the world food crisis of 2008 and soaring prices, which added urgency to already acute problems. Looking for rapid and short-term responses seemed the order of the day.

In the first part of the chapter I examine how the FAO became a controversial actor in national food politics 'clomping in like an elephant on the national level' (McKeon 2009: 141), bringing in the UN agenda and UN criteria when it drew up for the Nicaraguan parliament a draft law on national food security that contradicted the work that Nicaraguan civil society and policy-makers had accomplished over several years.

In the second part, I look at how the FAO acts as a development broker in the south of Nicaragua, carrying out the Food Facility Programme decided upon and financed by the European Union with the aim of combating rapidly and effectively the most pressing effects of the World Food Crisis of 2008. I will analyse the effects of the programme that distributed large amounts of chemical fertilisers, along with seed varieties that only grow well with external inputs, on local farming practices and political structures of local self governance.

In the third part I analyse how the FAO Special Programme for Food Security in the north of Nicaragua attempts through the method of 'participatory diagnosing' to systematise alternative approaches to agriculture and fit them into the global programme for food security. Normative systems and diagnostic tools become, in this process, not only part of a system of constraints but are also treated and circulated as resources which legitimise institutional interventions (see also Peter Bille Larsen's chapter in this volume).

PROVIDING 'TECHNICAL ADVICE' ON NICARAGUA'S FOOD SOVEREIGNTY LAW

The FAO has the global mandate if not to solve, then at least to alleviate, the problem of providing sufficient and healthy food for the 1 billion people who suffer from chronic or temporary hunger. To solve the problem of hunger is part of the Millennium Goals that thus set what seems like a moral imperative for intervention. In November 2004 the FAO Council adopted voluntary guidelines on the right to food with the objective of providing 'practical guidance to States in their implementation of the progressive realisation of the right to adequate food' (FAO 2005: iii). The guidelines are an attempt by governments to interpret on the international level the right to food that is inscribed in Article 11 of the International Covenant on Economic, Social and Cultural Rights (ICESCR) signed in 1966, and to recommend actions to be taken by individual governments (FAO 2005: i). These guidelines are part of what Peter Bille Larsen (this volume) termed an emerging guidelines culture. Guidelines have become one of the most prominent governance tools of international organisations. Guidelines allow actors to suggest and to recommend in contexts where constraint and obligation are impossible to impose but they nevertheless have concrete effects for national and international policy-making. They imply that the one who guides has the superior technical knowledge over the one who is guided. The guidelines for the right to food based on the ICESCR can thus claim a superior moral authority that stands beyond and above political interest. Guidelines are supposed to be technical, apolitical and moral at the same time.

Yet within the consensus on the global level that combating hunger is a priority, two internationally legitimated development paradigms coexist: one that promotes high-tech solutions, agro-chemicals, genetically modified seeds and production for the market, and another that encourages small scale agriculture, auto-consumption, agro-biodiversity and the preservation of soil fertility. While the first goes together with a discourse of urgency and speed, the other emphasises slowness and care (Adam 1998).

The publication in 2008 of the International Assessment of Agricultural Knowledge, Science and Technology for Development (IAASTD) report (McIntyre and Beverly 2008), which had been commissioned by the UN to advise countries on the best way of ridding the world of hunger, has not been able to solve the conflict between these two paradigms but has rather exacerbated them. The report, co-authored by 400 scientists, criticised the agro-industrial model, cautioned against GMOs (genetically modified organisms) and emphasised that traditional work-intensive farming practices could be as productive per acre farmed, if not more so, than forms of high-input agriculture which were costly and damaging to the environment. In its high degree of unanimity among scientists, the report can be compared to the fourth international assessment report on climate change (Pachauri and Reisinger 2007). To mark their dissent, agro-food corporations pulled out of the process in the last month of writing up and since then the IAASTD report is heralded not as a consensual but as an alternative discourse to the Green Revolution model in the international realm.

At the level of the FAO headquarters the confrontation between these two approaches is presented as a neutral technology debate for which the FAO offers a 'forum'. In this 'forum' contrasting views are supposed to be expressed and a consensus achieved with regard to the common goal of feeding the hungry in the world. The FAO wants to offer in this forum a voice to peasant and environmental organisations advocating for alternative and critical approaches to the dominant paradigm of high-input chemical dependent agriculture, while it continues to cooperate with donor countries and foundations that promote Green Revolution varieties and biotechnology. By rendering conflicting political and economic interests technical, it attempts to provide a gloss of harmony and to produce coherent policy narratives (Müller 2011). This does not mean, however, that all of the FAO's staff share this position. Already in the 1970s members of staff went on strike – the first in UN history – to protest that FAO 'masqueraded' as a neutral technical forum while it was promoting Green Revolution technologies (McKeon 2009: 20). On the national level, and in actual practice, the masks fall when the FAO undertakes development projects in one or the other logic and becomes an actor, or rather it seems to behave as several actors with different agendas who nevertheless claim to pursue the same supreme goal of combating hunger.

The intervention of the FAO on the Nicaraguan Law on Food Sovereignty and Food Security shows the strength and also the paradoxical use that can be made of such a mechanism of international governance. In 2006, still under the liberal government of Enrique Bolanos, a law on food sovereignty and food security, elaborated by a commission composed of elected representatives and members of seventy-five national and twenty-five international NGOs was introduced into the Nicaraguan parliament.[1] The law contained several articles that attributed an important regulatory role to national government and were in contradiction with the usual recipes of structural adjustment promoted by the World Bank and the International Monetary Fund (IMF). The proposal stipulated concrete measures. They included: the development of improved seed from traditional varieties (Art. 5.1), the distribution of not only individual but also communal land titles (Art. 5.3), strict control on food imports and the refusal of genetically modified food aid (Art. 5.8), the establishment of state grain reserves and the possibility of national food price regulation (Art. 5.9), the shortening of the food chain between producer and consumer (Art. 5.10).

With the law on food sovereignty the Nicaraguan parliament wanted to establish an effective instrument that would attenuate the effects of international trade agreements and the world market. In the letter introducing the project of law (paragraph II), the members of the Special Committee for Poverty Reduction affirmed that Nicaragua's signing of international trade agreements had pushed consumerism without allowing for a strategy of food sovereignty that would guarantee food security. Defining the concept of food security the committee referred to the Final Declaration of the World Forum on Food Sovereignty, convened by civil society organisations in Cuba in 2001 and not the FAO voluntary guidelines on the right to food:

Food security is the people's right to define their own policies and strategies for the sustainable production, distribution and consumption of food that guarantees the right to food for the entire population, on the basis of small and medium-sized production, respecting their own cultures and the diversity of peasant, fishing and indigenous forms of agricultural production, marketing and management of rural areas, in which women play a fundamental role.[2]

The emphasis that parliament placed on developing traditional seed varieties that were adapted to local conditions and able to grow without chemical inputs contrasted with the public plant breeding done by the Instituto Nacional de Tecnología Agropecuaria (INTA) that had so far focused on high-yield input-dependent varieties in its breeding programmes. It also antagonised foreign companies like Monsanto that have an aggressive presence in the Nicaraguan seed market. When Nicaragua, with the support of the FAO introduced the programme Libra por Libra in 2002, which urged farmers to exchange their traditional varieties of maize and beans for varieties that were higher yielding when they received sufficient chemical inputs, three of the six corn varieties distributed to the farmers came from the multinational corporation Monsanto. In contrast, by inscribing their commitment to supporting the improvement of traditional varieties in the food sovereignty law, the parliament affirmed its intention to increase Nicaragua's independence from imports of seeds and chemicals.

Inscribing the refusal of transgenic crops as food aid into the food sovereignty law, the parliament also directly attacked US interests, since the US insists that its food aid worldwide should be offered in kernel form and not be tested for GMOs.[3] In Nicaragua, the World Food Programme distributes, among other crop varieties, corn from the US in kernel form that contains GMOs.[4] Corn that is not milled not only enters the food chain but may also be used as seed. There were, in fact, many voices among both international aid workers and Nicaraguans who criticised the surreptitious way that transgenic corn was thus introduced into a country that did not authorise the cultivation of genetically modified corn varieties until 2012 when the biosecurity law was passed,[5] and that possesses a rapidly dwindling wealth of traditional corn varieties. Their justifiable fear was that food aid was being used as a Trojan Horse for the introduction of GMOs. Other aspects of the food sovereignty bill were equally unwelcome to transnational agrobusiness. The creation of state grain reserves and national food price regulations are controversial measures in international food policy-making which go against the credo of market liberalism and most conditions of structural adjustment programmes. In addition, inscribing the shortening of the food chain between producer and consumer into law posed a threat to the supermarket chains that, in Nicaragua, are almost exclusively owned by the US-based multinational WalMart.

On 7 June 2007, when the Sandinistas had already gained a relative majority in parliament, the food sovereignty law was passed by the National Assembly on its first reading in almost all points. However, it failed to pass its second reading because the Liberals refused to endorse the article prohibiting the import of transgenic food aid. At the demand of the liberal deputies the FAO then drafted a counter-proposal, which did away with all concrete measures, replacing them with vague formulations that came straight out of the voluntary guidelines. The counter-proposal provoked an outcry among the civil society organisations that had cooperated to create a draft law. In an interview Eduardo Vallecillo, coordinator of the government-commissioned Working Group on Food Sovereignty and Food Security (GISSAN) commented:

> certain administrators of the FAO don't like the subject of food sovereignty.... There are the voluntary guidelines ... they are practically a format that the FAO has already established. To talk about food sovereignty is a concept that goes beyond the established model. It is something very new that has to do with the dignity of the people. We introduce this subject not as an isolated subject, but as a model for intervention.... The FAO says, many things that they eliminated from our proposal should be included in a bylaw. But past experiences, for example in Guatemala,[6] tell us that this makes it unpredictable and often this instrument prevents a true application of the concept of sovereignty and food security. We want a law that sustains programs that really get to the people. (Trucchi 2007)

When challenged by civil society organisations over why the proposal had not been discussed with the working group beforehand, the director of FAO Nicaragua allegedly responded that she was providing technical assistance as requested by the National Assembly and that it was not her role to enter into a political debate. 'How can it be possible to solve a political problem with a technical law?' Vallecillo concluded (Trucchi 2007).

It took another two years before the law on food sovereignty was finally approved by parliament. The name remained the same but the content was streamlined to fit with the FAO proposal. As a reward, the FAO thanked and commended the National Assembly of Nicaragua.[7]

As the example of the Nicaraguan law shows, the voluntary guidelines took on a life of their own that weakened their initial intent. As an albeit small area of common ground among a number of politically and ideologically diverse nation states, and as universally agreed minimum standard, the voluntary guidelines were a real achievement of international policy-making. However, the voluntary guidelines had never been intended to replace national law-making. They were the baseline, and every state was supposed to do better than that and to decide on concrete measures and principles that would fill vague formulations such as Article 4.1: 'States should take into account the shortcomings of market mechanisms in protecting the environment and public good' (FAO 2005: 14). However, in the final text whose content had been streamlined to fit with the FAO proposals, Article 5.9 of the draft law that stipulated that the state should establish grain reserves and have the possibility to regulate prices was replaced by Article 9.a that stipulated that the state should have 'the right to define its own politics and sustainable strategies of food production, transformation, distribution and consumption … without prejudice to the exercise of the right to free enterprise and trade'. Grain reserves and price fixing, attacked by all structural adjustment programmes, were thus off the table. Article 5.8 of the draft law that forbade receiving 'food aid that contained genetically modified materials' was replaced by Article 9.b: 'Precaution. Guarantee the safety of the internal production of food, as well as of imports and donations, if they are damaging to production and human consumption.' Before refusing food aid containing GMOs, Nicaragua was thus supposed to prove that they were damaging to human health and the environment. What is more, the emphasis in the actual food sovereignty law, voted for on 18 June 2009, on free market and free enterprise, thus fell back even behind the careful formulations of the Voluntary Guidelines to support the progressive realisation of the right to adequate food in the context of national food security adopted by the 127th Session of the FAO Council in November 2004. It conceded in Article 4.1 that market mechanisms *could* have their shortcomings that the state *should* address (emphasis added). While the voluntary guidelines of the FAO admitted that market mechanisms could fail and that state intervention might become imperative, the new Nicaraguan food sovereignty law subordinated 'food sovereignty' to the right of free enterprise and free trade (Art. 9.a).

Was the FAO thus interfering directly in essential policy-making of the Nicaraguan parliament giving it a (neo)liberal spin? Governance by international organisations is more subtle than that. Although the FAO definitely 'clomped like an elephant on the national level' (McKeon 2009: 19) it did not intervene in the internal affairs of the Nicaraguan state without being invited to do so. As Gerhard Anders

(2005) showed, even the IMF only suggests structural adjustment measures, if the national governments call them in to do so. National governments use international policy guidance for their own purposes;[8] for example, they may pass laws that are unpopular at home under the supposed pressure from international organisations. A food sovereignty law devoid of concrete measures may well have been in the interest of the Nicaraguan government, absolving it from the legal obligation to intervene in volatile agro-food markets and confront foreign donors of food aid. Instead of antagonising foreign interests the government could act as a generous patron towards the hungry population.[9]

What makes the FAO influential in receiver countries is its broker role when donor countries launch larger agricultural development programmes, not so much its claim to moral and technical superiority. The FAO has become, over the last twenty years, more and more dependent on donor countries as funding to the institution itself has been constantly reduced. Losing part of its institutional autonomy, it has thus started to act as a 'broker' between food-exporting donor countries and food-insecure receiver countries. The funding of specific projects and programmes by donor countries has thus become vital to the authority and the survival of the FAO itself.

'A NEUTRAL BROKER': THE FOOD FACILITY PROGRAMME

One of the programmes for which the FAO acted as a broker was the worldwide 1 billion euros European Food Facility Programme, decided on in December 2008, which distributed in twenty-seven countries for two years (summer 2009 to summer 2011) the Green Revolution package of high-yielding varieties and fertilisers according to a global methodology determined by the donor. It dedicated 3 million euros to Nicaragua to fulfil three objectives: increase productivity of the farmers by 15 percent, reduce post-harvest losses from 30 percent to 14 percent and improve the self-organisation of farmers as 'entrepreneurs' acting in the market.[10] The discourse of urgency was complemented here by a rhetoric of empowering smallholder farmers to feed themselves and produce for the market. The programme was to be executed through legally constituted cooperatives growing staples like maize and beans and ready to accept new members. The programme was intended to empower cooperatives that had a weak organisational structure and that would need FAO's technical and logistical assistance for setting up, accounting and commercialisation. The cooperatives were encouraged to sell for a low price or lend the donated high-yielding varieties and fertilisers to local producers and thereby create revolving funds (Interview with the first national programme coordinator, November 2009).

The director of FAO Nicaragua enthusiastically welcomed the programme; it was deployed in the poorest parts of Nicaragua, which, incidentally, also have the most precarious environmental conditions, including steep hills, too much or too little rain, and thus problems of erosion. Farmers in these areas have practised slash-and-burn agriculture, pushing the agricultural frontier to its limit. Productivity per acre has basically remained the same, or gone down, although many development projects by Nicaraguan governments, NGOs and the FAO itself have promoted the same package of technologies that the Food Facility Programme brought to the country. The director, a fervent advocate of Green Revolution varieties, explained the failures of previous projects in the old development idiom of peasant resistance to change. It was their 'culture' that prevented people taking advantage of simple economic incentives (Crewe and Harrison 1998: 1): 'The traditional thinking of many peasants makes it difficult to make the step towards a new agriculture' (Interview November 2009). He was persuaded that the problem of hunger in Nicaragua could be rapidly solved if only the Nicaraguan farmers, big and small, would adopt high-yielding varieties, purchase certified seed every year and use sufficient fertiliser. Also, the problem of erosion in hilly areas could be solved by cultivating with low soil disturbance using herbicides to kill weeds. The director of the FAO thus contributed to the construction of the rural subjects who hardly ever acted as they should. For the farmers themselves, however (Müller 2010), development discourses, with their 'tales of triumph' (Gupta 1998: 41) and of overcoming hardship and poverty:

> appear as fictions providing the ruling regimes with their chief legitimating function that helps to keep them in power. Most farmers I talked to in Nicaragua experienced their individual lives not as a progression, a trajectory of potential improvement outlined in development discourses, but rather as a wheel that turns constantly and that can crush one's existence in the process. (Müller 2010: 271)

In 2011, I was able to observe how the Food Facility Programme was evolving in practice and what effects it had on the ground in a village – let's call it la Quebrada – where I had done fieldwork prior to the arrival of the programme from April to November 2009. In 2009 the farmers in this hilly and relatively dry part of Carazo felt the repercussions of the worldwide economic crisis. Young migrant workers had returned from work in Costa Rica and from the maquilladoras, and many mouths had to be fed. In spite of their economic difficulties I sensed a certain defiance among the families that had a hard time feeding the additional mouths. Some of them told me that the economic crisis was out there and affected the rich countries more than it affected them. As they did not have anything, they also did not have anything to lose. Some of the older farmers even seemed more glad than worried to see some of their children return to the land. As there was no cash to buy chemical fertilisers, farmers talked about changing their production techniques to preserve the land for future generations. They explained that chemical fertilisers used in the past had burned the land, exacerbating the effects of the still frequent practice of burning the residue on fallow land before cultivation. Moreover, slash-and-burn cycles had become shorter and shorter as more and more people lived from the same piece of land, and as a result the soil had become eroded and was 'tired'. The policy 'Don't burn the land!' (No quema!) received legal backing from national and municipal government and became more widely accepted by the farmers. In 2009 some farmers used the then available family labour to weed the crops instead of buying herbicides, and became interested again in techniques of green manure that had been introduced twenty years earlier by associations close to the farmer self-help movement called Campesino a Campesino (Holt-Gimenez 2006). Also, traditional varieties of maize and beans became more popular choices for farmers. When I left the village in 2009, a small but active minority of farmers had decided to preserve and exchange their traditional varieties of maize and beans and to create a seed bank.

When I came back in 2011 the Food Facility Programme had arrived in the village and not only the situation but also the discourse had changed considerably. Some of the farmers who had created the seed bank for traditional varieties in 2009 and who had experimented with green manure were now busy distributing fertiliser and Green Revolution varieties; they had also withdrawn from the activities of the agro-ecologically minded farmers' cooperative. Another cooperative that had been set up by ten of the wealthier farmers in 2007[11] but had laid dormant most of the time since, had now become the centre selected by the FAO to distribute seeds and fertiliser and one grain bin for 8 quintales[12] to the farmers in the area and beyond. The first thing I saw when I arrived back in the village in 2011 was a solid storage shed with a massive metal door and a huge lock that the FAO had built to store the seeds and fertilisers. Next to it were two drying beds with small roofs (2 ×4 metres) big enough to dry 1 quintal of beans at a time. The shed was now empty but for three empty metal bins that could hold 30 quintales each. I was immediately told that an endless procession of ox carts, riders and small pick-up trucks had carried away hundreds of bags of fertilisers and seeds. 'And what has remained for us?' people in the village asked reproachfully. 'Why did they give the seed and fertiliser away to people as far away as Nandaime?' And 'Who gave the right to this cooperative to sell seeds and fertilisers, if we have an elected village council (CPC), that could do the distribution?'[13]

The decision by the FAO to make a weak and malleable cooperative the carrier of the programme made the programme unaccountable to the elected village council. One of the declared objectives of the programme had been to select deliberately weak agricultural cooperatives and develop their governance structure, provide them with high-yielding seed varieties, fertilisers and technical assistance, and teach them how to administer their farms, and conserve and process their products. With this choice the FAO artificially constructed an organisational void on the village level, which it could fill with its own objectives and priorities. Instead of strengthening existing structures of local self-governance the programme ignored and weakened them. As a consequence, the FAO was able to enjoy autonomy from a village council that wanted first and foremost to defend the interests of the village. While the village council was left out of the distribution of fertiliser and seed, the municipality to which the village belonged happily accepted the programme as it alleviated pressure on the municipal budget, which the mayor used to spend in part on gifts of fertilisers for his electorate.

There were various shortcomings in the execution of the programme, partly because of extremely unfavourable weather conditions, and partly because of organisational failures on the local, national and international level. Waiting for the 'improved' seeds and fertilisers to be distributed made the farmers, once again, dependent on centralised structures of aid and assistance which they had just started to overcome in the previous year. When the thousands of quintales of seeds and fertilisers finally arrived late for the first growing season in June 2010, a private auditing firm hired by the FAO made farmers wait even longer, checking the product, counting, recommending. In the first cultivation cycle of 2010 many farmers were thus unable to seed their crop at the right time. They paid 200 cordobas[14] for the package of the first cultivation cycle and 250 cordobas for the second cycle and were supposed to give back 1 quintal of maize and 1 quintal of beans. However, torrential rains destroyed the bean harvest of 2010 and most farmers were unable to return any beans at the end of year. They also lost the maize harvest because the seeds of the ameliorated corn variety NB6 distributed through the programme were defective. Farmers did not know that the quality control of the distributed varieties was inadequate, took the chance of growing them without a germination test and lost. Many villagers were thus reluctant or unable in 2011 to pay even more, namely 600 cordobas, for their next package.[15] As the members of the cooperative had to prove to the programme administrators that all the seed and fertiliser were distributed and nothing was left in the storage shed, they distributed them to people outside the programme area. As a result, the ten members of the cooperative accumulated, somewhat unintentionally, capital of 300,000 cordobas (US $15,000).

The money accumulated through the programme brought into the open the ambiguity of the idea of good governance that the FAO had to offer: the money was privately held but should serve the common good. It should incite the entrepreneurial spirit of the members of the cooperative and improve the nutritional situation of the entire village population. One of the ideas to use the money to the advantage of the entire community was to create a community grain board, where farmers could sell their grain at harvest time and where it would be stored until prices increased. The price advantage achieved by storing the grain would then be shared between the cooperative and the farmer member, after a fee for maintenance and storage was deducted that would be paid to the people looking after the stored grain. The idea had been discussed in the village even before the programme arrived. Such a structure would alleviate dependence on volatile prices and deceitful grain merchants. The new storage shed, the grain bins and the capital accumulated, all seemed ideal for realising the plan. The essential obstacle, however, was the governance structure introduced through the programme, which left it to the cooperative to dispose of the fund as they wished and did not make it mandatory to open up the membership. Most members agreed in principle to use the fund to buy up grain, but some disagreed with opening up the cooperative to new members and wished to keep all the profit made from distributing the grain for the members of the cooperative. When the programme finished and the FAO withdrew on 31 July 2012, no decision as to the use of the money had been taken. Most villagers observing the heated conflicts in the cooperative expected that the fund would simply be squandered and would not be used in the general interest.

At the national level, the programme encountered the typical problems of a short-term assistance project. As the coordinator hired for the two years of the programme duration expressed it:

> Urgency! Urgency! Urgency is never a solution! I understand them, I understand all of them, but you will never solve the problem of poverty in this country with reactive programmes. Drought! Fshuuuu! All help! The drought finishes, already everything is gone! Floods!!! Bbbrrrr! Everybody!

Compared with programmes he executed for USAID, he thought that the FAO was slow and excessively bureaucratic. For any spending over US$100,000 they needed to get the budgetary approval of the Headquarters in Rome, which involved writing dozens of letters. His initiative to get plastic tunnels fabricated, so that individual producers could store and dry freshly harvested beans and maize, met with innumerable bureaucratic obstacles. When the tunnels finally arrived in la Quebrada, the producers were not instructed how to use them and I saw the metal arches standing at harvest time without their plastic covers. Most villagers thought they were perfectly useless.

While the national programme coordinator insisted that the most tragic paradox was to have good productivity, bad commercialisation and a lot of post-harvest losses, he did not support local initiatives such as the community marketing board or a board at the municipal level which would have strengthened the position of the most fragile local producers in the local market. As he did not take the village or the municipal council into account he felt he would have to manage it alone. 'I alone with four thousand and some beneficiaries.... I am not superman! Impossible!' Instead, he acted as an intermediary between the WalMart processing plant and some of the larger cooperatives supported by the programme that collected and cleaned in some regions the bean production of several smaller cooperatives. He took the buyer of WalMart to the cooperative so that he could instruct the administrators in the criteria of traceability and quality required by the multinational company and offer them fast cash.[16] Structurally, the deal with WalMart lengthened and centralised the food chain instead of favouring local markets as the Food Facility Programme had promised.

The unfolding of the Food Facility Programme in Nicaragua resembles the development dramas that are unfolding in a similar fashion all over the world. The programme was undertaken in a well-meaning spirit of urgency and arrived from the outside – and top down – in a local community that did not ask for it, undermining local initiatives to improve local self-sufficiency and to reduce the purchase of chemical inputs. Ultimately, only the more privileged farmers profited from it, those who already had enough to eat. In spite of its shortcomings, the programme was heralded as a success by the mayor of the municipality and of course by the members of the cooperative. 'I will defend the FAO wherever I go', a dedicated and usually quite critical community leader told me after he had been invited by the FAO to fly to a regional meeting of programme beneficiaries in Guatemala. The programme successfully embedded itself into a network of reciprocal favours, which tied together the FAO, the national government, the municipality and the cooperative to the detriment of the local community and the poorest farmers, and it claimed that FAO was offering here an example of best practice, to be followed by other agencies.

'PARTICIPATORY DIAGNOSING': THE SPECIAL PROGRAMME FOR FOOD SECURITY

In apparent contrast to this top-down intervention was the pilot project for the Special Programme for Food Security that FAO developed in a village in the north of Nicaragua: let's call it el Guanacaste. The Special Programme for Food Security (SPFS), is one of the high-priority initiatives of the FAO which aims to help fulfil the agreements of the two World Summits on Food (in 1996 and 2002), and the commitments of the Millennium Declaration to reduce world hunger by half by 2015. Its implementation follows a dual approach: at the national level it supports and promotes policy and institutional reforms, such as the law on food sovereignty and food security that I analysed above. It also takes:

a territorial approach, with field activities to identify and promote best practices of agricultural production and marketing ... and activities to improve organisational capacity at the community level and the nutrition practices of the households to assist States in meeting their international commitments.[17]

The village el Guanacaste was one of the first where the methodology of the programme was to be tested and refined over two years, from 2008 to 2010.

The method, called participatory diagnosing, combined the expression of subjective desires with objective measures and was supposed to generate shared values and principles. The FAO extension agent in the north, who was responsible for the programme, explained to me in 2009 that he was teaching the inhabitants of el Guanacaste to discover their own necessities and to act on them. The method he employed was to convoke a meeting of the villagers and make them 'dream' together about the changes they would like to see: sufficient food, healthy children, fertile fields. Their 'dreams' were then checked against and reconciled with objective scientific measures of food deficiencies. To evaluate the efforts to improve nutrition, the FAO cooperated with the Ministry of Health to weigh and measure the village children periodically. As the FAO administrator responsible for the programme on the national level expressed it: 'We are investing in human capital and informal leadership. We don't want to ask, what do you *need*, but what do you *have*?' (Interview April 2009). After collecting their 'dreams' the extension agent taught the villagers to establish nutrition charts and to translate their dream of sufficient tasty food into the need for proteins and vitamins. Together they decided that the villagers needed house gardens, for producing vegetables, goats to give milk to the undernourished children, a stock of high-yielding corn and bean varieties and bags of fertilisers, herbicides and pesticides, which were to become the foundation of a seed and fertiliser bank. They then designated a small number of families as the first beneficiaries of the programme and selected five promoters (for house gardens, goats, agro-forestry and ecological production methods and the seed bank) and one coordinator. The villagers who participated in producing the diagnosis would not necessarily be those who benefited from the programme. The FAO provided an initial stock of 'improved' seed varieties and chemical fertiliser, herbicides and pesticides for the seed and fertiliser bank, a goat for the families with undernourished small children, and vegetable seeds. The villagers were to give back after the harvest two bags of seeds for each one bag borrowed and to pay for the chemicals, and thus develop a collective capital fund.

Very soon the limitations of dreaming became apparent. As the villagers were unable to fulfil their dream of setting up gardens around their houses, because these were built on solid rock, the FAO extension agent brought them lorry tires to be put on wooden scaffoldings 150 cm above the ground, where they planted commercial varieties of tomatoes, peppers, carrots, beetroots and herbs during the dry season that had to be watered from wells. These cultivations were in constant danger of attack from the goats that had quickly reproduced themselves. The villagers were proud of their mini-gardens, and also of their goats, although the increasing numbers of roaming goats caused conflicts with the garden owners. They proudly showed their gardens and goats to each of the many FAO delegations that visited them. The FAO, on the other hand, dreamed of making villagers sell their vegetables and goat meat at the market in the next town and having them set up marketing plans for a production which, however, was not even sufficient for auto-consumption. In the end, the villagers cooperated in this 'dream' and sold their precious vegetables and goat meat at the local fairs set up by the FAO and the municipality. When I returned in 2011 there were virtually no goats left in the village. More than half the villagers who had taken seeds from the seed bank did not give them back and even more were unable to pay for the chemicals and fertilisers. The promoters thus decided to stop distributing chemicals through the seed bank. Some of them wanted the FAO to bring them traditional corn and bean varieties from other villages that would need fewer chemical inputs to grow, rather than Green Revolution varieties: a wish that was not fulfilled.

The SPFS claimed to have arrived in the village in a void, in a place untouched by previous development projects: abandoned, poor, unorganised and helpless. The story was well supported by the villagers who used the SPFS to strengthen their economic and social position in the village. However, this version did not correspond to the reality. The village had a long history of agricultural and health projects, starting in the 1970s with the *escuela radiofonica*, which promoted agro-ecological cultivation methods through radio programmes. Several farmers in the village had participated in these programmes. In the 1980s the village supported the Sandinistas and organised its own self-defence against the contra-revolutionary guerrillas controlling the area, and participated in the Sandinista land reform. A humanitarian NGO from Baltimore financed small projects then and continued to do so in the 1990s as well, when the village felt abandoned by the authorities because it continued to be a Sandinista stronghold. The NGO taught the villagers to build fuel-efficient stoves and provided them with rainwater cisterns. In 2004, the NGO from Baltimore joined a network of NGOs called Fedicamp, which promoted agro-ecological production using the methods of the Campesino a Campesino movement: nurseries for fruit trees, stone walls and plantations to retain the soil, dykes to channel rainwater and the conservation of seeds not only from population varieties of the main staple crops maize, beans and millet, but also from a wide range of local vegetables (pipian, chayote, hard squash, malanga, yucca, etc.). Fedicamp encouraged the farmers to cooperate with others in the village and to exchange fruit trees, vegetable seeds, seeds for green manure, medicinal herbs, etc. with farmers from other villages and regions, but they had almost no hand-outs to offer. Some farmers learned to build raised beds on the rocky land around their houses and plant vegetables more efficiently. They started to produce different types of compost that they used to fill the raised beds and the lorry tyres. In their field plots, the farmers used increasingly both traditional and new agro-ecological methods to preserve soil fertility.

Soon, these already existing initiatives became mingled with and appropriated by the FAO project. The compost heaps appeared on FAO films to promote the Food Security Programme. The house gardens were at last able to thrive because the villagers astutely played the two organisations that competed with each other, asking FAO to provide them with fences to keep the goats and chickens out of the gardens they had developed with the Fedicamp. They obtained material from FAO to build a storage shed to store the seeds from the FAO seed bank but also the traditional varieties that the other project had introduced. Both the FAO and the Fedicamp promoted agro-forestry, encouraging the farmers to leave some trees standing in the cultivated plots. However, while the FAO advised the farmers to stop growing maize, beans and millet in the same plot and to seed a single crop more densely, the Fedicamp promoted companion cropping and the use of green manure and cover crops. While the agricultural technicians of both organisations emphasised that they were in principle pursuing the same objectives, they never directly cooperated. The FAO did not acknowledge the work of Fedicamp and its impact upon the success of the programme. Its long-term involvement was simply officially ignored. As the agricultural advisor of Fedicamp put it:

We are representing continuity here. It is not that I want to be mean with respect to the programmes, but if you carry a heavy sack from the town to the village and somebody takes it from you at the village health centre and brings it here, who is going to get the praise? Not the one who carried it all the way from town ... (Interview October 2009)

Only the consistent and patient efforts of a well-respected village leader, who was coordinating not only the Food Security Programme but also collaborating actively with the Fedicamp, prevented the active members of the community from splitting into two groups: those that were 'with the FAO' and who jealously guarded, for example, the privilege of travelling in the FAO truck to meetings and fairs on the regional and national level, and those who were working with the Fedicamp and were invited to visit farming experiments in other communities.

In spite of their divisions, most villagers appreciated the personal engagement of the FAO project leader, who would actually deliver what he had promised and who made sure that the materials he brought were put to good use. From his experience in el Guanacaste and other villages he produced a methodological guideline which was supposed to be used by other development projects and would help implement the Law on Food Sovereignty and Food Security on the national level. Several promotional films were made in the village and the diagnostic tools used here were put on the FAO website. A careful analysis of the film material allows us to discern the ambiguities of how the FAO conceives of the governance of food security on the local and municipal level. In one of the films, the villagers and also the representatives of the municipality were presented as the initiators of the programme who had asked the FAO for organisational and technical support. The second film showed how the mayor, together with the municipal council and the FAO, picked out communities neglected by development projects to which the programme should provide organisational and technical support. This reading was contradicted by the local leader coordinating the programme in the village who explained in the same film:

Before there were plenty of organisations that came and just passed over our heads. They did not take us into account and planned their activities somewhere at a desk at the municipality and then came and said: 'Here, this and that will be done.' Today it is different. Today they take us into account and invite us. They invite us to a meeting and tell us: 'Look comrades, we want your support! You have a good organisational network.'

He affirmed that lots of organisations had already come to the village before and that the village was selected because it already had a good organisational structure. In his interpretation it was not so much that the programme was supporting *the villagers* but *the villagers* were supporting the programme and allowing it to become a success.

I have shown that the inhabitants of el Guanacaste were indeed no simple recipients of the SPFS; rather, they contributed to its success by shaping it to fit their needs. In the promotion that the FAO gave to the programme, elements of agro-ecological production methods practised in spite of FAO's initial technical guidance – such as the reduction of chemical use and preservation of population seed varieties – were mentioned, though only parenthetically. It seems that the FAO not only wants people to think and act in a certain way but also wants to present as *its* guidance the way people decided to organise anyway. For the FAO it seemed important not to surrender the field to others when practices became standardised. As farmers successfully adopted certain practices and shared them with others, it became important for the visibility of the organisation to have the FAO label put on it. To show a flourishing village had a strong publicity effect for the FAO. Moreover, the publicity that the FAO gave to the community attracted new potential donors looking for a place where they could develop a successful project. Since 2009 the NGO Vision Mundial signed up most of the children of the village for sponsorships from Germany. The FAO guidelines were taken up and transformed by other organisations like Vision Mundial that, however, hardly consulted with the villagers on the projects they were going to implement.

CONCLUSION

To what extent are the realities in a village like el Guanacaste becoming part of the FAO *dispositif*, the world of figures and collections of facts (Ilcan and Phillips 2003). Susan Ilcan and Lynne Phillips tell us that new social movements have challenged the hegemony of the UN world of figures and collections of fact that structure perceptions and act on reality. We could say the same of local practices, such as those developed in el Guanacaste. Similar projects to the one developed in el Guanacaste can be found in other parts of Nicaragua, where they might not be quite as successful and visible but where the objective of the farmers is the same: to make themselves as much as possible independent from buying inputs on the market and from debt.

This is, however, an uphill battle in a country where chemical fertilisers and herbicides are not only promoted as best agricultural practice but are also used as tokens to buy voter support. The role that the FAO plays in this context is ambivalent. The organisation appears to act on the national level like an octopus that undoes with one arm what it did with the other. It slowly integrates agro-ecological production methods into its repertoire and officially advocates the empowerment of local producers. However, when the Food Facility Programme showers the farmers with seeds and fertilisers for two years, agro-ecological production methods are hard to sustain. The farmers may improve their yields thanks to chemical fertiliser for two years, but then have to manage with a lesser crop, a chemical dependency and possibly debt after that. If one looks at how the different methodologies are promoted by the FAO, one also has to look at the relative power and resources that the different initiatives have at their disposal. What are the conditions of possibility and impossibility of the FAO itself? The approach represented by the Food Facility Programme is omnipresent in the ministries and state organisations and can count on the support of the big agro-chemical corporations, which see the millions of small peasants as millions of potential small customers. Agro-ecological production methods only very slowly gain some influence among government extension agents and are mainly promoted by the Campesino a Campesino movement inside the Unión Nacional de Agricultres y Ganaderos (UNAG) and by small development NGOs that can, however, be found all over the country. These methods are work-intensive and their effects are not immediate. They thus require a considerable amount of diligence, care and will to experiment which are hard to reconcile with the short-term programmes that the FAO carries out.

FAO guidelines, programmes and projects directly affect the capacities of local and national actors in Nicaragua to follow their own agendas. When Nicaragua formulated its food sovereignty law the FAO became a potent political actor by proposing internationally agreed voluntary guidelines for a legal blueprint to be used by the Liberal Party in order to weaken the legal frame that the Nicaragua parliament had elaborated to secure national food sovereignty. The FAO's claim to moral and technical superiority was thus used to protect the political agenda of liberalism (free trade, no grain stocks, introduction of patented transgenic varieties). On the local level, the FAO had to rely on existing governance structures, but nevertheless assumed an organisational void and a need to 'empower'. The FAO did not work through elected local community representatives; rather, they selected promoters and coordinators whose legitimacy came from the programme and the funds it distributed and who, arguably, the organisation could more easily control. The two programmes I observed in action thus had a divisive rather than an integrative effect on local self-governance.

The FAO claims not to take sides in the global agricultural policy debate between agro-ecology and Green Revolution. On the local level, however, it tends to simplify the challenges faced by farmers as they try to adapt their agricultural practices to population growth, erosion, variety loss, climate change, and dwindling fossil resources. The FAO continues to promote as a 'one size fits all' remedy the use of agro-chemicals and an extremely narrow range of Green Revolution varieties. The two programmes distributed the same variety of maize and the same variety of beans in la Quebrada in the south of Nicaragua and in el Guanacaste in the north, in spite of the fact that participatory breeding programmes now exist in Nicaragua that develop and improve traditional population varieties adapted to different local conditions without reducing their genetic diversity (Almekinders 2011). What is presented as 'lived experience' and 'best practice' on websites and in promotional films is obviously a simplification. It does not show the real achievements in practices of soil conservation, the renewed interest in traditional fruit and vegetable varieties, and the collective effort to produce compost. Instead it presents a utopian fast track and neoliberal success story that makes believe that it is possible to evolve from hunger and malnutrition to market production of vegetables grown in lorry tyres in only two years. What the films don't show are the controversies among those farmers who count on external financial resources, mostly obtained from migrant work, in order to pay for herbicides and fertilisers and those who count as much as possible on local resources and invest their work in agro-ecological production methods. These controversies are global ones and the political and economic interests and power relations underlying them need to be openly voiced, and be acknowledged from the local to the global level. Friction and conflicting interests exist in all polities. The problem arises when they are glossed over, presented as a homogeneous worldview or a technical problem. On the global level, the recent reform (2009) of the FAO Committee for Food Security, which opened up its political arena to the critical and informed input of civil society organisations active on the local and national levels is an important step in breaking the cunning rule of harmony.

NOTES

1. See: http://legislacion.asamblea.gob.ni/Diariodebate.nsf/1e91f0054ac77a850 62572e50067fde4/a6843a78d5801a25062576b00070e67a?OpenDocument (consulted 13 November 2012).
2. Ley de soberanía y seguridad alimentaria y nutricional, Dictamen 5.10.2006, Managua: Nicaragua. Available at: http://legislacion.asamblea.gob.ni/sileg/ iniciativas.nsf/01c00d5076037b5b062572d00072bee8/caf29f2bb00d13dd 06256886005796dc?OpenDocument&ExpandSection=3&TableRow=3.1 (accessed 9 April 2013).
3. See, for example, the controversies around food aid to Zimbabwe and Zambia.
4. See: http://nicaraguaymasespanol.blogspot.fr/2012/02/transgenicos-ya-entraron-nicaragua.html
5. Ley 705: Ley Sobre Prevención de Riesgos Provenientes de Organismos Vivos Modificados por Medio de Biotecnología Molecular, 2012.
6. The Guatemalan law on food security was designed jointly by the government, civil society and the UN in 2005.
7. The FAO commended the Nicaraguan National Assembly on 27 October 2009 for passing the food security and sovereignty law. The commendation was given during a special session of the Assembly on World Food Day. The FAO representative thanked the delegates for passing the law which, according to National Assembly President, had been before the body for two years. A cooperation accord between the FAO and Nicaragua was signed following the session. See: http://www.nicanet.org/?p=857 (consulted 13November 2012).
8. Shalini Randeria calls it the 'cunning state'.
9. With the Productive Food Programme (Programa Productivo Alimentario), initiated in June 2007, the new Sandinista government provided thousands of smallholder families with productive assets, a favour it could hope they would reciprocate by voting for them in the next election.
10. Interview with the FAO programme director, November 2009.
11. The members of this cooperative were: the richest farmer in the village, his wife who worked in Costa Rica, his mother and his son, a female farmer and her son, the head of the village council and his son, the head of the village council of a neighboring village and the son of a rather wealthy landowner in another village.
12. One Nicaraguan quintal is the equivalent of 46 kg.
13. The CPC (Consejo Popular Comunitario) was introduced by the new Sandinista government and had nine elected members who fulfilled various functions in the community being responsible for health, young people, education, water, etc.
14. The exchange rate is 20 cordobas to US$1.
15. This would have been worth 4,000 cordobas on the open market.
16. I was unable to find out at what price the deal was concluded.
17. See: http://www.pesacentroamerica.org/pesa_ca/que_es.php (consulted 24 May 2012).

BIBLIOGRAPHY

Adam, Barbara (1998) *Timescapes of Modernity* (London: Routledge).

Almekinders, Conny (2011) 'The joint development of JM-12,7: A technographic description of a bean variety', *NJAS Wageningen Journal of Life Sciences* 57: 3–4.

Anders, Gerhard (2005) 'Good governance as technology: Toward an ethnography of the Bretton Woods institutions', in David Mosse and David Lewis (eds) *The Aid Effect* (London: Pluto Press).

Crewe, Emma and Elizabeth Harrison (1998) *Whose Development? An Ethnography of Aid* (London: Zed Books).

de Certeau, Michel (1990) *L'Invention du quotidien*, vol. I, *Arts de faire* (Paris: Gallimard).

FAO (2005) *The Right to Food: Voluntary Guidelines to Support the Progressive Realization of the Right to Adequate Food in the Context of National Food Security* (Rome: FAO).

Foucault, Michel (1975) *Surveiller et punir: naissance de la prison* (Paris: Gallimard).

Foucault, Michel (1994 [1977]) 'Le jeu de Michel Foucault', in *Dits et écrits*, vol. 2, pp. 298–329 (Paris: Gallimard).

Gupta, Akhil (1998) *Postcolonial Development: Agriculture in the Making of Modern India* (Durham, NC: Duke University Press).

Holt-Giménez, Eric (2006) *Campesino a Campesino: Voices from Latin America's Farmer to Farmer Movement for Sustainable Agriculture* (New York: Perseus/Food First Books).

Ilcan, Susan and Lynne Phillips (2003) 'Making food count: The global governance of food and expert knowledge', *Canadian Review of Sociology and Anthropology* 40(4): 441–461.

Larsen, Peter Bille (2013) 'Guidance culture and the politics of technicality in environmental governance', in Birgit Müller (ed.) *The Gloss of Harmony: The Politics of Policy Making in Multilateral Organisations* (London: Pluto Press).

Li, Tania Murray (2007) *The Will to Improve: Governmentality, Development and the Practice of Politics* (Durham, NC: Duke University Press).

McIntyre, Beverly D. (ed.) *IAASTD (International Assessment of Agricultural Knowledge, Science and Technology for Development) Global Report* (Washington, DC: Island Press).

McKeon, Nora (2009) *The United Nations and Civil Society: Legitimating Global Governance – Whose Voice?* (London: Zed Books).

Mosse, David (2005) *Cultivating Development: An Ethnography of Aid Policy and Practice* (London: Pluto Press).

Müller, Birgit (2010) '*Favores, ayuda y robo*: Views of continuity in systemic change in Nicaragua', *Anthropologica* 52(2): 259–272.

Müller, Birgit (2011) 'The elephant in the room: Multi-stakeholder dialogue on agricultural biotechnology in the Food and Agriculture Organization', in Davide Però, Cris Shore and Sue Wright (eds) *Policy Worlds: Anthropology and the Anatomy of Contemporary Power* (Oxford: Berghahn).

Pachauri, Rajendra K. and Andy Reisinger (eds) (2007) *Climate Change 2007: Synthesis Report. Contribution of Working Groups I, II and III to the Fourth Assessment Report of the Intergovernmental Panel on Climate Change* (Geneva: IPCC).

Trucchi, Giorgio (2007) 'Nicaragua: La soberania alimentaria es una definición política estrategica, y no une especulación tecnocrática', *ecoportal*, available at: http://www.ecoportal.net/content/view/full/74237 (consulted 13 November 2012).

10
Nature for Money
The Configuration of Transnational Institutional Space for Environmental Governance

Kenneth Iain MacDonald

Shaheen raised his hand and pointed across the river valley. 'Look ... there ... ibex – a small group.' We were high up in a glaciated valley, just a few hundred metres below a towering tongue of ice. I squinted and looked across the river valley. I couldn't see anything that looked like a mountain goat. Shaheen pointed again and tried to verbally guide my eyes to the right spot. All I saw were a few grey rocks against the bleak grey-brown scrub covered slope. And then, no bigger than an ant on the horizon, one of the grey rocks moved. It was no more than a flicker, but it moved. Shaheen sat for an hour watching them graze. He took in the surroundings, calculated their movements and planned the following day's hunt. Six days after leaving the village, we returned with an ibex – and the ritual sharing of meat began. The ibex is loaded with cultural significance for peoples in northern Pakistan (MacDonald 2004). As the spirit of fertility in the former animist belief system, it retains a symbolic potency in these agro-pastoral societies. One manifestation of this potency lies in the offerings of meat given by the hunters to figures of authority in the village and poorer households as an expression of commitment to the social reproduction of the village polity. This is one among a number of practices that define socio-natural relations in northern Pakistan. It is also a practice that defines Shaheen.

A number of years later during a break in a meeting of the Working Group on Access and Benefit Sharing, a body of the Convention on Biological Diversity (CBD), I spoke with Salim a negotiator for Pakistan, about the sustainable use initiatives designed to restrict ibex hunting in northern Pakistan, Rather than demonstrating any familiarity with the sites affected by his work, he was more familiar with the institutional spaces of the CBD, and the cities around the globe they periodically occupy. Even as the text he inserted into the Convention and his work in shaping the decisions of the Convention and its programme of work had a substantive potential to affect peoples' lives by seeking to reconfigure their understanding of biodiversity, restructuring access and use rights, or redefining their historical use of biodiversity as criminal; Salim and his ilk were not only physically, but ideologically and subjectively, distanced from these places and the effects of their work and what it is to engage with 'nature' in those places – the meaning of a particular species, the affective dimensions of holding centuries of accumulated knowledge of a species or an ecosystem, the idea of an 'ecosystem' as a productive landscape.

Indeed, the work of Salim is not in any affective, or physical way engaged with people like Shaheen and the spaces they inhabit. Even as he claims to represent them, he is not accountable to them; he does not travel into their communities to tell them about the intent of the CBD, its programme of work, or even of its existence. And yet, his ideas, his knowledge, his hopes, aspirations, desires and frustrations, and those of thousands of others like him have been brought into relation, and at least partially shaped by, the existence of the CBD. Even as Salim and Shaheen are unknown to each other, they are bound together through the nexus of interests that have sought to define and address 'global environmental problems' through the institutionalised context of statist mechanisms like the CBD.

Over the past three decades the institutional and organisational environments in which biodiversity conservation is imagined, planned and practised have grown significantly and become increasingly integrated. The CBD has effectively brought into being a new locus around which new power relations and scales of governing nature have been reconfigured. In doing so it has also served to entrench state sovereignty over nature (Corson 2010; MacDonald 2010a). As the CBD has become a source of material support and legitimacy for conservation organisations, it has also created an incentive for conservation organisations to align their activities with the interests of parties to the CBD and the programme of work developed through the Convention; and to articulate their practices and objectives with those of the CBD.

In this chapter I link the translocal spaces and actors involved in a seemingly simple conservation project in northern Pakistan to stress that a focus on the scalar dimensions of power relations is integral to understanding the role of agency in the ideological production of nature and the material practices that derive from it. Central to understanding these relations is a process of longitudinal ethnographic research that relies on multi-scaled and multi-sited ethnography (Marcus 1998). As people and environments, localised in space, become increasingly subject to the demands of so-called global organisations, like the International Union for Conservation of Nature (IUCN) and as the practice of these organisations is structured by institutions like the CBD, it becomes necessary to understand a great deal more about the politics, processes and practices that shape the agenda of these institutions. To be focused, this must start from a long-term engagement with communities subject to such institutional processes and work outward to comprehend how the 'globalisation of everyday life' – taken to mean the subjectivities and material effects produced through willing or unwilling participation in ever-expanding socio-spatial relations – in such places is tied to the political discursive resources, social relations and material practices housed in 'global' organisations and institutions (Boli and Thomas 1999). An understanding of this relation demands that an ethnographic lens be turned on these sites and mechanisms (Watts 2001; West 2001). From this position it becomes possible to witness, comprehend and translate the relations and mechanisms that imaginatively bring into being the communities and environments upon which they act. It is through this multi-sited work – the locating of ethnographic practice in the para sites and meta sites[1] of conservation policy, planning and practice – that it becomes possible to situate case study analyses in a fuller understanding of the systemic conditions of biodiversity conservation that increasingly define biodiversity in terms of 'natural capital' and structure conservation practice in terms of the capacity to realise capital gains (Brockington et al. 2008; Buscher et al. 2012; Sullivan in press).

In what follows, I use an example of the interventionist practices of a 'global' conservation organisation – the IUCN – in northern Pakistan to illustrate how the material ecological relations shaped by that intervention are structured in relation to the dynamic history and politics of an institution, the CBD. These practices configure transnational institutional space, but they also reflect how diverse interests in nature bring relations and sites of power into being and it is, I think, these relations and sites that must be identified, accessed and studied *in relation* to better understand how the contemporary ideological production of nature and possibilities of intervention are bound to a simultaneous production of scale. Even though the spaces of the CBD are far removed from those sites in northern Pakistan, their capacity to act across space is a function of how the transnational quality of constructs of 'the environment' and 'global environmental governance' produce ecological relations that are decidedly 'trans-local'.

THE SITE: PRODUCING TRANS-LOCAL ECOLOGIES

The term trans-local implies a relation of scale. By trans-local ecologies I refer to material human–environment relations that emerge through the spatial reach of transnational institutions, organisations and capital into the everyday social and ecological relations of communities previously removed, to varying degrees, from those forces. For something to be trans-local is for an object or set of relations to have moved beyond or transcended boundaries, real or imagined, that define it as local. To some extent, this is an illusion. Few hard and fast boundaries separate one locale from another. Perhaps some of the most durable, however, are social boundaries that delimit who may or may not belong to a community (Barth 2000; Cohen 2000). Though these have, to some extent, become more permeable within the socio-economic relations of late capitalist societies, they still resonate strongly in small-scale agricultural societies around the world where survival continues to depend upon gaining access to resources that exist beyond the reach of state control. Such is the case in northern Pakistan, where I first began thinking about the concept of trans-local ecologies. The Karakoram mountain communities that I have worked in are very much 'local' in the sense that I have outlined above. Membership is typically through marriage or birth and, while infrequent out-migration occurs, in-migration does not. Land throughout the mountain range is strictly delimited as belonging to particular communities, and few non-community members (exceptions include state representatives, local political elites and military personnel) can gain access to 'local' community-controlled resources. Human–environmental relations historically have been beyond the regularised influence of extra-local organisations such as state departments of forestry, wildlife or agriculture. Certainly these relations have been historically structured by institutional concerns – say the need to pay taxes or tribute, or the resource demands of political elites or colonial officials – but direct intervention on the part of these institutional actors was rare and where it did occur was based on exacting what could be claimed out of the productivity of human–environment interactions rather than altering those interactions. Where alteration was attempted (e.g. state sanctions on subsistence hunting) these were, more often than not, ignored locally as the reach of state surveillance did not breach the social boundaries of 'the village'. These same communities, however, have long been trans-local in a number of ways. For over a century they have supplied porter labour for mountaineering expeditions, and have come to acquire significance within the global mountaineering and mountain tourism 'community' as that 'community' has invested stakes of identity and capital in 'conquering' high peaks (MacDonald 1998). This significance and the interaction it entails impact localised ecological relations in a number of ways, but again this is indirect and unplanned 'intervention'. More recently, however, localised environmental knowledge and practice have become the object of action for transnational development and conservation organisations, which explicitly strive to alter them in ways that satisfy institutional agendas. Particular among these actors are IUCN and the World Wide Fund for Nature (WWF).

Hushe, a small community of about 100 households at the head of one of the outermost valleys of mountainous northeast Pakistan, is one site where the 'global' reach of these organisations and their objectives is made apparent through their project-based interventions. As part of an agro-pastoral society Hushe controls access to lands and resources in much of the uninhabited regions that extend northeast from the village toward the Chinese and Indian borders. In 1994, IUCN approached leaders in Hushe with a plan meant to conserve the officially endangered stock of Himalayan Ibex (*capra ibex sibirica*), a wild mountain goat that is native to the region. The plan, in line with the market ideology of many contemporary conservation initiatives, was essentially a 'cash for wildlife' swap. Based on ill-grounded assumptions that village-based hunting was responsible for an assumed but undemonstrated decline in ibex numbers, IUCN offered to generate cash for the village by selling a limited number of hunting permits to foreign hunters in exchange for an agreement from village leaders that villagers would discontinue hunting ibex for subsistence purposes. The project, accepted by village leaders, carried with it a number of unexpected, or at least unstated, outcomes. The effective capitalisation of ibex set in motion a new shift in the localised meaning of 'nature' (MacDonald 2004). It redefined what had been an important symbolic and social activity (hunting) into, at least on the part of some proponents of the project, a crime against the community rather than the state. It also inserted tensions within an admittedly fragmenting social structure; allowed some villagers – those with access to capital resources – to capture and distribute the benefits of the project in particularised ways; strained long-standing reciprocal relations between Hushe and neighbouring villages; and created the incentive for directing changes in ecological practice that would encourage the containment of what is essentially a fugitive resource, ibex (MacDonald 2005).

While these localised outcomes can partially be explained through an absence of careful social and ecological research by the institutional and organisational proponents of the project, much more of the explanation can be read through the texts of project documents that, at least superficially, provide insight into the conceptual apparatus used in project formulation. Read as a map of social relations and the ideological representations that influence them, the project proposal navigates away from the particularised and localised context of Hushe to include actors drawn together as part of a wider $6 million Global Environment Facility (GEF) initiative entitled 'Maintaining Biodiversity in Pakistan with Rural Development'. This initiative provided the impetus for the project in Hushe and linked the government of Pakistan with three transnational non-governmental organisations (NGOs) – the GEF, the United Nations Development Programme (UNDP), and the implementing agency, the IUCN (Ahmed and Hussain 1998; Government of Pakistan n.d.).

THE PARA-SITE: BIODIVERSITY, ORGANIZATIONS AND THE PRODUCTION OF SCALE

The goal of biodiversity protection and the role of the IUCN – 'the world's oldest and largest global conservation body' – rely on an appeal to a global image of an interconnected web of life. It is this appeal, and the assertion that transnational organisations know best how to coordinate responses to an environment understood as such, that are used to claim wildlife, like the Himalayan Ibex, as global property and increasingly subject their protection to market devices. In effect, it is the appeal to the 'global' significance of individual species and localised environments that is used to deterritorialise those species and their habitats from their historical interaction with human communities (Jamison 1996). It is also this appeal that legitimates the intervention of transnational conservation organisations that set about restructuring human–environment relations and reterritorialising them in modified, but 'planned', forms (Luke 1999).

In the case of environmental decision-making, including 'policy-making', 'planning' and implementation, a realm or regime of distanced practice has developed over the past 150 or so years emerging out of colonial-era administrations or private elite organisations which have subsequently evolved into contemporary transnational environmental organisations (Adams 2004; Goldman 2003, 2005; Vogler 2003; Young 1994). The ability of organisations to exercise this spatial and governmental 'sphere of authority' has much to do with the rise of environmentalism as a political force over the same time period. However, as the emergence of the field of environmental (in)justice has taught us, a concern with the environmental consequences of action has never been divorced from the subject positionality of those acting. Value judgements regarding the knowledge and capacity of actors have always factored into considerations of the source and significance of environmental impact.[2]

Certainly in the case of Hushe, the representation of an incapable local population is used to try to legitimate the intervention of the IUCN, an organisation that effectively uses a discourse of global ecology to accumulate political authority within the network of state and trans-state actors and institutions that constitute 'global environmental governance' (Flitner 1999; MacDonald 2003, 2010a). But, at root, access to Hushe is structured through inequity: a desire on the part of at least some villagers for cash to satisfy the wish for the long-promised benefits of 'development', and the ability of the organisation to provide access to this cash. Absent this leverage of 'booty', it is unclear how intervention would have been facilitated in Hushe. Similar relations of inequity can be seen to facilitate state sanction of IUCN activities. Given that the government of Pakistan assumes sovereign jurisdiction over all environmental resources contained within its borders, the IUCN cannot operate in Pakistan without the sanction of the state. But in many cases the government is pleased to have the IUCN assume responsibility for implementing environmental programmes. Indeed, the *Pakistan National Conservation Policy*, a document that guides internal environmental research and policy formation, was written largely by representatives of, or consultants hired, by the IUCN, WWF and the Canadian International Development Agency (CIDA) (Government of Pakistan and IUCN – The World Conservation Union 1992). Some of the reasons for this willingness to cede authority are fairly straightforward. It allows a fiscally beleaguered state to shift a financial burden onto an NGO, which in turn contributes to its ability, for example, to meet the public spending reduction demands of International Monetary Fund dictates and help satisfy the cost of debt servicing, or devote fiscal resources to more immediate concerns of the state (see Steinberg 2003). All of this can be accomplished without ceding the legal authority to curtail NGO activities where they are seen to contradict or conflict with state interests.

NGOs, however, do not have the fiscal resources that governments command and need to develop not only dependable sources of funding but also cross-sector legitimacy to take on work that was historically the province of the state. And it has become increasingly clear that both of these needs came to be satisfied through a gradual embrace of the commodification of nature under neoliberalism (Buscher et al. 2012; MacDonald 2010a). Organisations sought to develop modes through which biodiversity could pay for its own salvation by extending the mechanisms through which nature could be 'conceived in the image of capital' into new spaces, and used this representation as the basis for the rational management of 'nature as capital' (Coronil 2000; O'Connor 1994: 131). In need of the funds that were increasingly channelled through an institutional structure in accord with neoliberalism, including the CBD, conservation organisations pursued projects that openly made conservation an instrument for the accumulation of capital and a vehicle through which capital interests could gain access to sites of 'nature as capital'. This typically occurred with the full support of relevant governments as they derived a share of revenue from what came to be known as 'market-based' incentive projects. With GEF and UNDP support, these projects quickly gained ground in the 1990s and trophy hunting, bioprospecting and ecotourism became the manifestation of a commoditised nature reoriented to serve elite and corporate interests but that would, under the rhetoric of 'community-based conservation' also provide a 'profit' for local communities (Hayden 2003; McAfee 1999; MacDonald 2004). The IUCN, then, developed as an organisation as it effectively pushed for an acceptance of the legitimacy of supra-national institutions in dealing with problems constructed as 'global' and has extended its spatial reach accordingly. Its ability to do this has been strategically facilitated by association with other transnational or supranational institutions such as the United Nations Environment Programme (UNEP), UNDP, the Global Environment Facility and the Secretariat for the CBD among others (MacDonald 2010a).

Through this alignment with dominant institutional actors, the IUCN, as an implementing agency, has become what Rosen (2000) calls a centre of calculation and accumulation – terms he uses to describe organisations, not simply as hierarchies but as sites (often multiple sites) where selective knowledge is accumulated and action designed. From these sites knowledge and action flow to distant places.[3] This flow, while not necessarily unidirectional or dominating as some, like Escobar (1995) or Smith (2005), assert, demands a response from those distant places. We can imagine this response as taking different forms. Individuals or social groups may resist categorisation; they may accommodate, but manipulate, assigned labels (Butz 2002; Carrier and West 2009). But the demand is persistent – to rationalise and then modify situated knowledge or practice within ideological boundaries of understanding subscribed to by transnational organisations like the IUCN. This organisational demand, and the localised responses it generates, delineate a network of relations that stretch across space to connect distant organisations and their ideational underpinnings with localised and particularised social and ecological communities. Based on regular longitudinal fieldwork, it is fairly straightforward to map these power relations.

At the outset of the Hushe project, the IUCN had already established a country office in Pakistan and was in the midst of establishing regional offices in the north of the country. In 1994, I was invited to a workshop to begin structuring a nomination of the Central Karakoram mountain range as a World Natural Heritage site (MacDonald 1995). Representatives from the IUCN were present because of their advisory role in the World Heritage Convention.[4] Notably, except for me, none of the people present at the meeting had been in the area they were proposing for World Heritage Site status. But prior to the meeting, on what he called 'a whim', the IUCN advisor took a side trip to Hushe, which bordered the proposed World Heritage Site. Thinking of possible development benefits that could be associated with World Heritage status he designated it as an appropriate project site and established contact with influential men in the village. Simultaneously contact was made with government officials in the district headquarters. Moving away from the village and into the main administrative centre of Skardu, an increasing number of actors entered the picture: connections were established between IUCN staff and local political elites. In this relationship, local IUCN staffs were relatively powerless in relation to political elites (e.g. vulnerable to bureaucratic stalling, or sanctions on their activities based on differing interpretations of cultural appropriateness). They also found themselves tied in to relations with more senior IUCN staff from the major offices in Islamabad and Karachi and with foreign consultants who had direct connections to major donors. To some extent, these sites of interface, sites where knowledge and action – as they flow from the centre of the organisation outward – can be translated or ideologically delimited, are observable, depending, of course, on issues of access. But moving away from the ostensible site of the project, the subject of observation becomes increasingly nebulous and difficult to bring into focus. This is where the invisibility of rule begins to take shape, not simply for observers, but also for people – mostly villagers – whose horizon of understanding is delimited by more circumscribed webs of power. The connections go on, of course, but it is not so easy to observe and map out power relations as 'the village' is brought into relation with the multiple sites of the organisation(s) and institutions responsible for conceiving and implementing the project.

The connections that I have sketched above express the physical and social distance between actors, but each set of actors exists similarly in locales that can be studied much as we study 'the community'. If I were to work only from within a village like Hushe, I could only guess at the broader context within which an organisation like the IUCN operates, and hence the network of actors and institutions in which they invisibly situate villages like Hushe; networks that include the CBD, GEF and other actors engaged in promoting a market orientation within organised biodiversity conservation (MacDonald 2010b). From this standpoint, understanding the ramifications of organisational intervention stops at a particular point – generally the borders of the village, perhaps extending to the regional market town. But when we realise that those borders are porous, that situated individuals are connected to others across much greater reaches of time and space, the borders of the village (or the ecosystem for that matter) as the bounds of study become less helpful in understanding how local material ecological relations are increasingly shaped by agendas formed at a significant spatial and ideological distance (Campbell 2007; Giddens 1990; Rankin 2003; Sundberg 1998).

It is important in addressing the connections involved in modifying localised human–environmental practice to understand how organisational actors engage in the production of scale and appeal to the authority of acting in the 'global' interest as a means of gaining access to particularised spaces. If we accept Rosen's definition of organisations as instruments for the attainment of goals and instruments of power underlain and mediated by cultural and ideational processes, we can begin to appreciate how the concept of scale is both an instrument in that accumulation and a basis for the formulation and attainment of goals (Jones 1998; McCarthy 2005; Smith 1992). Bruno Latour's (1987, 1999) work offers insights into understanding the effects of producing scale. These centre mostly on mechanisms of abstraction and representation used by organisational actors and the ways in which these mechanisms, derived from disciplinary knowledge, provide the possibility for re-definition and degrees of certainty. In addressing questions of scale, Latour implicitly asks what it is that allows the passage from conditions of ignorance to certainty among organisational actors. He locates one answer in the capacity of organisational actors to reference pre-existing modes of abstracting and categorising knowledge, what others might call labelling practices. In relation to the project I am dealing with in Pakistan, for example, it is clear that the IUCN has a categorical 'map' that guides their passage from ignorance to certainty in understanding the 'place' they will work upon. This is revealed in part through the apparent absence of the need to conduct local research prior to project formulation or the development of goals.[5] Some of this 'absence' can be ascribed to the simple capacity of the organisation to intervene based on a history of privileged position, and often backed by the coercive power of the state. More significant, though, is their subscription to a set of ontological objects that are taken to be universal and thus not open to question (e.g. biodiversity, ecology, wildlife, community). These serve as uniform and universal labels for the organisation of information and provide a frame of certainty that allows organisations like the IUCN to design interventions with a minimum of investment in grounded research. But in doing so, often for reasons of administrative expediency, transnational organisations tend to annihilate context. 'Community', for example, a categorical object common to many 'conservation-as-development' projects, is typically treated as a monolithic entity with little attention paid to the very real tensions and divergent interests that operate to structure proximal social relations in particular ways (Brosius et al. 1998; MacDonald 2001). The organisational perspective on community, however, is delimited by the institutional agendas reflected in project goals or objectives, formed at a distance from the communities to be affected by those goals. Project documents certainly represent the village under consideration, but they do so selectively. Only those objects of concern that are of interest to the organisational actor (according to their pre-set filters) make it into policy, project documents and implementation plans. This process of selectivity is directly related to an engagement in institutional tasks that are deeply embedded in scales of knowledge production and consequent action.

This spatial and social distance from their sites of intervention is characteristic of many transnational organisations, but this is not an accidental gap. Rather, 'distance' from the people and places directly affected by those interventions, or what is often benignly labelled as an 'objective perspective', Latour reminds us, allows the operation of a unifying 'gaze' which, rather than recognise distinct qualities of discrete sites through research or enquiry, constructs those sites by equating them with other sites in the organisational archive. And it is this facility for consultation, comparison and the construction of unity and conformity under a single organisational gaze that facilitates the emerging prevalence of dominating notions such as 'best practice' or 'capacity-building' – the application of a managerial logic that annihilates context. In the act of comparison, the observer/practitioner can disassemble the elements of observations made in a particular locale – 'the facts' – and reassemble them in ways that align with the categorical 'boxes' related to the epistemological domains of the organisation. They can turn interpretations into facts through a process of vetting and categorising. Ibex in the mountains surrounding Hushe, for example, become removed from a historical context that has 'governed' their human interaction and assume meaning structured by the epistemological metrics of taxonomic science, wildlife ecology and conservation biology. More importantly, they assume significance in relation to the mandate of a transnational institution and the objectives of organisations that secure funding and institutional legitimacy by aligning with that mandate. All of this amounts to what Latour (1999) calls oversight – which he defines as domination by sight – at once looking at things from above and selectively accommodating or ignoring elements of what is observed. The capacity for oversight, of course, implies the ability to 'look' from a distance that allows the observer to take in a wide view.

Under such a gaze, as 'integrated conservation and development' projects are imagined into being and implemented, situated communities often find themselves and their ecological practices detached, separated, preserved (if we take preservation to imply an interpreted condition of stasis), classified and tagged (for certain ends) by organisational practices. They are represented in terms of their relevance to criteria set by the organisation and subsequently classified as a particular type of community relative to the goals of the project (Li 2007; West 2006). People and the situated environments that surround them are described and re-assembled in organisational reports, and in the imagination of those who produce and consume those texts, according to the principles and goals of the observer/practitioner and the organisation they represent And just as two-dimensional representations of place sacrifice detail for area, so too are the details of 'community' sacrificed in processes of abstraction that allow comparability between communities and facilitate the application of a managerial logic.

In this move – this abstraction – organisational actors are not simply abstracting from the materiality of community to produce a representation of community, they are replacing a complex dynamic entity composed of continuous and multiple socio-ecological interactions with few definitive boundaries (i.e. a community as it exists) with a discrete unity locatable in space through x/y coordinates, and represented by fixed boundaries (i.e. a geographical community created for the purposes of interventions like the project described here). Here then, an inequitable relation which is temporally liminal and spatially marginal (i.e. the relation between organisational actors operating in centres of accumulation and calculation, and villagers) strips 'community' of context and creates a homogeneity in which individuals are conceptually removed from a social structure which is unseen or ignored by those intervening in it and inserts them en masse into a new social structure created out of the organisation's cognitive resources, which include historical, ideological representations of people and place that position local actors as incapable of effectively managing their surroundings (including wildlife) and situating them both as the source of an ecological 'problem', and, with appropriate alterations in local ideologies of nature, elements of the 'solution' (MacDonald 2005; cf. Agrawal 2005; Rosen 1991). This is neatly phrased in the proposal to the project described above:

> Government agencies have a very limited capacity to enforce wildlife laws, making it virtually impossible to control rural people's use of wild resources – especially when they need these resources to meet their subsistence requirements. The problem will become more acute with increasing human population if mechanisms are not provided for rural people to acquire the

technical skills to manage wild resources. An alternative approach
is needed that involves rural people in the solution rather than
considering them the cause. (Government of Pakistan n.d.: 23)

My point here is that organisations like the IUCN not only engage
in processes of abstraction to legitimate intervention (i.e. distant
organisations act on localised environments), but that in doing so
they actively work to create the 'realities' they claim only to describe.
In the case of organisations that position and represent themselves
as 'global', the political force of an ontology of scale works to create
the institutional 'realities' it claims only to describe (Kelly, 1999),
providing them with the capacity and the authority to act 'globally'
on 'local' spaces. It is this increasing ability to act from a distance
that highlights the importance of studying organisations as they
produce the networks of interactions – the spaces of engagement
(Cox 1998) – that allow them to operate trans-locally. As these
transnational organisations use inequity and the emergence of
globalising discourses to help them represent and gain access
to 'localised' environments, and as they strive to implement
normative, standardised practice, an appreciation of context, in
all its complexity, is increasingly deemed irrelevant at best and
as an obstruction at worst.[6] In the case of the Hushe project, for
example, no research had been done on hunting patterns or on the
demographics or population dynamics of ibex, and the proponents
had no knowledge of the social structure, social organisation or
cosmology of the community. It did not matter that they could
not use evidence to demonstrate that there was, in fact, a problem
to be addressed. The point of the proposal was not to address a
problem. The problem was presumed in the existence of the GEF
programme for funding. The point of the proposal was to 'frame'
reality – to define a problem that would satisfy the objectives of
the GEF programme and secure funding (and legitimacy) for the
IUCN. Through this framing, the project in practice reflected an
exercise in making actors in northern Pakistan confirm with IUCN
objectives structured through the CBD programme of work and the
directives of its funding mechanism, the GEF. It is this process of
alignment and articulation that highlights the importance of turning
the observational lens to the meta-site.

THE META-SITE: ALIGNMENT AND ARTICULATION

While ethnographic methods have been used to highlight the
mechanisms through which localised ecologies become subject to

global environmental governance, there is less understanding of how this occurs through the standard operating mechanisms of organisations and institutions involved in the field of environment and development. Certainly village-level ethnographic case studies can reveal the unfolding of conservation projects in and across communities, the impact on ecological dynamics and social relations, and the ways in which villagers negotiated the tensions produced by these projects. And textual analysis of project documents can highlight how ontological concepts such as wildlife, ecology and community are adopted and used rhetorically to legitimate certain practices of intervention. But the insights developed through these approaches do little to help understand the organisational processes that bring these projects into being, the knowledge upon which they are based, the everyday processes and interactions through which projects are developed, the ideological and material pressures that act upon the organisations and encourage their alignment with institutional configurations of power, and the ways in which these alignments produce new bases for justifying organisational actions and interventions.

To understand these relations and how localised communities are linked to distant institutional objectives, there is a need to observe and assess how institutions draw actors into new configurations of power and produce social relations that structure acts of alignment and articulation used to legitimate interventions. In particular, there is a need to uncover the structure, philosophies and practices of organisations; how operational concepts like biodiversity, conservation and development are conceptualised by organisational actors; how specific communities, as the targets of projects, are conceptualised within organisations; but, more importantly, how actors within organisations become ontologically complicit with the knowledge categories of the institutional field (e.g. the field configured by actors and interests associated with the CBD) that structures and provides the material resources and legitimacy needed to support the organisation's existence.

In the case of the project I've described in this chapter, for example, it is now clear from statements in the proposal, conversations with those who devised the project, and being able to track IUCN staff as they travel to policy setting venues, that the IUCN was aligning with the objectives of the CBD and seeking to produce projects that would articulate the organisation with a new source of institutional legitimacy and material resources. Indeed, the CBD, with a great deal of input from the IUCN, emerged from the 1992

Earth Summit with the sustainable use of biodiversity as one of its 'pillars'. By 1995 the parties had introduced sustainable use initiatives into the programme of work, which provides direction to GEF funding programmes. But it is significant that this only became clear after I had written and shared my analysis of the project with others and found that what I had observed in northern Pakistan was being repeated under the guise of Integrated Conservation and Development Programmes and sustainable use initiatives around the world. Clarity could only come after I began to ask a different set of questions that revolved around the interests and forms of knowledge translation responsible for mobilising projects like the one I had witnessed in Hushe, and situated myself in different 'field sites'. The first of these sites was the organisation. In turning the ethnographic lens on the organisation – the para-site – rather than the village, I gained access to a number of venues through which I could observe the ways in which organisational dynamics shifted within the IUCN. Observations during meetings, interviews with current and former staff, tracking actors and interests as they emerged within the organisation, all provided opportunities to identify how particular forms of knowledge were translated and gained legitimacy and traction, and the mechanisms through which particular interests were able to secure organisational privilege. What became clear during that time was the degree to which a conflation of nature and capital – apparent in the speed and ease with which the rhetoric of natural capital was adopted – established itself as a dominant view within the IUCN. Other signs include the organisational effort which the IUCN put into the development of new forms of coordinated production and investment that promote programmes to create markets for ecosystem services, venture capital programmes designed to facilitate the growth of small biodiversity businesses and offset programs to compensate for concentrated biodiversity impacts, among other initiatives. These shifts stem from an acceptance of eco-modernist equations of sustainable development with continued expansion in economic productivity, a recognition of the threat that environmental degradation poses to conventional modes of production, and a belief that imagining into being new markets and opportunities for accumulation is the basis for addressing these problems (MacDonald 2003, 2010a). It also became clear that these shifts were happening as the IUCN was drawn into a new configuration of power relations brought into being by the CBD.

There is a dry history of the CBD, the rehearsal of facts and figures. It goes like this. An outcome of the 1992 United Nations (UN) Earth Summit, the CBD entered into force in 1993 and has 191 party members. At its biennial Conference of the Parties (COP), these parties come together to review progress, identify priorities and establish work plans, as well as provide direction to the GEF, which is the financial mechanism of the CBD, and the Subsidiary Body on Scientific, Technical and Technological Advice, which provides scientific advice to the CBD. COP meetings encompass the formal plenary; two main working groups in which delegations state their positions on various decisions before the COP; break-out groups of smaller contact groups or friends-of-the-chair sessions, in which selected delegations negotiate specific text for presentation to the working groups; 'side events', or topical workshops, often organised by NGOs and intergovernmental organisations; press briefings; and high-level, closed-door meetings, open primarily to parties.

But there is a more dynamic history of the CBD. The CBD is not a monolithic institution. Rather, the 'lived reality' of the CBD is defined by a shifting network of relationships, imbued with continually changing power dynamics among parties, NGOs, intergovernmental organisations, representatives of indigenous and local communities and associated advocacy organisations, corporate representatives, trade associations, lobbyists, scientists and others (MacDonald 2010a). Even as relations among these actors are continually changing, these relations exist largely because the CBD represents an intensive institutionalisation of conservation practice and policy that was absent prior to 1992. While conservation organisations have always been articulated with institutions, the structure of the institutions of environmental governance that emerged out of the 1992 UN Conference on Environment and Development consolidated state authority, redirecting state and donor resources away from multilateral relations with conservation organisations and aligning them with the CDB programme of work and the funding of that programme through the GEF. This consolidation of state authority under the guise of internationalism reconfigured power relations within the field of biodiversity conservation, effectively prioritising state sovereignty and drawing actors into relations structured around and within the mechanisms of the CBD (MacDonald 2010a). The CBD effectively reconfigured the funding landscape of biodiversity conservation. Building on the neoliberal-inspired cutbacks to environmental funding that led to intensified relations between conservation organisations and the private sector (Brechin 2009; MacDonald 2010a) the CBD channelled state resources into the GEF in support of the CBD programme of work, which is defined by state parties to the Convention. The CBD then has the capacity to both direct material resources of its state members to organisations and provide a 'stamp' of legitimacy for organisations that align and articulate with that programme of work (Corson and MacDonald 2012; MacDonald 2010a). Accordingly, organisations reshape their conservation planning and practice to align with the decisions of the parties, the directives of the programme of work and the allocation of funding through the GEF. In doing so, they respond to or draw upon dominant ideologies within the CBD, and contribute to their hegemony.

This move signifies that the organisational constraints around a new institutional environment involve not only a concern with continuing access, but also the legitimacy needed to continue to secure increasingly important project-based funding. It also indicates that a significant part of gaining this legitimacy includes the willingness and capacity to develop 'working alliances'. In an institutional environment shaped by neoliberalism that increasingly accommodates and privileges the interests of business in pursuing an eco-modernist version of sustainable development, access to the resources allocated through CBD relies on an organisation visibly and legibly aligning its activities, capacities and objectives with the ideological and material interests of the dominant actors within that institutional context. Given these structural parameters, it is not surprising that many of the so-called integrated conservation and development programmes developed during the 1990s focused on the sustainable use of biodiversity and were oriented toward addressing the funding initiatives of GEF/UNDP and not based on empirically informed understandings of grounded problems in sites where they were implemented (MacDonald 2005). This shift in an external environment and the subordinate position of conservation NGOs within that environment helps to explain why 'partnerships' between conservation organisations and corporate actors and the broader involvement of conservation organisations in the promotion of business and biodiversity initiatives are growing so quickly, despite a long history of warranted distance.

These acts of alignment and articulation, however, require their own process of production. This is the importance of treating the CBD ethnographically, as the institution is also constituted by bundles of social relations and power dynamics that produce the mechanisms of the Convention, particularly its mandated meetings, as active political spaces – arenas in which interests may be negotiated and new social relations configured around those negotiations (see Strathern 2000). These arenas can provide creative opportunities for new, and previously excluded, groups to gain access, but they also create a context in which privileged positions and perspectives can be consolidated and codified in ways that structure policy and practice.

The political space of the CBD, for example, has multiple locales. The most obvious are the biannual meetings of the COPs convened by the Secretariat of the CBD, and the interim meetings of a variety of committees and ad hoc working groups that are open not only to CBD signatories but also to a variety of civil society and private sector actors. The COP, however, is much more than simply a meeting of the parties. It is more apt to call it a stage – a space in which the range of interests that constitute a major element of environmental politics today perform and communicate their messages. It regularly convenes a variety of actors – indigenous peoples, individual investors and the representatives of states, private companies and NGOs among others. As it circulates and sanctions representations of nature that render new definitions of biodiversity and its conservation as acceptable and desirable, it also orchestrates a realigning of state, market and civil society actors and becomes a site for the restructuring of international conservation governance so as to enrol conservation in a variety of larger projects from state-building to the expansion of capital accumulation (Corson and MacDonald 2012).

We can think of these institutional spaces as what some management scholars refer to as field-configuring events (Lampel and Meyer 2008): events that temporarily bring actors together and construct arenas for demonstrating, displaying and promoting perspectives, mechanisms, techniques and practices, and provide the institutional context and opportunity to transform contestation into legitimated outcomes,[7] and in so doing, shape disparate organisations and individuals into a 'community' that shares a common meaning system (Scott et al., 2000).

In this context, the ratification of the CBD produced, in effect, not so much an instrument to highlight the problems of biodiversity loss, but a centre of accumulation and allocation that provided institutional spaces and mechanisms within and through which to contest, define, direct and codify the project of biodiversity conservation. It configured power relations around mechanisms for achieving biodiversity conservation; and it provided a new source of organisational legitimation. As a result, if conservation organisations wanted to retain the favour of state actors and secure a share of the diminishing material resources to do their work, they needed to be responsive to, and align with, the decisions of the CBD and the programme directives of its associated financing arm, the GEF. It is this pressure to align and articulate that created the project I initially started studying in northern Pakistan – a project not grounded in any empirical research or demonstrable problem, but created out of an organisational need to align with a new configuration of power brought into being by the CBD. In doing so they also reconfigure, restructure and re-articulate the scale of biodiversity conservation, articulating small villages in the mountains of northern Pakistan with the multiple sites of the CBD and bringing new social relations into being in those villages as the interests shaping the CBD programme of work become expressed through projects like the one I have described here.

CONCLUSION: SHIFTING THE EMPIRICAL LENS

Organisational and institutional ethnography, especially when motivated by a politics of field experience, implies more than simply coming to an understanding of the organisational domain. It implies knowing 'the subject' from a new geographical and epistemological standpoint – that of the distant set of agents that choose to act upon 'the subject'. This reveals a particular view of institutions and organisations as mechanisms through which the dynamic meaning assigned to ideas, values and beliefs is continually brokered (see Goldman 2001, 2005). This is what makes ethnography so suitable for the study of organisations and institutions, for it demands a standpoint from which to see beyond the conventional rationalist understanding of institutions and organisations and to apply a perspective aimed at exploring how the social meaning system of organisational actors is (re)produced (Harper 1998; Hirsch and Gellner 2001; Lewis et al. 2003).

Just as 'field researchers' would attend to who is moving through a village or a neighbourhood, paying attention to who or what is moving through an organisation, where they are from, and the purpose of their visit can provide insight into the wider context in which organisations operate. This relational understanding is significant, for it is this wider context that legitimates the aims organisations pursue and sets limits to the ways in which they operate. It is in this wider context – what has become the institutional and organisational network that constitutes 'global environmental governance' – that we can locate a dialectical relation (among say the IUCN, WWF, UNDP, GEF) oriented toward the production of consent to believe and participate in the 'ecological realities' that are agreed upon by these 'big-picture' players (Rosen 2000). This dialectical relation, and its association with the need for funding, the demands of donors and capitalist markets, political competition for resources, the need to demonstrate results through measurable indices, all influence the ideological and practical orientations of, and tell us much about the functioning of boundaries around and within organisations.[8]

There is an empirical need to appreciate how relations of power configured around institutions like the CBD influence the formation and subsequent development of environmental policy and practice and configure new scales of biodiversity conservation (see MacDonald 2010b). Treating an organisation such as the IUCN and the CBD as a 'community' vested with 'culture' exposes how the privileging of standpoint operates to affect decisions regarding the viability of projects, the validity of information, the priority of relationships and the mechanisms of structuring localised human–environment relations.

My concerns regarding the study of organisations are not new, nor are my thoughts regarding the value of such study. Many of these resemble what Nader (1972) articulated when she called for anthropologists to study the 'culture of power'. By this she meant the ways in which hierarchies that govern our lives remain invisible; how their distancing mechanisms operate; the cultural constraints felt by members of organisations; and the ways in which 'clients' are manipulated. It is here that I think the value of organisational and institutional ethnography lies. It not only allows a critical examination of the institutional configurations of power that coordinate 'local' worlds and practices, but it opens to view discursive configurations that legitimate this coordination, and the mechanisms of alignment and articulation through which it is put into action. More than that, it exposes to view the relations and practices of domination that are central to an explanation of how people – differently positioned – contest the meaning of a situation, and how they use economic and institutional resources to dominate the material outcome of that contest (Asad 1979).[9] It allows an examination of the rationalising practices used by individuals within organisations to legitimate their structures of knowledge, their actions and their favoured mechanisms and metrics, and how those rationalisations can assume authority through processes of institutionalisation. This is fruitful ground for political ecology, for if we recognise that institutional power and agency have a direct effect on the ideological production of nature, on human–environment relations and on ecological 'reality', then we need to understand what shapes the directives flowing out of organisations to bring 'communities' within the sphere of authority of actors that are invisible to them. We need to situate the political ecological context not simply in conventional sites but in the para- and meta-sites of organisations and institutions. If we understand 'ecological reality' to be a product of the interaction across these sites (forced though it often is) surely we need to study dominant 'communities' – organisations like the IUCN and institutions like the CBD – as much and probably more than 'local' communities.

In this sense, then, institutional and organisational ethnography is not so much a study of institutional mechanisms as it is an exploration of the cultural logics that underlie those mechanisms. For underneath the surface of seemingly objective registers of, say, 'sustainability', 'self-reliance' or 'capacity-building' that characterise the kind of project I have described in this chapter, lie meaning-laden concepts, symbols, systems of morality, and practical tasks and techniques oriented to value-based goals that operate to the disadvantage of many of the people they are intended to benefit. And these people, like many villagers in Hushe, who may well be adept at monitoring and negotiating meaning in face-to-face interaction, suffer an erosion of political entitlement when the conceptual and symbolic grounds for interaction are obscured by either the appearance of bureaucratic 'neutrality' and appeals to 'global' significance, or when those grounds retreat behind the walls of organisations like the IUCN or institutions like the CBD that operate at a distance and become simply invisible.

NOTES

1. I use 'para site' to refer to the multiple spaces of organisations like the IUCN that implement conservation projects, whereas 'meta sites' are the institutional mechanisms (like the CBD) in which actors like those organisations are brought into alignment and articulated with dominant ideologies, political projects and interests that structure what constitutes biodiversity and biodiversity conservation at any point in time. There can clearly be an overlap between para and meta sites.
2. It is in these judgements that we can locate much of the current emphasis on knowledge transfer, capacity-building and 'best practice' within environment and development institutions that operate in much of the so-called 'third world'.

3. Using the IUCN as an example, we can consider it to be a site of accumulated knowledge incorporating a diverse subject matter related to issues of conservation. Of course this material is selected and archived according to particular ideologies of environment, nature and conservation, and we must recognise that the IUCN is also subject to the 'authority' of associated institutions and their handlers such as UNDP UNEP, UNESCO, GEF, all of whom Rosen would call 'big-picture' players aimed at achieving and managing consent.

4. This includes evaluating sites nominated for World Heritage Status, monitoring the sate of existing sites, implementing capacity-building initiatives, and providing technical advice to the convention.

5. In the case of IUCN's project in Hushe, for example, no research was undertaken to validate the assumed decline in ibex numbers, no research was undertaken to gain an appreciation of localised social structure or social relations, and no research was undertaken to understand the material and symbolic significance of wildlife within the community.

6. Again, these are goals established by organisations, presumably arising from the need to control and direct efforts in an efficient way and from the demand for standardisation and centralisation that makes results uniformly comprehensible by other participating institutions.

7. For example, the writing of favoured projects like 'The Economics of Ecosystems and Biodiversity' (TEEB) into CBDCOP decisions is a process of institutionalisation that privileges certain perspectives and encourages other actors to articulate themselves with the project due to its sanctioned and legitimating authority.

8. As Raymond Williams (1974) reminds us, cultural forms such as organisations and institutions do not stand alone. They are tools that can be used in a variety of ways. What is important is to understand how and why they are used in particular circumstances as well as to understand who uses them and under what conditions.

9. For an example of such work, see a special issue of Conservation and Society edited by Peter Brosius and Lisa Campbell (2010) describing the outcome of a recent collaborative event ethnography at the 2008 World Conservation Congress. The methodology applied there was refined and applied at the 10th Conference of the Parties to the Convention on Biological Diversity in October, 2010 (see MacDonald and Corson 2012).

BIBLIOGRAPHY

Adams, W.M. (2004) *Against Extinction: The Story of Conservation* (London: Earthscan).

Agrawal, A. (2005) *Environmentality: Technologies of Government and the Making of Subjects* (Durham, NC: Duke University Press).

Ahmed, J. and S. Hussain (1998) 'Community-based natural resource management in northern Pakistan'. Paper presented at the International Workshop on Community-based Natural Resource Management, Washington, DC, 10–14 May.

Asad, T. (1979) 'Anthropology and the analysis of ideology', *Man* 14: 607–627.

Barth, F. (2000) 'Boundaries and connections', in A.P. Cohen (ed.) *Signifying Identities: Anthropological Perspectives on Boundaries and Contested Values*, pp. 17–36 (London: Routledge).

Boli, J. and G. Thomas (1999) 'INGOs and the organization of world culture', in J. Boli and G. Thomas (eds) *Constructing World Culture*, pp. 13–49 (Palo Alto, CA: Stanford University Press).

Brechin, S.R. (2009) 'Corporate contributions to transnational conservation NGOs: Private international transfers or transactions?', *International Studies Review* 11: 423–430.

Brockington, D., R. Duffy and J. Igoe (2008) *Nature Unbound: Conservation, Capitalism and the Future of Protected Areas* (London: Earthscan).

Brosius J.P., A.L. Tsing and C. Zerner (1998) 'Representing communities: Histories and politics of community-based natural resource management', *Society and Natural Resources* 11(2): 157–168.

Brosius, J.P. and L. Campbell (2010) 'Collaborative event ethnography: Conservation and development trade-offs at the fourth World Conservation Congress', *Conservation and Society* 8(4): 245–255.

Buscher, B., S. Sullivan, K. Neves, J. Igoe and D. Brockington (2012) 'Towards a synthesized critique of neoliberal biodiversity conservation', *Capitalism Nature Socialism* 23(2): 4–30.

Butz, D. (2002) 'Resistance, representation and third space in Shimshal village, northern Pakistan', *ACME* 1: 15–34.

Campbell, L. (2007) 'Local conservation practice and global discourse: A political ecology of sea turtle conservation', *Annals of the Association of American Geographers* 97(2): 313–334.

Carrier, J.C. and P. West (2009) *Virtualism, Governance and Practice: Vision and Execution in Environmental Conservation* (Oxford: Berghahn).

Cohen, A.P. (2000) 'Discriminating relations: Identity, boundary and authenticity', in A.P. Cohen (ed.) *Signifying Identities: Anthropological Perspectives on Boundaries and Contested Values*, pp. 1–13 (London: Routledge).

Coronil, F. (2000) 'Towards a critique of globalcentrism: Speculations on capitalism's nature', *Public Culture* 12: 351–374.

Corson, C. (2010) 'Shifting environmental governance in a neoliberal world: US AID for conservation', *Antipode* 42(3): 576–602.

Corson, C. and K.I. MacDonald (2012) 'Enclosing the global commons: the Convention on Biological Diversity and green grabbing', *Journal of Peasant Studies* 39(2): 263–283.

Cox, K. (1998) 'Spaces of engagement, spaces of dependence and the politics of scale, or: Looking for local politics', *Political Geography* 17(1): 1–23.

Escobar, A. (1995) *Encountering Development: The Making and Unmaking of the Third World* (Princeton, NJ: Princeton University Press).

Flitner, M. (1999) 'Biodiversity: Of local commons and global commodities', in M. Goldman (ed.) *Privatizing Nature: Political Struggles for the Global Commons*, pp. 144–166 (New Brunswick, NJ: Rutgers University Press).

Giddens, A. (1990) *The Consequences of Modernity* (Cambridge: Polity Press).

Goldman, M. (2001) 'The birth of a discipline: Producing authoritative green knowledge, World Bank style', *Ethnography* 2(2): 191–217.

Goldman, M. (2003) 'Constructing an environmental state: Eco-governmentality and other transnational practices of a "green" World Bank', *Social Problems* 48(4): 499–523.

Goldman, M. (2005) *Imperial Nature: The World Bank and Struggles for Social Justice in the Age of Globalization* (New Haven, CT: Yale University Press).

Government of Pakistan (n.d.) *Maintaining Biodiversity in Pakistan with Rural Community Development: PCII* (Islamabad: Environment and Urban Affairs Division).

Government of Pakistan and IUCN – The World Conservation Union (1992) *The Pakistan National Conservation Strategy: Where We Are, Where We Should Be and How to Get There* (Islamabad: Environment and Urban Affairs Division).

Harper, R.H.R. (1998) *Inside the IMF: An Ethnography of Documents, Technology and Organizational Action* (San Diego, CA: Academic Press).

Hayden, C. (2003) *When Nature Goes Public: The Making and Unmaking of Bioprospecting in Mexico* (Princeton, NJ: Princeton University Press).

Hirsch, E. and D.N. Gellner (2001) 'Introduction: Ethnography of organizations and organizations of ethnography', in D.N. Gellner and E. Hirsch (eds) *Inside Organizations: Anthropologists at Work*, pp. 1–18 (Oxford: Berg).

Jamison, A. (1996) 'The shaping of the global environmental agenda: The role of non-governmental organisations', in S. Lash, B. Szerszynski and B. Wynne (eds) *Risk, Environment and Modernity: Towards a New Ecology*, pp. 224–245 (London: Sage).

Jones, K.T. (1998) 'Scale as epistemology', Political Geography 17(1): 25–28.

Kelly, P. (1999) 'The geographies and politics of globalization', *Progress in Human Geography* 23(3): 379–400.

Lampel, J. and A.D. Meyer (2008) 'Field-configuring events as structuring mechanisms: How conferences, ceremonies, and trade shows constitute new technologies, industries, and markets', *Journal of Management Studies* 45(6): 1025–1035.

Latour, B. (1987) *Science in Action: How to follow Scientists and Engineers through Society* (Boston, MA: Harvard University Press).

Latour, B. (1999) *Pandora's Hope: Essays on the Reality of Science Studies* (Boston, MA: Harvard University Press).

Lewis, D., A.J. Bebbington, S. Batterbury, A. Shah, E. Olson, M.S. Siddiqi et al. (2003) 'Practice, power and meaning: Frameworks for studying organizational culture in multi-agency rural development projects', *Journal of International Development* 15: 1–17.

Li, T.M. (2007) *The Will to Improve: Governmentality, Development, and the Practice of Politics* (Durham, NC: Duke University Press).

Luke, T.W. (1999) 'Environmentality as green governmentality', in E. Darier (ed.) *Discourses of the Environment*, pp.121–151 (Oxford: Blackwell).

MacDonald, K.I. (1995) 'A critical review of the central Karakoram World Heritage site workshop', in S. Fuller (ed.) *Proceedings of the Central Karakoram World Heritage Site Workshop*, pp. 29–44 (Karachi: IUCN – The World Conservation Union).

MacDonald, K.I. (1998) 'Push and shove: Spatial history and the construction of a portering economy in northern Pakistan', *Comparative Studies in Society and History* 40(2): 287–317.

MacDonald, K.I. (2001) 'Where the wild things are: Capitalised nature and the cultural politics of "community" in northern Pakistan', paper presented at the Annual Meeting of the American Anthropological Association, Washington, DC, November (available from author).

MacDonald, K.I. (2003) 'IUCN: A history of constraint', address given to the Permanent Workshop of the Centre for Philosophy of Law Higher Institute for Philosophy of the Catholic University of Louvain (UCL), Louvain-la-neuve.

Available at: perso.cpdr.ucl.ac.be/maesschalck/MacDonaldInstitutional_
Reflexivity_and_IUCN-17.02.03.pdf (consulted April 2013).

MacDonald, K.I. (2004) 'Developing "nature": Global ecology and the politics of conservation in northern Pakistan', in J.G. Carrier (ed.) *Confronting Environments: Local Environmental Understanding in a Globalising World*, pp. 71–96 (Lanham, MD: AltaMira).

MacDonald, K.I. (2005) 'Global hunting grounds: Power, scale and ecology in the negotiation of conservation', *Cultural Geographies* 12(3): 259–291.

MacDonald, K.I. (2010a) 'The devil is in the (bio)diversity: Private sector "engagement" and the restructuring of biodiversity conservation', *Antipode* 42(3): 513–550.

MacDonald, K.I. (2010b) 'Business, biodiversity and new "fields" of conservation: The World Conservation Congress and the renegotiation of organizational order', *Conservation & Society* 8(4): 256–275.

MacDonald, K.I. and C. Corson (2012) '"TEEB begins now": A virtual moment in the production of natural capital', *Development and Change* 43(1): 159–184.

Marcus, G. (1998) *Ethnography Through Thick and Thin* (Princeton, NJ: Princeton University Press).

McAfee, K. (1999) 'Selling nature to save it? Biodiversity and the rise of green developmentalism', *Environment and Planning D: Society and Space* 17: 133–154.

McCarthy, J. (2005) 'Scale, sovereignty, and strategy in environmental governance', *Antipode* 37(4): 732–753.

Nader, L. (1972) 'Up the anthropologist – Perspectives gained from studying up', in D.H. Hymes (ed.) *Reinventing Anthropology*, pp. 284–311 (New York: Pantheon).

O'Connor, M. (1994) *Is Capitalism Sustainable? Political Economy and the Politics of Ecology.* (New York: Guilford Press).

Rankin, K.N. (2003) 'Anthropologies and geographies of globalization', *Progress in Human Geography* 27(6): 708–734.

Rosen, M. (1991) 'Coming to terms with the field: Understanding and doing organizational ethnography', *Journal of Management Studies* 28(1): 1–24.

Rosen, M. (2000) *Turning Words, Spinning Worlds: Chapters in Organizational Ethnography* (Amsterdam: Harwood Academic).

Scott, W.R., M. Ruef, P.J. Mendel and C.A. Caronna (2000) *Institutional Change and Health Care Organizations. From Professional Dominance to Managed Care* (Chicago: University of Chicago Press).

Smith, D.E. (2005) *Institutional Ethnography: A Sociology for People* (Lanham, MD: Alta Mira Press).

Smith, N. (1992) 'Geography, difference, and the politics of scale', in J. Doherty, E. Graham and M. Malek (eds) *Postmodernism and the Social Sciences*, pp. 55–79 (London: Macmillan).

Steinberg, P. (2003) 'Understanding policy change in developing countries: The spheres of influence framework', *Global Environmental Politics* 3(1): 11–32.

Strathern, M. (2000) 'Multiple perspectives on intellectual property', in K. Whimp and M. Busse (eds) *Protection of Intellectual, Biological and Cultural Property in Papua New Guinea*, pp. 47–61 (Canberra: Asia Pacific Press at the Australian National University).

Sullivan, S. (2013) 'Banking nature? The spectacular financialisation of environmental conservation', *Antipode* 45(1): 198–217.

Sundberg, J. (1998) 'NGO landscapes in the Maya Biosphere Reserve, Guatemala', *Geographical Review* 88(3): 388–412.

Vogler, J. (2003) 'Taking institutions seriously: How regime analysis can be relevant to multilevel environmental governance', *Global Environmental Politics* 3(2): 25–39.

Watts, M. (2001) 'Development ethnographies', *Ethnography* 2(2): 283–300.

West, P. (2001) 'Non-governmental organizations and the nature of ethnographic inquiry', *Social Analysis* 45(2): 55–77.

West, P. (2006) *Conservation Is Our Government Now: The Politics of Ecology in Papua New Guinea* (Durham, NC: Duke University Press).

Williams, R. (1974) *Television: Technology and Cultural Form* (Hanover, NH: Wesleyan University Press).

Young, O.R. (1994) 'The problem of scale in human–environment relationships', *Journal of Theoretical Politics* 6(4): 429–447.

Notes on Contributors

Irène Bellier is a political anthropologist, a senior director of research at the National Centre for Scientific Research (CNRS) and head of LAIOS (the Laboratory for the Anthropology of the Institutions and Social Organisations) in Paris. Trained both in political science and in the anthropology of the Amazon, after her PhD on gender issues among the Mai huna, she developed the anthropology of administrative and political institutions. She has carried out fieldwork at various sites, including the National School of Administration (ENA); the European Commission, where she studied the impact of multilingual practices and multicultural policies on the making of the European project; and at the United Nations. At the UN, she focused on the human rights sector, particularly the indigenous peoples international movement. In 2010, she received a Senior Advanced Research Grant from the European Research Council, to coordinate as principal investigator the research project on 'Scales of Governance: The UN, the States and Indigenous Peoples – Self-determination at the Time of Globalisation' (www.sogip.ehess.fr).

Regina F. Bendix is Professor of Cultural Anthropology/European Ethnology at the University of Göttingen, Germany. She has carried out research on tourism and culture, heritage and cultural property, as well as work on the history of knowledge production in fields of cultural research. She is co-editor of *Ethnologia Europaea*. Among her works is the monograph *In Search of Authenticity* (1997); most recently, she has co-edited *A Companion to Folklore* (with Galit Hasan-Rokem, 2012) and *Heritage Regimes and the State* (with Aditya Eggert and Arnka Peselmann, 2012).

Jane K. Cowan is Professor of Social Anthropology in the Department of Anthropology at the University of Sussex, Brighton (UK), where she has taught since 1991. She is currently working on two major, interrelated projects regarding rights and international institutions. First, in a project that has received funding from the Macarthur Foundation and the British Academy-Leverhulme, she is tracing a longer-term history of intersections between claims for rights to difference and international mechanisms. This project focuses on the interwar League of Nations' 'supervision' of minority treaties. A second project, funded by the British Academy, examines the Universal Periodic Review at the Human Rights Council in Geneva, focusing on the social processes and contested meanings of this new human rights monitoring mechanism among the actors engaged in it. Her publications include *Culture and Rights: Anthropological Perspectives* (co-edited with Marie-Bénédicte Dembour and Richard A. Wilson, Cambridge University Press, 2001).

Marion Fresia is Assistant Professor at the Institute of Anthropology, University of Neuchâtel. In the past, her research focused on how Mauritanian refugees experienced forced displacement, life in refugee camps, exile and return (*Les Mauritaniens réfugiés au Sénégal: une anthropologie critique de l'asile et de l'aide humanitaire*, 2009). After working for two years with the United Nations High Commissioner for Refugees, she began ethnographic research on the social worlds of 'asylum makers', exploring the institutional fabric and circulation of refugee experts, norms and policies both at the national and global levels ('Une élite transnationale: la fabrique d'une identité professionnelle chez les fonctionnaires du HCR', *REMI*, vol. 25, 2010; *Les Rouages de l'asile en Suisse: regards ethnographiques sur une procédure administrative*, with D. Bozzini and A. Sala, SFM Studies, 2013).

Brigitta Hauser-Schäublin is Professor of Anthropology, University of Göttingen (Germany). She has been visiting professor at Columbia University, The New School for Social Research, Dartmouth College and École des Hautes Études en Sciences Sociales, Paris. She has carried out extensive fieldwork among the Iatmul and Abelam peoples in Papua New Guinea (between 1972 and 1983), in Bali, Indonesia (since 1988), and in Cambodia (since 2008). Many of her publications focus on the ritual and political organisation of space and the relationship between politics and religion. More recently she has dealt with the topic of the 'propertisation' of culture and the implications the certification of culture – such as the UNESCO World Heritage listings – has for local populations (*World Heritage – Angkor and Beyond: Circumstances and Implications of UNESCO Listings in Cambodia*. Göttingen Studies in Cultural Property, vol. 2. Göttingen: Universitätsverlag, 2011).

Tobias Kelly is a Reader in Social Anthropology at the University of Edinburgh. His research interests include human rights and legal anthropology. He has carried out fieldwork in Israel/Palestine, the UK, and at the UN. He has published two monographs: *Law, Violence and Sovereignty* (Cambridge University Press) and *This Side of Silence: Human Rights, Torture and the Recognition of Cruelty* (University of Pennsylvania Press).

Peter Bille Larsen is a lecturer in the Department of Anthropology at the University of Lucerne and currently a visiting fellow in the Department of International Development at the University of Oxford. His main fields of interest are human and environmental relationships, environmental governance and sustainable development issues. He has a strong interest in the intersections between environmental conservation and social equity concerns. This has led to work on socially inclusive conservation approaches, indigenous rights and the role and practice of international organisations and NGOs. Primary fieldwork sites include the Peruvian Amazon, Viet Nam and global-level processes. He has worked extensively with international organisations, NGOs and community-based organisations, seeking to deepen anthropological analysis of institutions and practices, while also seeking to translate anthropological insights into public policy innovation and better practice on the ground. Theoretically, his interests span environmental anthropology, political ecology and political anthropology.

Kenneth Iain MacDonald teaches in the Department of Geography and Program in Planning at the University of Toronto. He is also core faculty in two interdisciplinary programs: International Development Studies and Diaspora and Transnational Studies. Most of his research is ethnographically grounded and he has ongoing research interests in a number of areas that seek to understand the role of transnational processes in the reproduction of cultural formations. Some of this work includes: (a) the role of transnationalism and transnational ideologies in the production of cultural identity; (b) the production and configuration of transnational cultural economies; (c) the postcolonial politics of development; (d) the cultural politics of biodiversity conservation; and (e) the ethnographic study of transnational institutions of environmental governance, primarily the Convention on Biological Diversity. This latter work has involved (with colleagues) the development of a new methodological approach called Collaborative Event Ethnography.

Birgit Müller is a senior researcher at the LAIOS/CNRS (Laboratoire de l'anthropologie des institutions et organisations sociales), at the École des Hautes Études en Sciences Sociales in Paris. She has worked extensively on social movements and societies in rapid transformation: on women's riots in colonial Nigeria, on alternative movements in West Germany, in Nicaragua during and after the Sandinista period, and on post-socialist transformations in East Germany, the Czech Republic and Russia. Her focus is on institutional change, mechanisms of domination and the unintended and intended consequences brought about by political and cultural contestation and economic struggles. Her books include: *Toward an Alternative Culture of Work: Political Idealism and Economic Practices in West Berlin Collective Enterprises* (Westview Press, 1991), *Disenchantment with Market Economics: East Germans and Western Capitalism* (Berghahn, 2007). She is currently undertaking a multi-sited research project on 'Food, Property and Power: Agricultural Technologies as Global Policies and Local Practices' with fieldwork in the Food and Agriculture Organisation of the United Nations, and among agricultural producers in Saskatchewan (Canada) and Carazo (Nicaragua). She is the coordinator of the EASA Network on the Anthropology of International Governance (http://www.easaonline.org/networks/aig/).

Index

Compiled by Sue Carlton

Printed and bound by CPI Group (UK) Ltd, Croydon, CR0 4YY

16/04/2025

14658481-0003